Capital Accumulation and Economic Growth in a Small Open Economy

Economic growth is an issue of primary concern to policy makers in both developed and developing economies. As a consequence, growth theory has long occupied a central role in economics. In this book, Stephen J. Turnovsky investigates the process of economic growth in a small open economy, showing that it is sensitive to the productive structure of the economy. The book comprises three parts, beginning with models where the only intertemporally viable equilibrium is one in which the economy is always on its balanced growth path. Empirical evidence suggests relatively slow speeds of convergence so the second part of the book looks at several alternative ways in which transitional dynamics may be introduced. In the third and final part, the author applies the growth model to the issue of foreign aid, focusing specifically on whether aid should be untied or tied to the accumulation of public capital.

STEPHEN J. TURNOVSKY holds the Castor Chair of Economics at the University of Washington. He is a fellow of the Econometric Society and a past president of the Society of Economic Dynamics and Control, and of the Society for Computational Economics. He is a former editor of the *Journal of Economic Dynamics and Control* and has served on or is currently serving on the editorial boards of several major journals. He is the author of several books, including *Macroeconomic Analysis and Stabilization Policy* (Cambridge University Press, 1977) and *Methods of Macroeconomic Dynamics* (2000).

The CICSE Lectures in Growth and Development

Series editor
Neri Salvadori, University of Pisa

The CICSE lecture series is a biannual lecture series in which leading economists present new findings in the theory and empirics of economic growth and development. The series is sponsored by the Centro Interuniversitario per lo studio sulla Crescita e lo Sviluppo Economico (CICSE), a centre devoted to the analysis of economic growth and development supported by seven Italian universities. For more details about CICSE see their website at http://cicse.ec.unipi.it/.

Capital Accumulation and Economic Growth in a Small Open Economy

STEPHEN J. TURNOVSKY

CAMBRIDGE
UNIVERSITY PRESS

CAMBRIDGE UNIVERSITY PRESS
Cambridge, New York, Melbourne, Madrid, Cape Town, Singapore, São Paulo, Delhi

Cambridge University Press
The Edinburgh Building, Cambridge CB2 8RU, UK

Published in the United States of America by Cambridge University Press, New York

www.cambridge.org
Information on this title: www.cambridge.org/9780521764759

© CICSE 2009

First published 2009

Printed in the United Kingdom at the University Press, Cambridge

A catalogue record for this publication is available from the British Library

Library of Congress Cataloguing in Publication data
Turnovsky, Stephen J.
Capital accumulation and economic growth in a small open economy /
Stephen J. Turnovsky.
p. cm.
Includes bibliographical references.
ISBN 978-0-521-76475-9 (hbk.)   1. Saving and investment–Developing
countries–Econometric models.   2. Endogenous growth (Economics)–Developing
countries–Econometric models.   3. Economic development–Developing
countries–Econometric models.   I. Title.
HC59.72.S3T87 2009
332'.041091724–dc22
2009017297

ISBN 978-0-521-76475-9 hardback

Contents

Figures

Tables

Preface

This book is an extension of three lectures presented as the first set of "Centro Interuniversitario Crescita & Sviluppo Economico (CICSE) Lectures on Growth and Development" in Lucca, Italy, in July 2007. When I was invited to present this series, I was delighted that CICSE asked me to lecture on capital accumulation and economic growth in a small open economy. Both international macroeconomics and the theory of economic growth have interested me for a long period, so this seemed like a good opportunity to discuss them in a unified way. Over the past two decades economic growth has evolved into an enormous area of research, drawing increasingly on contributions from other areas of economics, as well as from other disciplines. The approach I adopt in these lectures is a traditional one, extending the standard models of capital accumulation to the open economy.

The lectures and this resulting short book draw heavily on research that I have undertaken in this area since the mid 1990s. At the appropriate places in each chapter, I have indicated the original source of the research from which the presentation has been adapted, although in many cases the material has been extensively revised. As will be seen from the appropriate references much of the research has been undertaken jointly and I am grateful to have had the opportunity to work with many talented coauthors over the years. I also want to express my appreciation to Stefan Schubert who worked through the manuscript and was helpful in eliminating errors and inconsistencies.

In developing the lectures and the book, I have tried to present the research in a progressive way. The first part (lecture) is devoted to setting out a basic canonical model and to analyzing the simplest version of it. This leads to a simple endogenous growth model, which has the characteristic that the only viable equilibrium is for the economy to always be on its balanced growth path. While this might serve as a convenient benchmark, it is obviously unrealistic, since empirical evidence suggests precisely the opposite, namely that most of the time economies are well away from their balanced growth paths. Hence the second part extends the model so that the long-run balanced growth equilibrium is reached only gradually along a transitional adjustment path. This structure can be accomplished in various ways, all of which involve augmenting the order of the underlying dynamics, and several alternative approaches are spelled out in Part II. The third part applies some of the models to an important practical subject, namely the granting of foreign aid. This is indeed a critical issue, having many dimensions. Within the framework we develop, we focus on a very specific, but widely debated, issue, namely the question of whether foreign aid should be "tied" to investment in infrastructure, say, or "untied," allowing the recipient economy to use the resources as it wishes. But even within this restricted framework the answer to this question is complex and involves detailed knowledge of the structural characteristics of the recipient economy. Moreover, the applications of the model are sufficiently complex that we need to supplement the formal analytics with numerical simulations. And so a by-product of Part III is the illustration of the use of these numerical methods in simple growth models of this kind.

Finally, I wish to thank Neri Salvadori for his invitation to present the 2007 CICSE Lectures on Growth and Development. It is indeed an honor to inaugurate the lecture series. I hope that it will be the start of a successful series, providing an avenue whereby the presentation of diverse approaches to the study of growth theory will enhance our understanding of this most important topic.

1

Introduction and brief overview

Economic growth is arguably the issue of primary concern to economic policy makers in both developed and developing economies. Economic growth statistics are among the most widely publicized measures of economic performance and are always analyzed and discussed with interest. As a consequence, growth theory has long occupied a central role in economics.

The study of economic growth illustrates the power of compound interest. A seemingly small growth differential can accumulate over time to substantial differentials in levels. To take one very simple example, suppose two countries begin with the same level of income. A sustained 1% growth differential in output between the two economies implies that in seventy years – just one lifetime – the output *level* of the faster-growing economy will be *double* that of the slower-growing economy. Indeed, the dramatic changes in relative incomes among the OECD countries that one can observe between the end of World War II and the present are in some cases the accumulated results of these seemingly small differences in growth rates.

1.1 Some background

Long-run growth was first introduced by Solow (1956) and Swan (1956) into the traditional neoclassical macroeconomic model by specifying a growing population coupled with a more efficient labor force. The direct consequence of this approach was that the long-run equilibrium growth rate in these models was ultimately tied to demographic factors, such as the growth rate of population, the structure of the labor force, and its productivity growth (technological change), all of which were typically taken to be exogenously determined. Hence, the only policies that could contribute to long-run economic growth were those that would increase the growth of population, and

1

manpower training programs aimed at increasing the efficiency of the labor force. Conventional macroeconomic policy had no influence on the long-run growth performance. It could, however, influence the transitional growth path and thus the long-run capital stock and resulting output. Moreover, the slower the economy's rate of convergence, the longer it remained in transition, and the more significant the accumulated level effects.

Over the last half-century, economic growth theory has produced a voluminous literature, doing so in two distinct phases. The Solow–Swan model was the inspiration for a first generation of growth models during the 1960s, which, being associated with exogenous sources of long-run growth, are now sometimes referred to as *exogenous growth models*. Research interest in these models tapered off abruptly around 1970 as economists turned their attention to shorter-run issues, perceived as being of more immediate significance, such as inflation, unemployment, and oil shocks, and the design of macroeconomic policies to deal with them. Beginning with the seminal work of Romer (1986), there has been a resurgence of interest in economic growth theory, giving rise to a second generation of growth models, and continuing to this day. This revival of activity has been motivated by several issues, which include: (i) an attempt to explain aspects of the data not discussed by the neoclassical model; (ii) a more satisfactory explanation of international differences in economic growth rates; (iii) a more central role for the accumulation of knowledge; and (iv) a larger role for the instruments of macroeconomic policy in explaining the growth process; see Romer (1994). These new models seek to explain the long-run growth rate as an endogenous equilibrium outcome of the behavior of rational optimizing agents, reflecting the structural characteristics of the economy, such as technology and preferences, as well as macroeconomic policy. For this reason they have become known as *endogenous growth models*.

One can identify interesting differences between the first and second generations of growth models, both in terms of the range of issues they address and the methodology they employ. The earlier models focused almost entirely on the role of physical capital accumulation as the source of economic growth, coupled with the exogenous growth in population and technology. The approach tended to be what one might call "sequentially structured," meaning that one begins with the simplest model and then augments it in various directions to incorporate additional aspects. This is well illustrated by Burmeister and Dobell (1970), which at the time of its publication was a state-of-the-art review of the literature. Beginning with the one-sector model, they first extend it by introducing technological change, then go on to two sectors, add a second asset, and subsequently advance to a range of multi-sector models, before culminating with a discussion of optimal growth.

In contrast, contemporary growth theory is more wide-ranging. While physical capital accumulation remains a central source of economic growth, many other aspects are discussed in parallel. These include the accumulation of human capital, knowledge and education, the role of public capital, the quality of health, demographic factors, and recently, the role of institutions, the political environment, and even religion. The transmission of techno-logical change and innovation is also assigned a central role. Recognizing that the spoils of growth are not shared equally among society, the relationship between economic growth, the level of development, and income distribution is a central issue that also has a long history. One consequence of studying growth from this broader perspective is that the study tends to be more motivated by empirical observation rather than by trying to develop a unity of structure as was more characteristic of the earlier literature.

One other contrast between the two generations of growth model is that whereas the old theory focused almost exclusively on closed economies, the new theory tends to have more of an international orientation; see e.g. Grossman and Helpman (1991). This may reflect the increased importance of the inter-national aspects in macroeconomics in general and the international linkages that exist throughout the economy. But it may also reflect the greater emphasis placed by the current literature on empirical issues and the reconciliation of the theory with the empirical evidence. In this respect, differential national growth rates and evolving differential national income levels are central topics and have given rise to the widely debated issue of the so-called convergence hypothesis. The question here is whether or not countries have a tendency to converge to a common per capita level of income, and if so, how long it takes.

As one assesses the new growth theory, one can identify two main strands of the theoretical literature, emphasizing different sources of economic growth. One class of models, closest to the neoclassical growth model, stresses the accumulation of (private) physical capital as the fundamental source of economic growth. This differs in a fundamental way from the neoclassical growth model in that it does not require exogenous elements, such as a growing population, to generate an equilibrium of ongoing growth. Rather, the equilibrium growth is internally generated, though in order to achieve that, certain restrictions relating to homogeneity must be imposed on the economic framework. Some of these restrictions are of a knife-edge character and have been the source of criticism; see e.g. Solow (1994).

In the simplest such model, in which the only factor of production is capital, the constant-returns-to-scale condition implies that the production

function must be linear in physical capital, being of the functional form
$Y = AK$. For obvious reasons, this technology has become known as the "AK
model." As a matter of historical record, explanation of growth as an
endogenous process in a one-sector model is not new. In fact it dates back to
Harrod (1939) and Domar (1946). The equilibrium growth rate characterizing
the AK model is essentially of the Harrod–Domar type, the only difference
being that consumption (or savings) behavior is derived as part of an intertemporal optimization, rather than being posited directly. These one-sector
models assume (often only implicitly) a broad interpretation for capital,
taking it to include both human, as well as nonhuman, capital; see Rebelo
(1991). This is necessary if the model is to be calibrated plausibly using "real-
world" data. A direct extension of this basic model is a two-sector investment-based growth model, originally due to Lucas (1988), that disaggregates
private capital into human and nonhuman capital. This has also generated an
extensive literature; see e.g. Mulligan and Sala-i-Martin (1993) and Bond,
Wang, and Yip (1996).

A second class of models emphasizes the endogenous development of
knowledge, or research and development, as the engine of growth. The
seminal contribution here is that of Romer (1990), which develops a two-
sector model of a closed economy, where new knowledge produced in one
sector is used as an input in the production of final output. The knowledge/
education sector has been extended in various directions by a number of
authors; see e.g. Aghion and Howitt (1992), Zhang (1996), Glomm and
Ravikumar (1998), Bils and Klenow (2000), and Blankenau (2005). A related
class of models deals with innovation and the diffusion of knowledge across
countries, and a comprehensive discussion is provided by Barro and Sala-i-
Martin (2000, ch. 8).

One is beginning to see a confluence of some aspects of the old and new
growth theories. The new growth models are often characterized as having
scale effects, meaning that variations in the size or scale of the economy, as
measured by population, say, affect the size of the long-run growth rate. For
example, the Romer (1990) model of research and development implies that a
doubling of the population devoted to research will double the growth rate.
Whether the AK model is associated with scale effects depends upon whether
there are production externalities that are linked to the size of the economy; see
Barro and Sala-i-Martin (2000). By contrast, the neoclassical Solow–Swan
model has the property that the equilibrium growth rate is independent of the
scale (size) of the economy; it is therefore not subject to such scale effects.

Empirical evidence does not support the existence of scale effects. For
example, Jones (1995a) finds that variations in the level of research

employment have exerted no influence on the long-run growth rates of the OECD economies. Backus, Kehoe, and Kehoe (1992) find no conclusive empirical evidence of any relationship between US GDP growth and measures of scale. These empirical observations are beginning to stimulate interest in the development of non-scale models. Such models are hybrids in the sense that they share some of the characteristics of the neoclassical model, yet their equilibrium is derived from intertemporal optimization as in the new growth models.[1] Jones (1995b) proposes a specific model, in which the steady-state growth rate is determined by the growth rate of population, in conjunction with certain production elasticities, in his case pertaining to the knowledge-producing sector.

1.2 Scope of this book

It is clearly beyond the scope of this book to present an exhaustive discussion of growth theory. For that the reader should refer to specialized textbooks, such as Grossman and Helpman (1991), Aghion and Howitt (1998), Barro and Sala-i-Martin (2000), and Acemoglu (2008), which provide comprehensive treatments of the subject from different perspectives. Nor is it a comprehensive treatment of international macroeconomic dynamics. This too is a broad area and discussed from various viewpoints by Frenkel, Razin, and Yuen (1996), Obstfeld and Rogoff (1996), and Turnovsky (1997a). Rather, the purpose of this book is to exposit investment-based growth models, but from an international perspective, and more specifically from a viewpoint that is more applicable to a small open economy. This means that numerous topics central to international macroeconomics are not addressed.

The book has three parts. We begin our discussion in Chapter 2 by expositing a canonical model of a small open economy that is sufficiently general to encompass alternative models that appear in the literature and that we shall discuss. The remainder of Chapter 2 and Chapter 3, which together make up Part I, develop models that have the property that the economy is always on its balanced growth path. It is important to stress that this characteristic is not assumed, but is derived as the only equilibrium that is intertemporally viable.

These initial models can be viewed as being alternative versions of the AK growth model. Such models have been extensively used to analyze the effects of fiscal policy on growth performance; see e.g. Barro (1990), Jones and

---

[1] Jones (1995a) refers to such models as "semi-endogenous" growth models.

Manuelli (1990), King and Rebelo (1990), Rebelo (1991), Jones, Manuelli, and Rossi (1993), Ireland (1994) and Turnovsky (1996a).[2] Most of these endogenous growth models have been developed for a closed economy, although several applications to an open economy now exist; see Rebelo (1992), Razin and Yuen (1994, 1996), Mino (1996), Turnovsky (1996b, 1996d, 1997c), van der Ploeg (1996), Baldwin and Forslid (1999, 2000), and Chatterjee (2007).

Section 3 of Chapter 2 begins with the simplest Romer (1986) model with fixed labor supply, characterizing in detail the equilibrium that is attained. Section 4 then discusses an open economy version of the Barro (1990) model, where government expenditure is productive, and analyzes optimal fiscal policy in that setting. Chapter 3 extends this basic model to the case where labor is supplied elastically. It emphasizes how going from one assumption to the other fundamentally changes the determination of the equilibrium growth rate and the impact of fiscal policy. Adjustments that are borne by the accumulation of capital when the labor supply is fixed, are accommodated by an adjustment in the capital–labor ratio, when labor is supplied elastically.

These initial models all abstract from transitional dynamics, so that in each case the economy is always on its balanced growth path. This implies that the economy fully responds instantaneously to any structural or policy change. While this may be pedagogically convenient, it is obviously implausible. It is also inconsistent with the empirical evidence pertaining to convergence speeds, which suggests that economies spend most of their time adjusting to structural changes. Part II therefore presents in some detail several natural ways that transitional dynamics may be introduced.

Chapter 4 discusses two ways of accomplishing this in a one-sector economy. Like much of international macroeconomics, the benchmark assumption being adopted is that the small country can borrow or lend as much as it wishes, at a fixed given interest rate. One way to introduce dynamics is to replace this assumption, which in any event is a polar one, with an assumption that the small economy has restricted access to world financial markets, in the form of borrowing costs that increase with its debt position. This is particularly likely to be relevant for a small developing economy, but it is also plausible as a general proposition. The second modification, which again is a move toward reality, is the introduction of

---

[2] There has been less research analyzing the effect of monetary policy on endogenous growth. Two studies that consider monetary aspects include van der Ploeg and Alogoskoufis (1994) and Palivos and Yip (1995).

government capital, so that in contrast to the Barro model, government expenditure influences production as a stock of public capital, rather than as a current expenditure flow.

Transitional dynamics can also be introduced in other ways, and these are discussed in the following two chapters. Chapter 5 treats the case where the production technology is augmented to two sectors, a traded and a nontraded sector, showing the nature of the dynamics that this introduces. The two-sector model, where the two sectors consist of physical (nonhuman) and human capital, respectively, was one of the original models of endogenous growth pioneered by Lucas (1988). Other authors who analyze the two-sector model include Mulligan and Sala-i-Martin (1993), Devereux and Love (1994), and Bond, Wang, and Yip (1996). This aspect is particularly relevant for international economies, where it is natural to identify the two sectors with nontraded and traded capital, as in the traditional dependent economy model.

As we have already noted, the endogenous growth model has been subject to criticism along two lines. First, it is often associated with "scale effects" meaning that long-run growth rates are linked to the size of the economy, a characteristic that is not supported by the empirical evidence. Second, it holds only if strict "knife-edge" conditions on the technology hold. In response to this, we have seen the development of non-scale growth models, which have the property that long-run growth rates are independent of the scale of the economy. This model is also associated with transitional dynamics and is discussed in Chapter 6. In particular, we show that if we combine this more general technology with the increasing cost of debt, introduced in Chapter 4 we are able to replicate quite complex behavior of debt, which in some cases was associated with the episodes of the Asian debt crisis in the 1990s.

Part III of this book combines some of the elements presented in Parts I and II and applies them to the issue of foreign aid. Specifically, we construct an endogenous growth model of a small developing economy that faces restricted access to the world financial market. The country is relatively poorly endowed with public capital, which it then receives in the form of foreign aid from abroad. The issue that the model addresses concerns the form that the aid should take. Should it be tied in the sense of being committed solely to public investment, or should it be untied, in the sense of being used for any purpose that the recipient country wishes, including debt reduction, consumption, or perhaps private capital formation? By combining the accumulation of public with private capital, together with costly debt accumulation, the macroeconomic equilibrium is represented by a higher-order dynamic system, the effective analysis of which can be conducted only numerically. Chapters 7 and 8 perform this in some detail, thus illustrating the use of straightforward numerical simulations to assist in our understanding of this process. We should emphasize that the answer to the basic question being posed here – the relative merits of tied versus untied foreign aid – is highly sensitive to many aspects of the economic structure, and for this reason we need to conduct substantial sensitivity analysis.

Throughout this book, our main objective is to exposit the structures of the various models in their basic form rather than to analyze any one in detail. The models provide powerful analytical tools that can be adapted to various needs and circumstances. One key issue that distinguishes the endogenous growth model from the non-scale model is the impact of policy on the long-run equilibrium growth rate. Before embarking further, we should acknowledge that the empirical evidence pertaining to this issue is mixed. If one takes the evidence on non-scale growth models seriously, and accepts that the long-run growth rate is determined as suggested by Jones (1995b), the scope for fiscal policy is limited, although less so than in the Solow model. Indeed, empirical evidence by Easterly and Rebelo (1993) and Stokey and Rebelo (1995) suggests that the effects of tax rates on long-run growth rates are insignificant, or weak at best. Stokey and Rebelo argue that their findings provide evidence against those models, such as AK models, that predict large growth effects from taxation. In order for the predictions of these models to be consistent with their evidence, these growth effects would have to be largely offset by changes in other determinants of the long-run growth rate. But other studies, such as Grier and Tullock (1989), Barro (1991), and Barro and Lee (1994), obtain negative relationships between growth and government consumption expenditure, while Barro and Lee also find that government expenditure on education has a positive effect on growth. Taken together, we do not view the empirical evidence as necessarily contradicting the ability of fiscal policy to influence the growth rate. It may well be the case that a higher income tax has a significant negative effect on the growth rate, but that this is roughly offset by a significant positive growth effect of the productive government expenditure it may be financing, thus yielding a small overall net effect.[3] Indeed, the welfare-maximizing rate of taxation in the simple Barro (1990) model of productive government expenditure coincides with the growth-maximizing tax rate, so that if the tax rate is in fact close to optimal there

---

[3] Kneller, Bleaney, and Gemmell (1999) argue that the results finding weak evidence for the effects of tax rates on growth are biased because of the incomplete specification of the government budget constraint.

should be little effect on the growth rate, precisely as the empirical evidence seems to suggest. But to understand this relationship, it is important to develop a model in which the various components of fiscal policy are introduced explicitly, and their separate and possibly conflicting effects on the growth rate analyzed. It is in this vein that we view the AK model as providing an instructive framework for analyzing the effect of fiscal policy on growth.

PART ONE

Models of balanced growth

2

Basic growth model with fixed labor supply

2.1 A canonical model of a small open economy

We begin by describing the generic structure of a small open economy that consumes and produces a single traded commodity. There are N identical individuals, each of whom has an infinite planning horizon and possesses perfect foresight. Each agent is endowed with a unit of time that is divided between leisure, l, and labor, $1 - l$. Labor is fully employed so that total labor supply, equal to population, N, grows exponentially at the steady rate $\dot{N} = nN$. Individual domestic output, Y_i, of the traded commodity is determined by the individual's private capital stock, K_i, his labor supply, $(1 - l)$, and the aggregate capital stock $K = NK_i$.[1] In order to accommodate growth under more general assumptions with respect to returns to scale, we assume that the output of the individual producer is determined by the Cobb–Douglas production function:[2]

$$Y_i = a(1 - l)^{1-\sigma} K_i^{\sigma} K^{\eta} \qquad 0 < \sigma < 1, \; \eta \gtrless 0 \qquad (2.1a)$$

This formulation is akin to the earliest endogenous growth model of Romer (1986). The spillover experienced by an individual from the aggregate stock of capital can be motivated in various ways. One is to interpret K as knowledge capital, as Romer suggested. Another is to assume N specific inputs (subscripted by i) with aggregate K representing an intra-industry spillover of knowledge. A negative exponent can be interpreted as reflecting congestion, along the lines of Barro and Sala-i-Martin (1992a) and is illustrated in Section 2.4 below.

---

[1] Since all agents are identical, all aggregate quantities are simply multiples of the individual quantities, $X = NX_i$. Note that since all agents allocate the same share of time to work, there is no need to index the individual agents' leisure, l.

[2] When production functions exhibit non-constant returns to scale in all factors, the existence of a balanced growth equilibrium requires the production function to be Cobb–Douglas, as assumed in (2.1a); see Eicher and Turnovsky (1999a).

Each private factor of production has positive, but diminishing, marginal physical product. To assure the existence of a competitive equilibrium the production function exhibits constant returns to scale in the two private factors (Romer, 1986). In contrast to the standard neoclassical growth model, we do not insist that the production function exhibits constant returns to scale; indeed total returns to scale are $1 + \eta$, and are increasing or decreasing, according to whether the spillover from aggregate capital is positive or negative.

As we shall show in subsequent chapters, the production function is sufficiently general to encompass a variety of models. For example, we shall demonstrate that the model is consistent with long-run stable growth, provided returns to scale are appropriately constrained. This contrasts with models of endogenous growth and externalities in which exogenous population growth can be shown to lead to explosive growth rates; see Romer (1990). We should also point out that the standard AK model emerges when $\sigma + \eta = 1$ and $n = 0$, and the neoclassical model corresponds to $\eta = 0$.

Aggregate consumption in the economy is denoted by C, so that the per capita consumption of the individual agent at time t is $C/N = C_i$, yielding the agent utility over an infinite time horizon represented by the intertemporal isoelastic utility function:

$$\Omega \equiv \int_0^\infty (1/\gamma)\left(C_i l^\theta\right)^\gamma e^{-\rho t} dt; \quad -\infty < \gamma < 1 ; \quad \theta > 0, 1 > \gamma(1 + \theta), \quad 1 > \gamma\theta \quad (2.1\text{b})$$

where $1/(1 - \gamma)$ equals the intertemporal elasticity of substitution, and θ measures the substitutability between consumption and leisure in utility.[3] The remaining constraints on the coefficients in (2.1b) are required to ensure that the utility function is concave in the quantities C and l.

Agents accumulate physical capital, with expenditure on a given change in the capital stock, I_i, involving adjustment (installation) costs that we incorporate in the quadratic (convex) function:

$$\Phi(I_i, K_i) \equiv I_i + hI_i^2/2K_i = I_i(1 + hI_i/2K_i) \quad (2.1\text{c})$$

This equation is an application of the familiar Hayashi (1982) cost of adjustment framework, where we assume that the adjustment costs are

---

[3] This form of utility function is consistent with the existence of a balanced growth path; see Ladrón-de-Guevara, Ortigueira, and Santos (1997). The specification in (2.1b) introduces leisure as an independent argument; they also consider the case where utility derived from leisure depends upon its interaction with human capital.

proportional to the *rate* of investment per unit of installed capital (rather than its level). The linear homogeneity of this function is necessary if a steady-state equilibrium having ongoing growth is to be sustained.[4]

Convex adjustment costs are a standard feature of models of capital accumulation in small open economies with tradable capital facing a perfect world capital market, being necessary for such models to give rise to non-degenerate dynamics; see Turnovsky (1997a). They are, however, less common in endogenous growth models of closed economies, which typically treat the accumulation of capital as being determined residually; see e.g. Barro (1990), Rebelo (1991).[5]

Adjustment costs turn out to have at least two important roles in this model, particularly in the basic AK version of the model to be discussed in Section 2.2. First, they may preclude the existence of a steady-state equilibrium growth path. Second, they introduce an important flexibility into the equilibrating process. In equilibrium, the after-tax rates of return on the two assets available to the economy, traded bonds and capital, must be equal. Given the linear technology, the marginal physical product of capital is also constant, so that the equality between these two after-tax rates of return in general constrains the feasible choice of tax rates. By contrast, the presence of adjustment costs introduces a variable shadow value of capital (the Tobin q), which equilibrates the rates of return on these two assets, for any arbitrarily specified tax rates.

For simplicity we assume that the capital stock does not depreciate, so that the net rate of capital accumulation is given by:

$$\dot{K}_i = I_i - nK_i \qquad (2.1\text{d})$$

In addition, agents have unrestricted access to a world capital market, being able to accumulate foreign bonds, B_i, which pay an exogenously determined fixed rate of return, r. We shall assume that income from current production is taxed at the rate τ_y, income from bonds is taxed at the rate τ_b, while, in addition, consumption is taxed at the rate τ_c. We shall illustrate the contrasting implications of different models by analyzing the purely distortionary aspects of taxation and assume that revenues from all taxes are

---

[4] Many applications of the cost of adjustment in the Ramsey model assume that adjustment costs depend upon the absolute rate of investment, rather than its rate relative to the size of the capital stock. They also often assume only that it is convex; the assumption of a quadratic function is made for convenience, simplifying the solution for the equilibrium growth rates in the endogenous growth model.

[5] There are some exceptions; see Turnovsky (1996c) in a closed economy. Baldwin and Forslid (1999, 2000) emphasize the q-theoretic approach in an open economy.

rebated to the agent as lump-sum transfers, T_i. Thus the individual agent's instantaneous budget constraint is described by:

$$\dot{B}_i = (1 - \tau_y)Y_i + [r(1 - \tau_b) - n]B_i - (1 + \tau_c)C_i - I_i\left(1 + \frac{h}{2}\frac{I_i}{K_i}\right) + T_i$$

(2.1e)

The agent's decisions are to choose his rates of consumption, C_i, leisure, l, investment, I_i, and asset accumulation, B_i, K_i, to maximize the intertemporal utility function (2.1b), subject to the accumulation equations (2.1d) and (2.1e). The discounted Hamiltonian for this optimization is:

$$H \equiv e^{-\rho t}\frac{1}{\gamma}\left(C_i l^{\theta}\right)^{\gamma} + \lambda e^{-\rho t}\left[(1 - \tau_y)Y_i - \Phi_i - (1 + \tau_c)C_i\right.$$
$$\left. + [r(1 - \tau_b) - n]B_i - T_i - \dot{B}_i\right] + q'e^{-\rho t}[I - nK_i - \dot{K}_i]$$

where λ is the shadow value of wealth in the form of internationally traded bonds and q' is the shadow value of the agent's capital stock. Exposition of the model is simplified by using the shadow value of wealth as numeraire. Consequently, $q \equiv q'/\lambda$ can be interpreted as being the market price of capital in terms of the (unitary) price of foreign bonds.

The optimality conditions with respect to C_i, l, and I_i are respectively:

$$C_i^{\gamma-1}l^{\theta\gamma} = \lambda(1 + \tau_c)$$

(2.2a)

$$\theta C_i^{\gamma}l^{\theta\gamma-1} = \frac{\lambda(1 - \tau_y)(1 - \sigma)Y_i}{(1 - l)}$$

(2.2b)

$$1 + h(I_i/K_i) = q$$

(2.2c)

Equation (2.2a) equates the marginal utility of consumption to the tax-adjusted shadow value of wealth, while (2.2b) equates the marginal utility of leisure to its opportunity cost, the after-tax marginal physical product of labor (real wage), valued at the shadow value of wealth. The third equation equates the marginal cost of an additional unit of investment, which is inclusive of the marginal installation cost hI_i/K_i, to the market value of capital. Equation (2.2c) may be solved to yield the following expression for the rate of capital accumulation:

$$\frac{\dot{K}_i}{K_i} = \frac{I_i}{K_i} - n = \frac{q-1}{h} - n \equiv \phi_i \tag{2.3}$$

With all agents being identical, equation (2.3) implies that the growth rate of the aggregate capital stock is $\phi = \phi_i + n$, so that:

$$\frac{I}{K} = \frac{\dot{K}}{K} = \frac{\dot{K}_i}{K_i} + n = \frac{q-1}{h} \equiv \phi \tag{2.3'}$$

This describes a "Tobin q" theory of investment, with $\dot{K} \gtrless 0$ according to whether $q \gtrless 1$. Starting from an initial capital stock, K_0, the aggregate capital stock at time t is $K(t) = K_0 e^{\int_0^t \phi(s)ds}$.

Optimizing with respect to B_i and K_i implies the arbitrage relationships:

$$\rho - \frac{\dot{\lambda}}{\lambda} = r(1 - \tau_b) - n \tag{2.4a}$$

$$\frac{(1 - \tau_y)\sigma Y_i}{qK_i} + \frac{\dot{q}}{q} + \frac{(q-1)^2}{2hq} = r(1 - \tau_b) \tag{2.4b}$$

Equation (2.4a) is the standard Keynes–Ramsey consumption rule, equating the marginal return on consumption to the growth-adjusted after-tax rate of return on holding a foreign bond. With ρ, r, and τ_b all being constants, it implies a constant growth rate of marginal utility, λ. In contrast to stationary models of intertemporal capital accumulation, in which, in order to ensure a finite steady-state equilibrium, we must set $\lambda = \bar{\lambda}$, for all t, implying a constant *level* of λ, the equilibrium is now consistent with a constant *growth* in λ; see Turnovsky (2002a). In most of our discussion we assume that $B > 0$, so that the agent is a net lender abroad, being taxed on his foreign income earnings. However, nothing rules out the possibility that $B < 0$, in which case the agent is a net borrower, and indeed in subsequent chapters this case is considered in the situation where the economy faces an upward-sloping supply curve of debt.

Likewise (2.4b) equates the after-tax rate of return on domestic capital to the after-tax rate of return on the traded bond. The former has three components. The first is the after-tax output per unit of installed capital (valued at the relative price q), while the second is the rate of capital gain. The third element, which is less familiar, is equal to $(qI - \Phi)/qK$. This measures the rate of return arising from the difference in the valuation of the new capital qI and the value of the resources it utilizes, Φ, per unit of installed capital. This component reflects the fact that an additional source of benefit from higher capital stock is the reduction of the installation costs (which depend upon I/K) associated with new investment.

Finally, in order to ensure that the agent's intertemporal budget constraint is met, the following transversality conditions must be imposed:[6]

$$\lim_{t\to\infty} \lambda B_i e^{-pt} = 0; \quad \lim_{t\to\infty} q' K_i e^{-pt} = 0 \tag{2.4c}$$

The government in this canonical economy plays a limited role. It levies income taxes on output and foreign interest income, it taxes consumption, and then rebates all tax revenues. In aggregate, these decisions are subject to the balanced budget condition:

$$\tau_y Y + \tau_b rB + \tau_c C = T \tag{2.5}$$

Aggregating (2.1e) over the N individuals, and imposing (2.5) and (2.1d) leads to:

$$\dot{B} = Y + rB - C - I[1 + (h/2)(I/K)] \tag{2.6}$$

which describes the country's current account. It asserts that the rate at which the economy accumulates foreign bonds equals its trade balance, $Y - C - I$ $(1 + (h/2)(I/K))$, plus the interest it is earning on its capital account.

The model can thus be summarized by the five optimality conditions (2.2a)–(2.2c), (2.4a), and (2.4b), together with the current account relationship (2.6). If, as many models do, we assume that labor is supplied inelastically, in that case the optimality condition for labor (2.2b), ceases to be operative.

2.2 The endogenous growth model

The investment-based endogenous growth model has been the subject of intensive research since Romer's seminal paper appeared in 1986. Most such models assume that labor is supplied inelastically and, as we shall demonstrate, the endogeneity, or otherwise, of labor is a crucial determinant of the equilibrium growth rate and its response to economic policy.

---

[6] The transversality condition on debt is equivalent to the national intertemporal budget constraint.

The key feature of the endogenous growth model is that it is capable of generating ongoing growth in the absence of population growth, i.e. $n = 0$. For this to occur, the production function (2.1a) must exhibit constant returns to scale in the accumulating factors, individual and aggregate capital, that is:

$$\sigma + \eta = 1 \qquad (2.7)$$

Substituting this into (2.1a), this implies individual and aggregate production functions of the form:

$$Y_i = a[(1-l)K]^{\eta}K_i^{1-\eta}; \quad Y = a[(1-l)N]^{\eta}K \qquad (2.8)$$

The individual production function thus has constant returns to scale in private capital, K_i, and in labor, measured in terms of "efficiency units" $(1-l)K$. Summing over agents, the aggregate production function is thus linear in the endogenously accumulating capital stock. Note that as long as $\eta \neq 0$ so that there is an aggregate externality, the average (and marginal) productivity of capital depends upon the size of the population. Increasing the population, indefinitely, holding other technological characteristics constant, increases the productivity of capital and the equilibrium growth rate. The economy is thus said to have a "scale effect"; see Jones (1995a). While productivity may increase with population until some critical population level is reached (i.e. there may be an optimal population level), this clearly cannot continue indefinitely, since congestion and other impediments to productivity will eventually set in. Such indefinite scale effects run counter to the empirical evidence and have been a source of criticism of the AK growth model; see Backus, Kehoe, and Kehoe (1992). These scale effects can be eliminated from the AK model if either (i) there are no externalities ($\eta = 0$), or (ii) the individual production function (2.1a) is modified to:

$$Y_i = a(1-l)^{1-\sigma}K_i^{\sigma}(K/N)^{\eta} \qquad (2.1a')$$

so that the externality depends upon the average, rather than the aggregate, capital stock; see Mulligan and Sala-i-Martin (1993). Henceforth, throughout this chapter, we shall normalize the size of the population at $N = 1$ and thereby sidestep the issue of scale effects.

2.2.1 Inelastic labor supply

Throughout the remainder of this chapter, we focus on the case where labor is supplied inelastically, i.e. $l = \bar{l}$. With population normalized, the individual and aggregate production functions are of the pure AK form:

$$Y_i = A K_i^{\sigma} K^{1-\sigma}; \quad Y = AK \tag{2.9}$$

where $A \equiv a(1 - \bar{l})^{1-\sigma}$ is a fixed constant. With the labor supply fixed, both the marginal and average productivity of capital are constant. The specification of the technology, consistent with ongoing growth, is a very strong knife-edge condition, one for which the endogenous growth model has been criticized; see Solow (1994).[7]

To determine the macroeconomic equilibrium, we first take the time differential of (2.2a), which with labor supplied inelastically implies:

$$(1 - \gamma)\frac{\dot{C}}{C} = -\frac{\dot{\lambda}}{\lambda}$$

and then combine the resulting equation with (2.4a) (and zero population growth):

$$\frac{\dot{C}}{C} = \frac{r(1 - \tau_b) - \rho}{1 - \gamma} \equiv \psi \tag{2.10}$$

An immediate consequence of (2.10) is that the equilibrium growth rate of domestic consumption is proportional to the difference between the after-tax rate of return on foreign bonds and the (domestic) rate of time preference. From a policy perspective, it also implies that the consumption growth rate varies inversely with the tax on foreign interest income, but is independent of all other tax rates. Solving this equation implies that the level of consumption at time t is:

$$C(t) = C(0)e^{\psi t} \tag{2.11}$$

where the initial level of consumption $C(0)$ is yet to be determined.

The critical determinant of the growth rate of capital is the relative price of installed capital, q, the path of which is determined by the arbitrage condition (2.4b). To analyze this further, we rewrite (2.4b) as the following nonlinear differential equation with constant coefficients:

$$\dot{q} = [r(1 - \tau_b)q - A\sigma(1 - \tau_y)] - \frac{(q - 1)^2}{2h} \equiv H(q) \tag{2.12}$$

---

[7] Note that the technology (2.9) is identical to that of the original Harrod–Domar model, of which the AK model is a modern counterpart. It was Harrod himself who originally referred to the "knife-edge" characteristics of his model.

In order for the capital stock domiciled in the economy ultimately to follow a path of steady growth (or decline), the stationary solution to this equation attained when $\dot{q} = 0$ must have (at least) one real solution. Setting $\dot{q} = 0$ in (2.12), implies that the steady-state value of q, $\tilde{q}$ say, must be a solution to the quadratic equation:

$$A\sigma(1 - \tau_y) + \frac{(q - 1)^2}{2h} = rq(1 - \tau_b) \qquad (2.13)$$

Equation (2.13) also emphasizes the importance of adjustment costs and the associated market price in equilibrating the rates of return. In the absence of such costs ($h \to 0$, $q \to 1$), (2.13) reduces to $A\sigma(1 - \tau_y) = r(1 - \tau_b)$. Since A and r are given constants, this condition imposes a fixed constraint on the two tax rates when capital is freely adjustable; in this case they cannot be set independently.[8]

A necessary and sufficient condition for the capital stock ultimately to converge to a steady growth path is that this equation have real roots, and this will be so if and only if:

$$A\sigma(1 - \tau_y) \leq r(1 - \tau_b)\left[1 + \frac{hr(1 - \tau_b)}{2}\right] \qquad (2.14)$$

The smaller the adjustment cost, h, the smaller must the marginal physical product of capital A be, in order for a balanced growth path for capital to exist. This is because there is a tradeoff between the first and third components of the rates of return to capital given by the left-hand side of (2.4b). The smaller the adjustment cost h, the greater the returns to capital due to valuation differences between installed capital and the embodied resources and the greater the incentives to transform new output to capital. If for a given h, A is sufficiently large to reverse (2.14), the returns to capital dominate the returns to bonds, irrespective of the price of capital, so that no long-run balanced equilibrium can exist where the returns on the two assets are brought into equality.

Figure 2.1 illustrates the phase diagram for the differential equation (2.12) in the case where (2.14) holds, so that a steady asymptotic growth path for capital does indeed exist. In this case, the real solutions to the quadratic equation (2.13) are:

---

[8] We may also point out that if the convexity of the adjustment costs is represented by a higher-order term than a quadratic, then (2.13) would have more solutions and quite plausibly a multiplicity of feasible solutions.

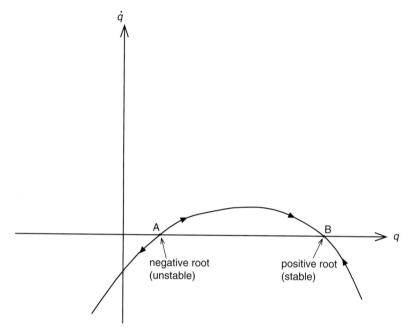

Figure 2.1 Phase diagram

$$q_1 = [1 + hr(1 - \tau_b)] - \sqrt{[1 + hr(1 - \tau_b)]^2 - [1 + 2hA\sigma(1 - \tau_y)]} \quad (2.15a)$$

$$q_2 = [1 + hr(1 - \tau_b)] + \sqrt{[1 + hr(1 - \tau_b)]^2 - [1 + 2hA\sigma(1 - \tau_y)]} \quad (2.15b)$$

indicating the potential existence for two steady equilibrium growth rates for capital. Two cases can be identified:

Case I: $r(1 - \tau_b) > A\sigma(1 - \tau_y)$, which implies $q_2 > 1 > q_1 > 0$
Case II: $r(1 - \tau_b) < A\sigma(1 - \tau_y)$, which implies $q_2 > q_1 > 1$

In either case it is seen from the phase diagram that the equilibrium point A, which corresponds to the smaller equilibrium value, q_1, is an unstable equilibrium, while B, which corresponds to the larger value, q_2, is locally stable. That is, if the system starts off with an initial value of q lying to the right of the point A, it will converge to B. Likewise, if it starts to the right of B, it will return to B. However, any time path for q which converges to B violates the transversality condition (2.4c). To see this, observe that:

$$\lim_{t\to\infty} q'Ke^{-pt} = \lim_{t\to\infty} q\lambda Ke^{-pt}$$

Solving equations (2.3′) and (2.4a), implies $K(t) = K_0 e^{\int_0^t \phi(s)ds}$; $\lambda(t) = \lambda(0)e^{(\rho - r(1-\tau_b))t}$, where K_0 is the given initial stock of domestic capital and $\lambda(0)$ is the endogenously determined initial marginal utility, so that:

$$\lim_{t\to\infty} q'Ke^{-pt} = \lim_{t\to\infty} q\lambda(0)K_0 e^{\left\{\int_0^t ([q(s)-1]/h)ds\right\} - r(1-\tau_b)t} \tag{2.16}$$

Substituting the larger root, q^2, from (2.15b) into this expression, it is seen that this limit diverges, thereby violating the transversality condition on the capital stock. Likewise, substituting the smaller root, q_1, from (2.15a), the transversality condition is shown to hold.[9] The behavior of q can thus be summarized by:

Proposition 2.1: The only solution for q that is consistent with the transversality condition is that q always be at the (unstable) steady-state solution q_1, given by the smaller root to (2.13). *Consequently there are no transitional dynamics in the market price of capital q.* In response to any shock, q immediately jumps to its new equilibrium value. Correspondingly, domestically domiciled capital is always on its steady growth path, growing at the rate $\phi = (q_1 - 1)/h$.

The domestic government is assumed to maintain a continuously balanced budget in accordance with (2.5), with all tax revenues being rebated back to the private sector, implying that the net rate of accumulation of traded bonds by the private sector, the current account balance, is described by (2.6). Substituting the expressions I and $K(t)$ from (2.3′) and $C(t)$ from (2.11) into (2.6), this accumulation equation can be written in the form:

$$\dot{B} = rB + \vartheta K_0 e^{\phi t} - C(0)e^{\psi t} \tag{2.17}$$

---

[9] There are some intermediate steps here that should be noted. If q were to converge to the larger (stable) root, q_2, it would do so along the stable adjustment path $q(s) = q_2 + (q(0) - q_2)e^{\mu t}$, where $\mu < 0$, is the corresponding stable eigenvalue. Along this path:

$$\int_0^t ([q(s) - 1]/h)ds = ([q_2 - 1]/h)t + ([q(0) - q_2]/\mu)(e^{\mu t} - 1)$$

Substituting this expression into (2.16), evaluating the expression, and letting $t \to \infty$ we verify that the transversality condition is indeed violated, as suggested in the text. In the case of the smaller (unstable) root there are no transitional dynamics; q is always at the unstable root and the fact that it satisfies the transversality condition can be verified by substituting $q(s) = q_1$ into (2.16) and evaluating the expression directly.

where ϕ and ψ are as defined in (2.3′) and (2.10) respectively, and:

$$\vartheta \equiv A - \frac{(q^2 - 1)}{2h} = q(r - \phi) + \left(A[1 - \sigma(1 - \tau_y)] - qr\tau_b\right) \quad (2.18)$$

The q appearing in (2.18) is the smaller root, q_1, reported in (2.15a), though for notational convenience the subscript 1 will henceforth be omitted.

The final step is to solve (2.17), which describes the accumulation of traded bonds. Starting from a given initial stock B_0, the stock of traded bonds at time t is given by:

$$B(t) = \left(B_0 + \frac{\vartheta K_0}{r - \phi} - \frac{C(0)}{r - \psi}\right)e^{rt} - \frac{\vartheta K_0}{r - \phi}e^{\phi t} + \frac{C(0)}{r - \psi}e^{\psi t} \quad (2.19)$$

In order to ensure national intertemporal solvency, the transversality conditions $\lim_{t \to \infty} \lambda B e^{-\rho t} = \lim_{t \to \infty} \lambda(0)B e^{-r(1-\tau_b)t} = 0$ must be satisfied, and this will hold if and only if:

$$r(1 - \tau_b) - \phi > 0 \quad (2.20a)$$

$$r(1 - \tau_b) - \psi > 0 \quad (2.20b)$$

$$C(0) = (r - \psi)\left(B_0 + \frac{\vartheta K_0}{r - \phi}\right) \quad (2.20c)$$

Condition (2.20a) is ensured by the solution q_1, while (2.20b) imposes an upper bound on the rate of growth of consumption. This latter condition reduces to $\rho > \gamma r(1 - \tau_b)$ and is certainly met in the case of a logarithmic utility function. The third condition determines the feasible initial level of consumption and if this condition is imposed, the equilibrium stock of traded bonds follows the path:

$$B(t) = \left(B_0 + \frac{\vartheta K_0}{r - \phi}\right)e^{\psi t} - \left(\frac{\vartheta K_0}{r - \phi}\right)e^{\phi t} \quad (2.21)$$

2.3 Equilibrium in one-good model

Equations (2.3′), (2.11), and (2.21), together with the solution for q and the initial condition (2.20c), comprise a closed-form solution describing the evolution of the small open economy starting from given initial stocks of traded bonds, B_0, and capital stock, K_0. One additional variable of importance is domestic wealth, $W(t) = B(t) + qK(t)$, which can be expressed as follows:

$$W(t) = (B_0 + qK_0)e^{\psi t} + \left(\frac{\vartheta}{r - \phi} - 1\right)K_0\left[e^{\psi t} - e^{\phi t}\right] \qquad (2.22)$$

A key quantity in the above solution is $(\vartheta/(r - \phi))$. From the definition appearing in (2.18), this equals $[q + (A[1 - \sigma(1 - \tau_y)] - qr\tau_b)]/(r - \phi)$ and represents the price of capital, adjusted for both taxes and the aggregate production externality. Thus we shall define $W_T(t) \equiv B(t) + (\vartheta/(r - \phi))K(t)$ to be "adjusted" wealth. Consequently, equation (2.20c) indicates that the initial consumption $C(0)$ is proportional to the initial adjusted wealth $W_T(0)$. Furthermore, combining (2.3′) and (2.21), we see that $W_T(t) = W_T(0)e^{\psi t}$, so that with consumption growing at the same rate, consumption is proportional to the adjusted wealth at all points of time.

The following three additional general characteristics of this equilibrium can be observed.

(i) Consumption and adjusted wealth on the one hand, and physical capital on the other, are always on their respective steady-state growth paths, growing at the rates ψ and ϕ respectively. The former is driven by the difference between the after-tax rate of return on foreign bonds and the domestic rate of time preference; the latter by q, which is determined by the technological conditions in the domestic economy, as represented by the marginal physical product of capital σA, and adjustment costs h, relative to the return on foreign assets. For the simple linear production function, the rate of growth of capital also determines the equilibrium growth of domestic output, $\dot{Y}/Y$.

Thus an important feature of this equilibrium is that it can sustain differential growth rates of consumption and domestic output. This is a consequence of the economy being small and open. It is in sharp contrast to a closed economy in which, constrained by the growth of its own resources, all real variables, including consumption and output, would ultimately have to grow at the same rate. In order to sustain such an equilibrium we shall assume that the country is sufficiently small that it can maintain a growth rate that is unrelated to that in the rest of the world. Ultimately, this requirement imposes a constraint on the growth rate of the domestic economy. If it grows faster than does the rest of the world, at some point it will cease to be small. While we do not attempt to resolve this issue here, we note that the question of convergence of international growth rates has been an area of intensive research activity; see e.g. Barro and Sala-i-Martin (1992b), Mankiw, Romer, and Weil (1992), Razin and Yuen (1994, 1996), Galor (1996), Quah (1996).

(ii) Holdings of traded bonds are subject to transitional dynamics, in the sense that their growth rate $\dot{B}/B$ varies through time. Asymptotically, the growth rate converges to $[\psi, \phi]$, and which it will be depends critically upon the size of the consumer rate of time preference relative to the rates of return on investment opportunities. In the case of the logarithmic utility function ($\gamma = 0$)

$$\text{sgn}(\phi - \psi) = \text{sgn}\left(\rho - \frac{1}{h}\sqrt{[1 + hr(1 - \tau_b)]^2 - [1 + 2hA\sigma(1 - \tau_y)]}\right) \quad (2.23)$$

Suppose that domestic agents are sufficiently patient (i.e. ρ is sufficiently small) that both expressions appearing in (2.23) are negative. Thus $\psi > \phi$ and in the long run domestic consumption will grow at a faster rate than the domestic capital stock or domestic output. Being patient, the agents choose to consume a small fraction of their tax-adjusted wealth. This enables them to accumulate foreign assets, running up a current account surplus and generating a positively growing stock of foreign assets. It is the income from these assets that permits the small economy to sustain a long-run growth rate of consumption in excess of the growth rate of domestic productive capacity. The opposite applies if $\psi < \phi$. In the long run, the country accumulates an ever increasing foreign *debt* (see [2.21]) and is unable to maintain a consumption growth rate equal to that of domestic output.[10]

(iii) The final feature of the equilibrium is that with all taxes being fully rebated, it is completely neutral with respect to the consumption tax, which has no effect on any aspect of the economic performance. In this circumstance, the consumption tax acts like a pure lump-sum tax. This is because the labor supply is assumed to be fixed so that we are excluding a possible labor–leisure choice, which in general causes the consumption tax to have real effects.

2.3.1 Taxes and growth

With the neutrality of consumption taxes, we can focus on the two forms of income taxation. Differentiating the solution for q_1, together with the

---

[10] The result that a patient country is able to sustain a higher long-run consumption growth rate than an impatient country is analogous to the result of Jones and Manuelli (1990), where they show that with identical rates of time preference, a country without taxes will grow at a faster rate than one with taxes. The parallel can be seen most directly from equation (2.10) where increasing patience (reducing ρ) is equivalent to reducing the tax rate. Jones and Manuelli also briefly discuss heterogeneous agents having different rates of time preference.

definition of the growth rate of capital we obtain

$$\frac{dq}{d\tau_b} = \frac{qr}{r(1 - \tau_b) - \phi} > 0 \tag{2.24a}$$

$$\frac{dq}{d\tau_y} = -\frac{A\sigma}{r(1 - \tau_b) - \phi} < 0 \tag{2.24b}$$

We may thus state:

Proposition 2.2: An increase in the tax on bond income increases the growth rate of capital and reduces the growth rate of consumption. An increase in the tax on capital income reduces the growth rate of capital, but leaves the growth rate of consumption unaffected.

Intuitively, an increase in the tax on bond income lowers the rate of return on bonds, thereby inducing investors to increase the proportion of capital in their portfolios, raising the price of capital and inducing growth in capital. In addition, this tax induces agents to switch from saving to consumption, increasing the ratio of consumption to tax-adjusted wealth. This slows down the rate of growth of consumption. An increase in the tax on capital income generates the opposite portfolio response, lowering the growth rate of capital. On the other hand, the growth rate (but not the level) of consumption is unaffected by the tax on capital income.

2.3.2 Taxes and welfare

A key issue concerns the effects of tax changes, on the level of welfare of the representative agent, when consumption follows its optimal path, namely the expression:[11]

$$\Omega = \int_0^\infty \frac{1}{\gamma} [C(0)e^{\psi t}]^\gamma e^{-\rho t} dt = \frac{[C(0)]^\gamma}{\gamma(\rho - \gamma\psi)} \tag{2.25}$$

Thus, the overall intertemporal welfare effects of any policy change depend upon their effects on (i) the initial consumption level, and (ii) the growth rate of consumption.

---

[11] The transversality condition (2.20b) implies that $\rho > \psi\gamma$ so that the integral in (2.25) converges.

Consider first a change in the tax on capital τ_y. Its effect on the initial level of utility $(1/\gamma)\,[C(0)]^\gamma$, say, is given by $[C(0)]^{\gamma-1}\,(\partial C(0)/\partial \tau_y)$. Starting from an initial situation of zero taxes:

$$\frac{\partial C(0)}{\partial \tau_y} = (r - \psi)\left[\frac{\partial q}{\partial \tau_y} + \frac{A\sigma}{r - \phi}\right] = 0 \qquad (2.26)$$

leaving initial welfare unaffected. It then follows from (2.25) that since it has no effect on the consumption growth rate, the capital income tax has no impact on the time profile of utility, leaving total overall discounted welfare unchanged as well.

The effect of a tax on bond income on welfare has two components. Starting from an initial zero tax equilibrium, its impact on initial consumption is:

$$\frac{\partial C(0)}{\partial \tau_b} = \frac{r}{1 - \gamma}\left[B_0 + \frac{\theta K_0}{r - \phi}\right] + (r - \psi)\left[\frac{\partial q}{\partial \tau_b} - \frac{qr}{r - \phi}\right] \qquad (2.27)$$

The first component reflects the fact that the higher tax on bond income raises the fraction of tax-adjusted wealth that is consumed and this is welfare-improving. The second component is the effect on the tax-adjusted price of capital and, as for the capital income tax, this is zero. Thus in the short run, a higher tax on bond income raises consumption and is therefore welfare-improving. However, its effect on the growth rate of consumption is negative, so that the short-run gains come at the expense of longer-run losses. Indeed, it is straightforward to establish that the net effects on the discounted utility measure (2.25) are exactly offsetting so that starting from zero taxes, the imposition of a tax on bond income (with appropriate rebating) has no effects on overall intertemporal welfare. All it does is to redistribute the time path of consumer welfare. We may summarize these results in:

Proposition 2.3: Starting from zero taxes, an increase in either form of income tax leaves the overall level of welfare unchanged. However, the two taxes do have fundamentally different effects on the time profile of consumer welfare.

2.3.3 Wasted tax revenues

An alternative assumption for separating tax from expenditure effects, introduced for example by Rebelo (1991), is that the tax revenues, instead of being rebated, are wasted on useless government expenditure which has no effect on the behavior of the private sector or the resources available to it. The components of the equilibrium determined by the optimality conditions characterizing the behavior of the representative agent remain unchanged. In particular, the equilibrium value of q and the growth of capital ϕ remain as described in Proposition 2.1. The equilibrium growth rate of consumption ψ, which is determined by: $\dot{\lambda}/\lambda$, also remains unchanged, as defined in (2.10). Because the tax revenues are no longer rebated, what changes is the level of consumption and the measure of wealth to which it is tied. Specifically, one can show that now the evolution of wealth and consumption are related by:

$$\dot{W} = r(1 - \tau_b)W - (1 + \tau_c)C(0)e^{\psi t}$$

The solution to this equation, together with the transversality condition, implies that the equilibrium consumption to wealth ratio is now the following constant:

$$\frac{C(t)}{W(t)} = \frac{\rho - \gamma\psi}{1 + \tau_c} \qquad (2.28)$$

and wealth grows at the same steady rate as consumption.

Tax rates impact on the various growth rates in much the same way as before. The tax on foreign bond income raises q and thus the growth rate of capital and domestic output, while it lowers the growth rate of total wealth and consumption. The tax on capital income lowers the growth rate of capital, but has no effect on the growth rates of consumption or wealth. The lack of impact on the growth of wealth is different from (2.22), which implied that with rebating, the capital income tax will influence the transitional path of wealth.

The consumption tax has no effect on any growth rate nor does it affect wealth. However, it does lower the consumption to wealth ratio and therefore the level of consumption at all points of time. In the absence of rebating this is unambiguously welfare-deteriorating. A tax on capital income leaves the consumption to wealth ratio unchanged. But by reducing the price of capital, q, it reduces wealth, thereby lowering consumption at all points of time, and it too is unambiguously welfare-deteriorating.

The tax on foreign bond income is less clear. By increasing q it raises wealth, while at the same time reducing the consumption–wealth ratio, and this may result in either a higher or lower level of consumption in the short run. But by reducing the growth rate of consumption it always induces long-run losses. The foreign bond tax will always be ultimately welfare-deteriorating if $\psi > \phi$, when the domestic economy is a net creditor. However, if $\phi > \psi$, so that the economy is ultimately a net debtor, then such a tax may become welfare-enhancing. The reason is simply that without rebating, in this case it represents a subsidy rather than a tax.

2.4 Productive government expenditure

Thus far we have focused on the taxation side of the government budget. But most tax revenues are used to finance government expenditures, which provide some benefits to the economy. We shall focus on government expenditure that enhances the productive capacity of the economy, identifying such expenditures as being on some form of infrastructure.

2.4.1 The Barro model

This model was first applied to a closed economy by Barro (1990) and, like Barro, we shall make the simplifying assumption that the benefits are derived from the *flow* of productive government expenditures.[12] In Chapter 4 below, we shall discuss in some detail the more plausible case where it is the accumulated *stock* of government expenditure that is the more appropriate measure of productive government expenditure.

We continue to abstract from labor (maintaining $l = \bar{l}$) and assume that the production function of the representative firm is now specified by:

$$Y_i = AG_s^\eta K_i^{1-\eta} \equiv A(G_s/K_i)^\eta K_i, \quad 0 < \eta < 1 \qquad (2.29)$$

where G_s denotes the flow of productive services enjoyed by the individual firm. As in Section 2.3, we assume that the population growth $n = 0$. Thus productive expenditure has the property of positive, but diminishing, marginal physical product, while enhancing the productivity of private capital.

We shall assume that the services derived from aggregate expenditure, G, are:

$$G_s = G\left(\frac{K_i}{K}\right)^{1-\varepsilon} \qquad (2.30)$$

where K denotes the aggregate capital stock. As Barro and Sala-i-Martin (1992a) have argued, most public services are characterized by some degree of

---

[12] In Turnovsky (1996b) we discuss the parallel case where government expenditure is on a utility-enhancing consumption good.

congestion; there are few pure public goods. It is straightforward to parameterize the degree of congestion. This is important since the degree of congestion is to some extent the outcome of a policy decision, and, once determined, congestion turns out to be a critical determinant of optimal tax policy. Substituting (2.30) into (2.29), the individual's production function can be expressed as:

$$Y_i = AG^\eta \left(\frac{K_i}{K}\right)^{\eta(1-\varepsilon)} K_i^{1-\eta} = AG^\eta K_i^{1-\varepsilon\eta} K^{-\eta(1-\varepsilon)} \qquad (2.31)$$

Equation (2.30) is one convenient formulation of congestion that builds on the public goods literature; see Edwards (1990). It implies that in order for the level of public services, G_s, available to the individual agent to remain constant over time, given his individual capital stock, K_i, the growth rate of G must be related to that of K in accordance with $\dot{G}/G = (1 - \varepsilon)\dot{K}/K$. Congestion increases if aggregate usage increases relative to individual usage, and a good example of this type of congestion is the service provided by highways. Unless an individual drives his car (uses his capital), he derives no service from a publicly provided highway, and in general, the service he derives depends upon his own usage relative to that of others in the economy, as total usage contributes to congestion.

The parameter ε can be interpreted as describing the degree of relative congestion associated with the public good, and the following special cases merit comment. If $\varepsilon = 1$, the level of services derived by the individual from the government expenditure is fixed at G, independent of both the individual's own usage of capital and aggregate usage. The good G is a non-rival, non-excludable public good that is available equally to each individual; there is no congestion. Since few, if any, such public goods exist, it is probably best viewed as a benchmark. At the other extreme, if $\varepsilon = 0$, then only if G increases in direct proportion to the aggregate capital stock, K, does the level of the public service available to the individual remain fixed. We shall refer to this case as being one of *proportional* (relative) congestion. In that case, the public good is like a private good, in that since $K = NK_i$, the individual receives his proportionate share of services. This can be seen by setting $\varepsilon = 0$ in (2.31).

In order to sustain an equilibrium of ongoing growth, government expenditure cannot be fixed at some exogenous level, but rather must be tied to the scale of the economy. This can be achieved most conveniently by assuming that the government sets its level of expenditure as a share of aggregate output, $Y = NY_i$:

$$G = gY \qquad (2.32)$$

In an environment of growth this is a reasonable assumption. Government expenditure thus increases with the size of the economy, with an expansionary government expenditure being denoted by an increase in g.

Summing (2.29) over the N identical agents and substituting (2.30) and (2.32), we obtain

$$G = (AgN^{\eta\varepsilon})^{1/(1-\eta)}K$$
$$Y_i = (Ag^{\eta}N^{\eta\varepsilon})^{1/(1-\eta)}K_i \qquad (2.33)$$
$$Y = (Ag^{\eta}N^{\eta\varepsilon})^{1/(1-\eta)}K$$

In equilibrium, each firm thus has the fixed AK technology, as does aggregate output, where the productivity of capital depends (positively) upon the productive government input. Notice that provided $\eta\varepsilon > 0$, the productivity of capital depends upon the size (scale) of the economy, as parameterized by the fixed population, N. This is because the size of the externality generated by government expenditure increases with the size of the economy, playing an analogous role to aggregate capital in the Romer (1986) model. As in that model, this scale effect disappears if $\varepsilon = 0$, so that there is proportional congestion and each agent receives his own individual share of government services, G/N.

We now re-solve the representative individual's optimization problem. In so doing, he is assumed to take aggregate government spending, G, and the aggregate stock of capital, K, as given, insofar as these impact on the productivity of his capital stock. Performing the optimization, the optimality conditions (2.2a), (2.2c), and (2.4a) remain unchanged. The optimality condition with respect to capital is now modified to:

$$\frac{(1-\tau_y)(1-\eta\varepsilon)Y_i}{qK_i} + \frac{\dot{q}}{q} + \frac{(q-1)^2}{2hq} = r(1-\tau_b) \qquad (2.4b')$$

The difference is that the private marginal physical product of capital is now proportional to $(1-\eta\varepsilon)$, depending both upon the degree of congestion and the productivity of government expenditure. The less congestion (the larger ε), the less the benefits of government expenditure are tied to the usage of private capital, thus lowering the return. The other modifications are to the government budget constraint (2.5) and the current account relationship (2.6), which are modified to:

$$\tau_y Y + \tau_b rB + \tau_c C = G \qquad (2.5')$$

and

$$\dot{B} = Y + rB - C - I[1 + (h/2)(I/K)] - G \qquad (2.6')$$

The key point to be made is that the equilibrium structure basically remains intact. The consumption growth rate is still given by (2.10). The growth rates of the capital stock and therefore output continue to be given by (2.3′) where q is the smaller root to the quadratic equation (2.4b′). It is clear from this relationship that the growth rate of production is affected by both the tax rates and government expenditure insofar as the latter influences the equilibrium productivity of capital, as indicated in (2.31).

2.4.2 Optimal fiscal policy

It is clear from Section 2.4.1 that in this model, growth and economic performance are heavily influenced by fiscal policy. This naturally leads to the important question of the optimal tax structure. To address this issue it is convenient to consider, as a benchmark, the first-best optimum of the central planner, who controls resources directly, against which the decentralized economy can be assessed. The central planner is assumed to internalize the equilibrium relationship $NK_i = K$, as well as the expenditure rule (2.32). The optimality conditions are now modified to:

$$C_i^{\gamma-1} = \lambda \qquad (2.2a')$$

$$1 + h(I_i/K_i) = q \qquad (2.2c')$$

$$\rho - \frac{\dot{\lambda}}{\lambda} = r \qquad (2.4a'')$$

$$\frac{(1-g)Y_i}{qK_i} + \frac{\dot{q}}{q} + \frac{(q-1)^2}{2hq} = r \qquad (2.4b'')$$

The key difference is that the social return to capital nets out the fraction of output appropriated by the government.

It is straightforward to show that the decentralized economy will replicate the first-best equilibrium of the centrally planned economy if and only if:

$$\tau_b = 0 \qquad (2.34a)$$

$$(1 - g) = (1 - \tau_y)(1 - \varepsilon \eta) \tag{2.34b}$$

The first condition follows from the fact that since there is no distortion to correct in the international bond market the optimal tax on foreign bond income should be zero. By contrast, government expenditure, by being tied to the stock of capital in the economy, induces spillovers into the domestic capital market, generating distortions that require a tax on capital income in order to ensure that the net private return on capital equals its social return.

To better understand (2.34b), it is useful to observe that the welfare-maximizing share of government expenditure is (Barro, 1990):[13]

$$\hat{g} = \eta \tag{2.35}$$

Substituting (2.35) into (2.34b) and simplifying, the optimal income tax can be expressed in the form:

$$\hat{\tau}_y = \frac{g - \eta \varepsilon}{1 - \eta \varepsilon} = \frac{g - \hat{g}}{1 - \eta \varepsilon} + \frac{\hat{g}(1 - \varepsilon)}{(1 - \eta \varepsilon)} \tag{2.34b$'$}$$

In order to finance its expenditures (2.5$'$), the government must, in conjunction with $\hat{\tau}_y$, set a corresponding consumption tax $\hat{\tau}_c$:

$$\hat{\tau}_c = \frac{\eta \varepsilon (1 - g)}{(1 - \eta \varepsilon)(C/Y)} \tag{2.34c}$$

Equation (2.34b$'$) emphasizes that the optimal tax on capital income corrects for two distortions. The first is due to the deviation in government expenditure from the optimum; the second is caused by congestion. Comparing (2.34b$'$) and (2.34c) we see that there is a tradeoff between the income tax and the consumption tax in achieving these objectives, and that this depends primarily upon the degree of congestion. In the case where $\varepsilon = 1$, so that there is no congestion, capital income should be taxed only to the extent that the share of government expenditure deviates from the social optimum. The tradeoff between the two taxes is seen most directly if g is set optimally in accordance with (2.35). In this case, if there is no congestion, government expenditure should be fully financed by a consumption tax alone; capital

---

[13] This is obtained by maximizing utility with respect to g. We can also show that setting g in accordance with (2.35) maximizes the output growth rate, just as it does in the closed economy. But in contrast to the closed economy, the consumption growth rate is given by (2.10) and is independent of government spending.

income should remain untaxed. As congestion increases (ε declines), the optimal consumption tax should be reduced and the income tax increased until, with proportional congestion, government expenditure should be financed entirely by an income tax.

It is useful to compare the present optimal tax on capital with the well-known Chamley (1986) proposition which requires that asymptotically the optimal tax on capital should converge to zero. The Chamley analysis did not consider any externalities from government expenditure. Setting $\eta = 0$, we still find that the optimal tax on capital is equal to the share of output claimed by the government ($\hat{\tau}_y = g$). The difference is that by specifying government expenditure as a fraction of output, its level is not exogenous, but instead is proportional to the size of the growing capital stock. The decision to accumulate capital stock by the private sector leads to an increase in the supply of public goods in the future. If the private sector treats government spending as independent of its investment decision (when in fact it is not), a tax on capital is necessary to internalize the externality and thereby correct the distortion. Thus, in general, the Chamley rule of not taxing capital in the long run will be non-optimal, although it will emerge in the special case where $g = \eta\varepsilon$, in which case there is no spillover from government expenditure to the capital market.

2.5 Two immediate generalizations

As we have noted, an equilibrium of ongoing growth will emerge only if the underlying preference and production functions yield an equilibrium in which the ratios of the endogenously growing quantities are constant. This involves severe restrictions, and indeed we have focused on the Cobb–Douglas production function and a constant elasticity utility function. Both of these specifications can be generalized to some degree, as we now briefly discuss.

2.5.1 More general production function

The critical feature of the production function is that it be homogeneous of degree one in the accumulating factors. Thus for example, the production function for the individual firm in (2.8) could be generalized to:

$$Y_i = F([(1 - l)K], K_i) \tag{2.36}$$

where $F(\cdot, \cdot)$ is homogeneous of degree one in its two arguments. Using the homogeneity, the equilibrium marginal product of capital (obtained by imposing the equilibrium condition $K_i = K$) is:

$$\frac{\partial Y_i}{\partial K_i} = f(1 - l) - (1 - l)f'(1 - l)$$

where $f(1 - l) \equiv F(1 - l, 1)$ and equilibrium aggregate output is:

$$Y = NY_i = F\left(\frac{(1 - l)K}{K_i}, 1\right)NK_i = f(1 - l)K$$

This structure enables all of the previous analysis to go through without imposing the Cobb–Douglas specification. An example of this more general specification is provided in the analysis involving public capital discussed in the latter part of Chapter 4. It is illustrated further in the numerical simulations carried out in Chapter 8, which employ the constant elasticity of substitution (CES) production function.

2.5.2 More general utility specification

Our analysis has focused on a single traded good, which again is a restriction and obviously precludes consideration of some of the key issues in international economics, pertaining to the real exchange rate, for example. While we shall take up this issue in greater depth in Chapter 5, where we develop a richer two-sector model, we shall indicate one straightforward extension of the present analysis that can easily accommodate two consumption goods, one produced domestically, the other imported. This type of specification has been extensively used in studying terms of trade shocks in the context of the Laursen–Metzler (1950) effect; see e.g. Obstfeld (1982).

Suppose that the instantaneous utility function is of the constant elasticity of substitution (CES) form:

$$U = \frac{1}{\gamma}\left(aC_D^{-\nu} + (1 - a)C_M^{-\nu}\right)^{-\frac{\gamma}{\nu}}$$

where $\varepsilon \equiv \frac{1}{1+\nu}$ is the elasticity of substitution in consumption between C_D, a domestically produced good, and C_M, an imported consumption good. Let us consider a small open economy which faces a fixed relative price, p, between these two goods. Dropping the index for the individual, we assume that the consumer's objective is to maximize:

$$\int_0^\infty \frac{1}{\gamma}\left(aC_D^{-\nu} + (1-a)C_M^{-\nu}\right)^{-\frac{\gamma}{\nu}} e^{-\rho t}\, dt \qquad (2.37a)$$

subject to the accumulation equation modified to:

$$\dot{B} = (1-\tau_y)Y + [r(1-\tau_b) - n]B - (1+\tau_c)[C_D + pC_M]$$
$$- I\left(1 + \frac{h}{2}\frac{I}{K}\right) + T \qquad (2.37b)$$

together with the previous production and capital accumulation conditions.

The difference arises with respect to the equilibrium conditions for consumption and we shall focus our attention on them, since all other conditions remain unchanged. There are now two optimality conditions for consumption:

$$\left(aC_D^{-\nu} + (1-a)C_M^{-\nu}\right)^{-\frac{(\gamma+\nu)}{\nu}} aC_D^{-\nu-1} = \lambda \qquad (2.38a)$$

$$\left(aC_D^{-\nu} + (1-a)C_M^{-\nu}\right)^{-\frac{(\gamma+\nu)}{\nu}} (1-a)C_M^{-\nu-1} = \lambda p \qquad (2.38b)$$

Dividing (2.38b) by (2.38a) yields:

$$(1-a)C_D^{\nu+1} = apC_M^{\nu+1}$$

Now define:

$$C^{1+\nu} \equiv C_D^{1+\nu} + pC_M^{1+\nu}$$

It then follows that:

$$C_D = a^{\frac{1}{1+\nu}}C \qquad (2.39a)$$

$$C_M = \left(\frac{1-a}{p}\right)^{\frac{1}{1+\nu}} C \qquad (2.39b)$$

With a, p being constant, we immediately have:

$$\frac{\dot{C}_D}{C_D} = \frac{\dot{C}_M}{C_M} = \frac{\dot{C}}{C} \qquad (2.40)$$

Now take the time derivative of (2.38a):

$$-(1+v)\frac{\dot{C}_D}{C_D} + (\gamma+v)\left[\frac{aC_D^{-v}(\dot{C}_D/C_D) + (1-a)C_M^{-v}(\dot{C}_M/C_M)}{aC_D^{-v} + (1-a)C_M^{-v}}\right] = \frac{\dot{\lambda}}{\lambda}$$

and combine this equation with (2.40) and (2.4a). This yields:

$$\frac{\dot{C}_D}{C_D} = \frac{\dot{C}_M}{C_M} = \frac{\dot{C}}{C} = \frac{r(1-\tau_b)-\rho}{1-\gamma} \qquad (2.41)$$

It thus follows that consumption of the two goods, the domestic and imported, grows at the same rate, as does aggregate consumption, $\hat{C} \equiv C_D + pC_M$. Moreover, since the growth rate of production is independent of consumption, the growth rate of capital and output will be unaffected by the presence of the second consumption good. Its impact will be on the accumulation of traded bonds as reflected in (2.37b).

3

Basic growth model with endogenous labor supply

3.1 Introduction

The endogenous growth model analyzed in Chapter 2 includes two interdependent critical knife-edge restrictions: (i) inelastic labor supply, and (ii) fixed productivity of capital. The structure of the equilibrium changes fundamentally when the labor supply is endogenized. This introduces two key changes. The first is that the production function is modified to (2.8), so that the productivity of capital now depends positively upon the fraction of time devoted to productive labor. Second, the fixed endowment of a unit of time leads to the requirement that the steady-state allocation of time between labor and leisure must be constant. This latter condition provides a link between the long-run rate of growth of consumption and the rate of growth of output, forcing them to grow at the same constant rate.

In this chapter we address the role of an elastic supply of labor in some depth, focusing particularly on the effectiveness of fiscal policy in such an economy. As in a closed economy, endogenizing labor supply leads to important changes in the equilibrium structure of the economy, and has important implications for fiscal policy. But in contrast to the closed economy, the introduction of an elastic labor supply yields a *less*, rather than a more, potent role for distortionary taxes in influencing the equilibrium growth rate. Not only do the taxes on wage income and consumption continue to have very limited effects, but now, in addition, the capital income tax ceases to have any effect on the growth rate of output and capital. All the adjustment to a capital income tax now takes place through the labor–leisure choice and the resulting adjustment in the capital–labor ratio. Indeed, with elastically supplied labor, the equilibrium growth rate of output becomes independent of almost all fiscal instruments, including government expenditure, the only instrument to have any influence being the tax on foreign interest income.

The fact that the equilibrium growth rate is invariant with respect to the main fiscal instruments is of interest to the recent debate regarding the empirical relevance of the AK endogenous growth model. Empirical studies by Easterly and Rebelo (1993), Jones (1995b), and Stokey and Rebelo (1995), which suggest that the effects of tax rates on long-run growth rates are insignificant, or weak at best, have been taken as evidence against AK models that predict large growth effects from taxation. However, the implications of the present model of a small open economy with endogenous labor supply turn out to be entirely consistent with these empirical findings, which may therefore be viewed as being supportive of this form of AK growth model.

Our analysis of fiscal policy focuses on two general issues. First, we conduct a number of comparative static exercises, analyzing the effects of distortionary tax changes and government expenditure changes (which we take to be on a productive good) on the equilibrium growth–leisure (employment) tradeoff. We find many striking contrasts between the effects of various policy changes in closed and open economies respectively. For example, an increase in the tax on capital income in the decentralized economy now leads to a decline in leisure (increase in labor supply), whereas in the analogous closed economy just the opposite occurs. Likewise, an increase in government expenditure in the present open economy, financed by a lump-sum tax, leads to an increase in leisure (decline in labor supply), again in contrast to the closed economy.

The key mechanism generating these results is the assumption that the small open economy has access to a perfect world capital market that pays a fixed rate of return, r. This rate of return, together with preference parameters, pins down the equilibrium growth rate. The equilibrium equality between the after-tax rates of return on domestic capital and foreign bonds then determines the equilibrium output–capital ratio, which is increasing in labor supply and government expenditure. An increase in the tax on capital income reduces the net return on capital and requires an increase in labor supply in order for the equilibrium arbitrage condition to hold. An increase in government expenditure raises the return to capital and requires a decrease in labor supply for this equilibrium condition to be maintained. For convenience, Table 3.1 summarizes the key qualitative differences of fiscal policy between open and closed economies, for both fixed and elastically supplied labor.

The second issue we address is optimal fiscal policy. If government expenditure is set optimally, then capital income should not be taxed, while consumption and leisure should be taxed uniformly. If government expenditure is not at its optimal level, it introduces a distortion to the

Table 3.1. *Summary of qualitative effects of fiscal shocks in a decentralized economy*

	Closed economy		Open economy		
	$\tilde{\psi}$	$\tilde{l}$	$\tilde{\psi}_c$	$\tilde{\psi}_k$	$\tilde{l}$
Increase in productive government expenditure, g					
Fixed labor	+	0	0	+	0
Endogenous labor	+	−	0	0	+
Increase in capital income tax, τ_k					
Fixed labor	−	0	0	−	0
Endogenous labor	−	+	0	0	−
Increase in labor income tax, τ_w, or consumption tax, τ_c					
Fixed labor	0	0	0	0	0
Endogenous labor	−	+	0	0	0

Note: $\tilde{\psi}_c$ and $\tilde{\psi}_k$ denote the equilibrium growth rates of consumption and capital (output) respectively. These are distinct for the open economy with fixed labor supply; they are identical in all other cases.

domestic capital market, requiring a tax on capital income for its correction. These optimal policies are essentially as in the analogous closed economy. This is hardly surprising since similar distortions are being corrected in the two cases. But, in addition, for the form of government expenditure rule being considered, foreign interest income should remain untaxed.

3.2 The analytical framework: centrally planned economy[1]

Given our emphasis on discussing optimal fiscal policy, it is convenient to begin by setting out the equilibrium for the centrally planned economy to serve as a benchmark. As in Chapter 2, the small open economy comprises *N* identical individuals, each of whom has an infinite planning horizon and possesses perfect foresight. Since we wish to focus on the endogenous growth equilibrium, population remains fixed over time. We shall also assume that the externality generating endogenous growth is due to productive government spending, thereby extending the Barro (1990) model discussed in Section 2.4 to incorporate endogenous labor supply. Thus,

---

[1] This material is adapted from Turnovsky (1999).

output of the individual firm, Y_i, is determined by the Cobb–Douglas production function:

$$Y_i = aG^\eta (1 - l)^\eta K_i^{1-\eta} \quad 0 < \eta < 1 \tag{3.1}$$

where K_i denotes the individual's capital stock, assumed to be infinitely durable, and G denotes the flow of services from government spending on the economy's infrastructure. We assume that these services are congestion-free so that G is a pure public good.[2] The individual firm faces positive, but diminishing, marginal physical products in all factors, constant returns to scale in the private factors, capital and labor, and constant returns to scale in private capital and in government production expenditure.[3] As noted in Chapter 2, to ensure ongoing growth, we shall assume that government claims a fraction, g, of aggregate output, Y, for expenditure on a productive activity (infrastructure), in accordance with:

$$G = gY \quad 0 < g < 1 \tag{3.2}$$

Thus, combining (3.1) with (3.2), and noting $Y = NY_i$, aggregate output in the economy is given by:

$$Y = (Ag^\eta)^{1/(1-\eta)} (1 - l)^{\eta/(1-\eta)} K \tag{3.3}$$

where $A = aN^\eta$. As in Section 2.4, the aggregate production function is an AK technology, though now the productivity of the aggregate capital stock depends positively upon the fraction of time devoted to work, as well as the share of productive government expenditure.

The representative agent's welfare is given by the intertemporal isoelastic utility function:[4]

$$\Omega \equiv \int_0^\infty (1/\gamma)(C_i l^\theta)^\gamma e^{-\rho t} dt = \int_0^\infty (1/\gamma)\left(\tfrac{C}{N} l^\theta\right)^\gamma e^{-\rho t} dt;$$
$$-\infty < \gamma < 1; \quad \theta > 0, 1 > \gamma(1 + \theta), 1 > \gamma\theta \tag{3.4a}$$

---

[2] Congestion can be introduced along the lines of Section 2.4.
[3] Recall that in order to assure ongoing growth the production function must be linearly homogeneous in the factors that are being accumulated. This requires that, in equilibrium, government expenditure be tied to the capital stock and that the production function have constant returns to scale in capital and government expenditure.
[4] In general the introduction of leisure will be consistent with a balanced growth equilibrium as long as the utility function is of one of the two following forms (see Ladrón-de-Guevara, Otigueira, and Santos, 1997):

$$u(C, l) = (1/\gamma)C^\gamma f(l), \gamma > 1, \gamma \neq 0 \text{ or}$$
$$u(C, l) = \ln C + f(l), \text{ for } \gamma = 0$$

The constant utility formulation being adopted here is of this class.

He also accumulates physical capital in accordance with the convex cost of adjustment function (2.1c) which, aggregating over the N individuals, leads to:

$$\Phi(I,K) = \frac{I + \frac{h}{2}I^2}{K} = I\left(1 + \frac{h}{2}\frac{I}{K}\right) \qquad (3.4b)$$

The aggregate economy accumulates net foreign bonds, B, that pay an exogenously given world interest rate, r, subject to the accumulation equation:

$$\dot{B} = Y + rB - C - I[1 + (h/2)(I/K)] - G \qquad (3.4c)$$

where we have substituted for the cost function $\Phi(I, K)$. We continue to assume that capital does not depreciate, so that the economy also faces the physical capital accumulation constraint:

$$\dot{K} = I \qquad (3.4d)$$

In this section, we consider the equilibrium generated in a centrally planned economy in which the planner chooses C, I, and l, together with K and B, to maximize the utility of the representative agent (3.4a), subject to the aggregate resource constraint of the economy (3.4c), the capital accumulation equation (3.4d), and the aggregate production function (3.3). We begin by assuming that the government's share of output used for production, g, is fixed arbitrarily; in Section 3.2.3 below we consider the case where g is set optimally, along with the other decision variables.

The optimality conditions with respect to C, l, and I, consist of the following:

$$N^{-\gamma}C^{\gamma-1}l^{\theta\gamma} = \lambda \qquad (3.5a)$$

$$N^{-\gamma}\theta C^{\gamma}l^{\theta\gamma-1} = \lambda(1-g)\left(\frac{\eta}{1-\eta}\right)\frac{Y}{1-l} \qquad (3.5b)$$

$$1 + h\frac{I}{K} = q \qquad (3.5c)$$

where q is the shadow price of capital, normalized by the marginal utility of wealth, λ.

Dividing (3.5b) by (3.5a) the first two equations can expressed as:

$$\theta \frac{C}{l} = (1 - g)\left(\frac{\eta}{1 - \eta}\right)\frac{Y}{(1 - l)}$$

On the left-hand side we see that with the allocation of time remaining bounded ($0 < l < 1$), the marginal rate of substitution between consumption and leisure grows with consumption. On the right-hand side we see that, given the fixed allocation of labor, the social return to labor (the wage rate) grows with output. Rewriting this equation as:

$$\frac{C}{Y} = \left(\frac{l}{1 - l}\right)\left(\frac{\eta}{1 - \eta}\right)\frac{(1 - g)}{\theta} \tag{3.6a}$$

we see that for these conditions to remain compatible over time, the equilibrium consumption–output ratio must remain bounded, forcing output and consumption ultimately to grow at the same constant rate.

From (3.6a) we see that an increase in leisure, l, both raises the marginal utility of consumption and reduces output, leading to an increase in the consumption–output ratio. An increase in the productivity of labor, η, raises the return to labor. This raises the marginal rate of substitution between leisure and consumption, so that given the fraction of time devoted to leisure, it induces an increase in the latter. Finally, an increase in the fraction of output absorbed by the government reduces the amount available for consumption, thus reducing the consumption–output ratio. Equation (3.5b), which is analogous to (2.3), may be immediately solved to yield the following expression for the rate of capital accumulation:

$$\frac{\dot{K}}{K} = \frac{q - 1}{h} \equiv \phi \tag{3.6b}$$

so that starting from an initial capital stock, K_0, the aggregate capital stock at time t is $K(t) = K_0 e^{\int_0^t \phi(s)ds}$.

Applying the standard optimality conditions with respect to B and K yields the analogous arbitrage relationships to (2.4a) and (2.4b):

$$\rho - \frac{\dot{\lambda}}{\lambda} = r \tag{3.7a}$$

$$\frac{(1 - g)(Ag^\eta)^{1/(1-\eta)}(1 - l)^{\eta/(1-\eta)}}{q} + \frac{\dot{q}}{q} + \frac{(q - 1)^2}{2hq} = r \tag{3.7b}$$

Finally, in order to ensure that the agent's intertemporal budget constraint is met, the following transversality conditions must be imposed:

$$\lim_{t\to\infty} q\lambda Ke^{-pt} = 0 = \lim_{t\to\infty} \lambda Be^{-pt} \qquad (3.7c)$$

3.2.1 Macroeconomic equilibrium

To derive the macroeconomic equilibrium, we begin by taking the time derivatives of: (i) the optimality condition for consumption (3.5a), (ii) the equilibrium consumption–output ratio (3.6a), and (iii) the production function (3.3). This leads to the relationships:

$$(\gamma - 1)\frac{\dot{C}}{C} + \theta\gamma\frac{\dot{l}}{l} = \frac{\dot{\lambda}}{\lambda} = \rho - r \qquad (3.8a)$$

$$\frac{\dot{C}}{C} - \frac{\dot{Y}}{Y} = \frac{\dot{l}}{l} + \frac{\dot{l}}{1-l} \qquad (3.8b)$$

$$\frac{\dot{Y}}{Y} = \frac{\dot{K}}{K} - \left(\frac{\eta}{1-\eta}\right)\frac{\dot{l}}{1-l} = \frac{q-1}{h} - \left(\frac{\eta}{1-\eta}\right)\frac{\dot{l}}{1-l} \qquad (3.8c)$$

Combining these equations with (3.3), (3.6), and (3.7), the macroeconomic equilibrium can be expressed by the pair of differential equations in q and l:

$$\dot{q} = rq - \frac{(q-1)^2}{2h} - (1-g)(Ag^{\eta})^{1/(1-\eta)}(1-l)^{\eta/(1-\eta)} \qquad (3.9a)$$

$$\dot{l} = \frac{1}{F(l)}\left[r - \rho - \frac{(1-\gamma)(q-1)}{h}\right] \qquad (3.9b)$$

where:

$$F(l) \equiv \frac{1 - \gamma(1+\theta)}{l} + \left(\frac{1-\gamma}{1-l}\right)\left(\frac{1-2\eta}{1-\eta}\right) > 0$$

.

The steady state to (3.9) is obtained by setting $\dot{q} = \dot{l} = 0$, and is therefore characterized by the relative price of capital, q, and the fraction of time devoted to leisure, l, both being constant. Linearizing (3.9) around its steady state, we can easily show that the two eigenvalues to the linearized approximation are both positive.[5] Hence the only bounded equilibrium is one in which both q and l adjust instantaneously to any structural or policy shock, to ensure that the economy is always on its balanced growth path (denoted by $\sim$), namely:[6]

$$\tilde{\psi} \equiv \frac{r - \rho}{1 - \gamma} = s(r - \rho) = \frac{\tilde{q} - 1}{h} \qquad (3.10a)$$

$$\frac{(1 - g)(Ag^{\eta})^{1/(1-\eta)}(1 - \tilde{l})^{\eta/(1-\eta)}}{q} + \frac{(\tilde{q} - 1)^2}{2hq} = r \qquad (3.10b)$$

where s denotes the intertemporal elasticity of supply and $\tilde{\psi}$ denotes the equilibrium growth rate. The transversality condition (3.7c) yields:[7]

$$\tilde{\psi} \equiv \frac{\tilde{q} - 1}{h} < r, \quad \text{i.e.} \quad \rho > r\gamma \qquad (3.10c)$$

Equation (3.10a) implies that the equilibrium is one in which domestic output, capital, and consumption all grow at a common rate determined by the difference between the world rate of interest and the domestic rate of time preference, all multiplied by the intertemporal elasticity of substitution. In effect the (common) equilibrium growth rate is driven by the consumption growth rate, and the form of the expression is analogous to the

---

[5] Linearizing (3.9) one can easily establish that the determinant, Δ, and the trace, Tr, to this linearized system satisfy:

$$\Delta = (1 - g)(\eta/(1 - \eta))(Y/K)((1 - \gamma)/h)1/F(l) > 0$$
$$\text{Tr} = r - (q - 1)/h > 0.$$

This implies that the two eigenvalues are real and positive.

[6] This local instability of the dynamic path depends in part upon our assumptions of a Cobb–Douglas production function and constant elasticity utility function, and justifies our focus on that equilibrium in the present analysis. For more general production functions one cannot dismiss the possibility that the dynamics have a stable eigenvalue, giving rise to potential problems of indeterminate equilibria. In a model with both physical and nonhuman capital, Benhabib and Perli (1994) and Ladrón-de-Guevara, Ortigueira, and Santos (1997) show how the steady-state equilibrium may become indeterminate. Other authors have emphasized the existence of externalities as sources of indeterminacies of equilibrium; see Benhabib and Farmer (1994).

[7] This is met under plausible conditions. It is certainly met if $\gamma < 0$, i.e. if the intertemporal elasticity of substitution is less than unity, a condition that the overwhelming majority (but not all) empirical studies confirm. For example, an early study by Hall (1988) estimates the intertemporal elasticity of substitution in consumption to be around 0.1. This result, obtained for the United States, is confirmed in a later study by Patterson and Pesaran (1992), who also obtain slightly higher estimates (0.4), for the United Kingdom. Guvenen (2006) provides a recent study that reconciles some of the conflicting evidence on the intertemporal elasticity of substitution.

equilibrium growth rate in the simplest AK model; see Barro (1990). The only difference is that for the small open economy the (fixed) marginal physical product of capital is replaced by the (given) foreign interest rate. Given this growth rate, (3.10a) determines the equilibrium price of capital, $\tilde{q}$, which will ensure that domestic capital grows at this required equilibrium rate. Having obtained $\tilde{q}$, (3.10b) then determines the fraction of time devoted to leisure (employment) such that the marginal physical product of capital ensures that the rate of return on domestic capital equals the (given) world rate of interest. Hence in this small open economy with elastically supplied labor, the growth rate of output and capital is independent of production characteristics such as the productivity parameter, A, and the marginal cost of adjustment, h. Changes in these parameters are reflected in the labor–leisure choice $\tilde{l}$. In order for the equilibrium to be viable, the implied fraction of time devoted to leisure must lie in the range $0 < \tilde{l} < 1$. This will be so if and only if:

$$0 < r + \left(\frac{h}{1-\gamma}\right)(r-\rho)\left[\frac{r(1-2\gamma)+\rho}{2(1-\gamma)}\right] < (1-g)(Ag^\eta)^{1/(1-\eta)} \qquad (3.11)$$

a condition that is plausibly met. For example, for the plausible parameter values $r = 0.06$, $\rho = 0.04$, $\gamma = -1$, $h = 16$, $a = 0.18$, $\eta = 0.08$, $g = 0.08$, inequality (3.11) reduces to $0 < 0.07 < 0.12$.

With the equilibrium growth rate, $\tilde{\psi}$, being determined exogenously by (3.10a), it immediately follows that an increase in the share of government expenditure claimed by the central planner has no effect either on the growth rate, or on the Tobin q that determines the growth rate of capital. Instead, an increase in g has two offsetting effects on the net social marginal physical product of capital. On the one hand, an increase in government expenditure raises the productivity of capital, while at the same time it absorbs some of the output. The effect on the net productivity of capital depends upon $(\eta - g)$.[8] In order to maintain the net marginal physical product of capital constant, so that the rate of return to capital remains equal to the (fixed) return on traded bonds, the supply of labor must adjust to offset this effect. That is, the fraction of time devoted to labor must decrease if $\eta > g$, and increase otherwise. Accordingly, the effect of an increase in g on the time devoted to leisure is given by:

---

[8] The effect of g on the net productivity of capital is given by
$$\partial[(1-g)(Ag^\eta)^{1/(1-\eta)}(1-\tilde{l})^{\eta/(1-\eta)}]\big/\partial g.$$

$$\mathrm{sgn}\left(\frac{\partial \tilde{l}}{\partial g}\right) = \mathrm{sgn}(\eta - g) \qquad (3.12)$$

We now need to address the implications of this for the country's external account. To do this we first note from (3.6a) that consumption at time t is given by:

$$\frac{C(t)}{K(t)} = \left(\frac{\tilde{l}}{1 - \tilde{l}}\right)\left(\frac{\eta}{1 - \eta}\right)\frac{(1 - g)}{\theta}\frac{\tilde{Y}}{\tilde{K}} \qquad (3.13)$$

where $\tilde{Y}/\tilde{K}$ is given by the production function (3.3). Thus, having determined the equilibrium fraction of time employed, (3.13) determines the constant consumption–capital ratio. Substituting (3.6) and (3.13) into the current account relationship (3.4c), the accumulation of foreign bonds by the economy is:

$$\dot{B} = rB + \left\{(1 - g)\left[1 - \left(\frac{\tilde{l}}{1 - \tilde{l}}\right)\frac{\eta}{\theta(1 - \eta)}\right]\frac{\tilde{Y}}{\tilde{K}} - \left(\frac{\tilde{q}^2 - 1}{2h}\right)\right\}K_0 e^{\tilde{\psi}t} \qquad (3.14)$$

Solving this equation and applying the transversality condition (3.7c), implies:

$$B_0 + \frac{K_0}{r - \tilde{\psi}}\left[(1 - g)\left[1 - \left(\frac{\tilde{l}}{1 - \tilde{l}}\right)\frac{\eta}{\theta(1 - \eta)}\right]\frac{\tilde{Y}}{\tilde{K}} - \left(\frac{\tilde{q}^2 - 1}{2h}\right)\right] = 0 \qquad (3.15)$$

This equation is the nation's intertemporal resource constraint. The initial value of its foreign bonds plus the capitalized value of the current account surplus along the balanced growth path must sum to zero. Having determined the equilibrium values of $\tilde{l}, \tilde{q}$ and Y/K, the intertemporal constraint (3.15) determines the combination of the initial capital stock, K_0, and the initial stock of foreign bonds, B_0, necessary for the equilibrium to be intertemporally viable. If the inherited stocks of these assets violate (3.15) we assume that the central planner can engage in an initial trade, described by: $dB_0 + \tilde{q}dK_0 = 0$, to bring about the correct ratio. Substituting (3.15) into the solution of (3.14) we see that the equilibrium stock of traded bonds accumulates at the common equilibrium growth $\tilde{\psi}$.

3.2.2 Comparison with two models

Small open economy fixed-employment AK model

The above model of the small open economy with elastic labor supply behaves very differently from the basic small open economy AK model with fixed labor supply discussed in Chapter 2. Consumption growth in that model remains as given by (3.10a), and is thus determined by domestic taste parameters and the world interest rate. Investment growth is given by (3.6b), where now $\tilde{q}$ is determined by:

$$\frac{(1-g)(Ag^{\eta})^{1/(1-\eta)}}{\tilde{q}} + \frac{(\tilde{q}-1)^2}{2h\tilde{q}} = r$$

In this case, $\tilde{q}$ is determined by the smaller root to this quadratic equation which can be shown to satisfy the transversality condition (3.10c).[9] The growth of domestic capital and output now depend upon the domestic production parameters, a and h, and are independent of the taste parameters. In general, consumption and capital (output) grow at different constant rates, with the difference being reconciled by the accumulation of traded bonds. These are subject to transitional dynamics, with the long-run growth rate of traded bonds converging to the larger of these two growth rates. This in turn depends upon the consumer rate of time preference relative to the rates of return on investment. With consumption being tied to output, it is no longer free to adjust so as to ensure international solvency of the economy. Instead, B_0 and K_0 must be adjusted in accordance with $dB_0 + \tilde{q}dK_0 = 0$, so as to ensure that the intertemporal viability condition (3.15) is met.

The flexibility of labor supply also has important consequences for the impact of government policy. Equation (3.10b) determining $\tilde{q}$ implies that in the fixed-employment open economy, the common equilibrium rate of growth of domestic output and capital, $\tilde{\varphi}$, satisfies:

$$\text{sgn}\left(\frac{\partial \tilde{\varphi}}{\partial g}\right) = \text{sgn}(\eta - g) \tag{3.16}$$

With labor supplied *inelastically*, the net effect of higher government expenditure is to raise the marginal physical product of capital if and only if $\eta > g$, thereby leading to an increase in the growth rate of capital and output. By contrast, when labor supply is *elastic*, the equilibrium adjustment to the higher government expenditure is borne entirely by the labor–leisure choice, with the equilibrium growth rate of capital remaining unchanged.

---

[9] As in Chapter 2, one can demonstrate from this equation that the presence of convex adjustment costs may plausibly preclude the existence of a balanced growth equilibrium. In contrast, with flexible labor supply, the corresponding equation (3.10b), yields a feasible solution for $\tilde{l}$ and therefore a balanced growth equilibrium for all but extreme parameters. For example, the transversality condition (3.10c) ensures that this will be so for all cases of positive equilibrium growth.

Closed economy endogenous labor supply model

The behavior of the small open economy model with elastic labor supply also contrasts sharply with that of the corresponding closed economy model. In that case, Turnovsky (2000) has established the following tradeoff between the effects of government expenditure on growth and leisure:

$$\text{sgn}\left(\frac{\partial\tilde{\varphi}}{\partial g}\right) = \text{sgn}(\eta - g); \quad \text{sgn}\left(\frac{\partial\tilde{l}}{\partial g}\right) = \text{sgn}(g - \eta)$$

Assuming, for example, $\eta > g$, higher government expenditure leads to more growth, as in the fixed-employment AK open economy. The higher growth rate raises the wage rate, thereby encouraging agents to substitute work for leisure. This *decline* in leisure in the closed economy is in direct contrast to the *increase* in leisure implied by (3.12) for the open economy.

3.2.3 Optimal government expenditure

Suppose now that the planner chooses the share of government expenditure, g, optimally in conjunction with C, l, B, and K. This leads to the additional optimality condition:

$$\hat{g} = \eta \tag{3.17}$$

That is, the optimal fraction of output claimed by the government (denoted by ˆ) should equal the elasticity of output with respect to the government input. This optimality condition is standard across all models. It obtains both in the fixed-employment and elastic labor supply closed economy models, as well as in the fixed-employment small open economy model. With elastically supplied labor, (3.13) and (3.17) imply that the effect of an increase in government expenditure on leisure depends upon whether government expenditure is above or below its social optimum. Finally, corresponding to the first-best optimal government expenditure policy (3.17), the overall first-best optimal consumption–output ratio is:

$$\left(\frac{\hat{C}}{Y}\right) = \left(\frac{\hat{l}}{1 - \hat{l}}\right)\frac{\eta}{\theta}$$

3.3 Decentralized economy

We now turn to an individual agent in a decentralized market economy. In order to highlight the decentralization aspect, we assume that the agent confronts a wage rate and asset returns that he takes as parametrically given.

With endogenous labor supply it now makes sense to decouple the tax on labor income from the tax on capital income since they influence the agent's decisions in very different ways. Thus, the agent purchases consumption out of the after-tax income generated by labor, his holdings of domestic capital, and foreign bonds. His objective is to maximize (3.4a) subject to his bond and capital accumulation equations:

$$\dot{B}_i = (1 - \tau_w)w(1 - l) + (1 - \tau_k)r_k K_i + (1 - \tau_b)rB_i$$
$$- (1 + \tau_c)C_i - I_i\left(1 + \frac{h\,I_i}{2\,K_i}\right) - T_i \tag{3.18a}$$

$$\dot{K}_i = I_i \tag{3.18b}$$

where r_k = return to capital, w = real wage rate, τ_w = tax on wage income, τ_k = tax on capital income, τ_b = tax on foreign bond income, τ_c = consumption tax, and T_i = agent's share of lump-sum taxes. As before, K_i refers to the individual agent's holdings of capital, and now C_i denotes the individual consumption level.

The production function remains as specified in (3.3), while the government continues to tie its expenditure levels to aggregate output as in (3.2). Aggregating the individual production functions (3.1), aggregate output is determined by:

$$Y = NY_i = aG^\eta[N(1 - l)]^\eta K^{1-\eta} = a(GL)^\eta K^{1-\eta}$$

where $L \equiv N(1-l)$ = aggregate supply of labor. The equilibrium real wage and rate of return on capital are determined by the marginal product conditions:

$$w = \frac{\partial Y_i}{\partial(1 - l)} = \eta\frac{Y_i}{(1 - l)} = \eta\frac{Y}{L} \tag{3.19a}$$

$$r_k = \frac{\partial Y_i}{\partial K_i} = (1 - \eta)\frac{Y_i}{K_i} = (1 - \eta)\frac{Y}{K} \tag{3.19b}$$

Carrying out the optimization for the consumer and aggregating over the N identical representative agents leads to the corresponding optimality conditions:

$$\frac{C}{Y} = \left(\frac{1 - \tau_w}{1 + \tau_c}\right)\frac{\eta}{\theta}\left(\frac{l}{1 - l}\right) \tag{3.6a'}$$

$$1 + h\frac{I}{K} = q \tag{3.6b'}$$

together with the dynamic efficiency conditions:

$$\rho - \frac{\dot{\lambda}}{\lambda} = r(1 - \tau_b) \tag{3.7a'}$$

$$(1 - \tau_k)(1 - \eta)(Ag^\eta)^{1/(1-\eta)}(1 - l)^{\frac{\eta/(1-\eta)}{q}} + \frac{\dot{q}}{q} + \frac{(q-1)^2}{2hq} = r(1 - \tau_b) \tag{3.7b'}$$

The parallels between (3.6a'), (3.6b'), (3.7a'), and (3.7b') in the decentralized economy, and (3.6a), (3.6b), (3.7a), and (3.7b) in the centrally planned economy are clear. The main difference is that in the decentralized economy the agent takes the size of government as given independently of his decisions, and responds to tax incentives. The fact that a higher tax on consumption reduces the consumption–income ratio is straightforward and familiar from models having inelastic labor supply. But in addition, a higher tax on labor income, for given leisure, l, also reduces the consumption–output ratio. This is because for given output a higher wage tax reduces the income available for private consumption. Equations (3.7a') and (3.7b') equate the net after-tax rate of return on bonds to the net after-tax private rate of return to capital and to the rate of return on consumption.

In the absence of debt, tax revenues and government expenditures must satisfy the balanced budget condition:

$$\tau_w N w(1 - l) + \tau_k r_k K + \tau_b r B + \tau_c C + T = gY \tag{3.20}$$

Summing (3.18a) over the N individuals and combining with (3.20) leads to the aggregate resource constraint (3.4b).

3.3.1 Macroeconomic equilibrium

Following the procedure set out in Section 3.2, the macroeconomic equilibrium in the decentralized economy may again be expressed as a pair of first-order differential equations in q and l. Again the two eigenvalues to the linearized system are positive, and both q and l adjust instantaneously to ensure that the system always lies on its balanced growth path, now expressed by:

$$\tilde{\psi} \equiv \frac{r(1 - \tau_b) - \rho}{1 - \gamma} = s(r - \rho) = \frac{\tilde{q} - 1}{h} \qquad (3.10a')$$

$$\frac{(1 - \tau_k)(1 - \eta)(Ag^\eta)^{1/(1-\eta)}(1 - \tilde{l})^{\eta/(1-\eta)}}{q} + \frac{(\tilde{q} - 1)^2}{2hq} = r(1 - \tau_b) \qquad (3.10b')$$

where the transversality condition now implies:

$$\tilde{\psi} \equiv \frac{\tilde{q} - 1}{h} < r(1 - \tau_b)$$

As before, these three equations jointly determine the steady-state equilibrium growth rate, the Tobin q, and leisure. Eliminating $\tilde{q}$ from (3.10a'), the equilibrium can be conveniently summarized by a pair of relationships between ψ and l, illustrated in Figure 3.1.[10]

The first of these, described by the horizontal locus RR expresses the equilibrium growth rate in terms of its determinants, namely the taste and interest rate parameters. The second, illustrated by PP, describes the tradeoff between the equilibrium growth rate and the fraction of time devoted to leisure that ensures the equality between the after-tax rate of return to capital and the after-tax rate of return to bonds. This curve is nonlinear (quadratic) as indicated in the figure. A feasible equilibrium, where $0 < l < 1$, will exist if and only if:[11]

$$0 < r(1 - \tau_b) + \left(\frac{h}{1 - \gamma}\right)(r(1 - \tau_b) - \rho)\left[\frac{r(1 - \tau_b)(1 - 2\gamma) + \rho}{2(1 - \gamma)}\right] \qquad (3.11')$$
$$< (1 - \tau_k)(1 - \eta)(Ag^\eta)^{1/(1-\eta)}$$

The viability of the equilibrium requires that the nation's intertemporal budget constraint (3.15) be met and this requires that the initial ratio of traded bonds, B_0, to capital, K_0, be set appropriately. In the decentralized economy we assume that this occurs through initial lump-sum taxation (if necessary), of the form $dT_0 + dB_0 + \tilde{q}dK_0 = 0$, whereby the private agent is forced to readjust his portfolio to attain the intertemporally viable ratio consistent with (3.15). Using the equilibrium conditions (3.19), the government's balanced budget (3.20) can be expressed as:

$$T = gY - \tau_w\eta - \tau_k(1 - \eta)K - \tau_b rB - \tau_c C \qquad (3.21)$$

---

[10] A similar graphical representation can also be given in the centrally planned economy.
[11] Assuming the parameter values applied to equation (3.11), and in addition the tax rates $\tau_k = \tau_b = 0.28$, (3.11') reduces to $0 < 0.04 < 0.09$.

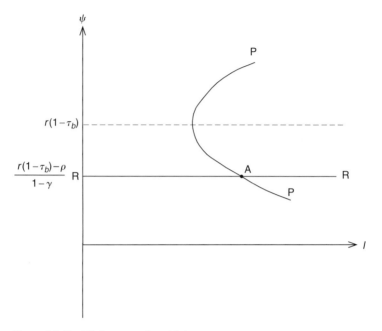

Figure 3.1 Equilibrium growth and leisure

thus determining the required level of lump-sum taxes at each point in time. Along the balanced growth path, this is of the form:

$$T(t) = (aK_0 + bB_0)e^{\tilde{\psi}t} \tag{3.22}$$

where a, b are constants, easily derived from the balanced growth equilibrium.

3.4 Fiscal shocks in the decentralized economy

This section uses the model to analyze the effects of various fiscal shocks.

3.4.1 Tax on capital income

This is illustrated in Figure 3.2. A higher tax on capital income shifts the PP locus to the left from PP to P′P′. The equilibrium thus moves from A to B. With the equilibrium growth rate, and the equilibrium price of capital, $\tilde{q}$, fixed, the higher tax on capital reduces the after-tax return to capital. In order

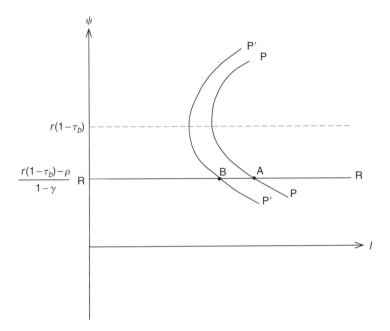

Figure 3.2 Increase in tax on capital

to maintain equilibrium among rates of return, the productivity of capital must be increased. This is achieved by an increase in the fraction of time devoted to labor, that is, by a decline in leisure.

This response contrasts with the fixed-employment open economy AK model, where the higher tax on capital reduces the equilibrium growth rate of output. It also contrasts with the analogous closed economy with endogenous labor, in which the higher tax on capital also reduces the growth rate, but is accompanied by a reduction in the time devoted to labor, i.e. an increase in the time allocated to leisure. Hence we conclude that the effect of a higher capital income tax on employment (leisure) depends critically upon whether the economy is open or closed.

3.4.2 Increase in government expenditure

This is illustrated in Figure 3.3 and operates in precisely the opposite way to a higher capital income tax. The move is represented by the increase in leisure from A to B, with the growth rate remaining unchanged. The contrast in this

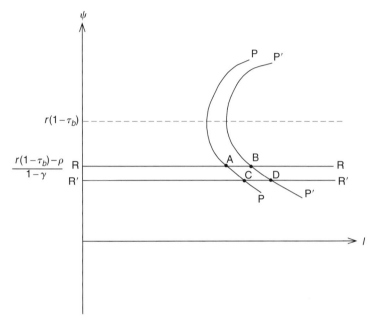

Figure 3.3 Increase in government expenditure and tax on foreign interest

response with both the fixed-employment small open economy and the endogenous labor closed economy continues to apply.

3.4.3 Tax on interest income

This is also illustrated in Figure 3.3 and leads to a downward shift in the RR curve together with a rightward shift in the PP curve. These two effects compound and the combined response is summarized by the movement from A to D. First, the higher tax on foreign interest reduces its net return and the equilibrium growth rate directly. If the after-tax rates of return on domestic capital and foreign bonds are initially in equilibrium, domestic capital now yields a higher net rate of return. To restore equilibrium the productivity of domestic capital must be reduced and this is achieved by a switch from work to leisure. This initial effect is reflected by the movement along AC in the figure. In addition, however, the lower growth rate means a reduction in the Tobin q. This further increases the rate of return on domestic capital relative to the net return on foreign bonds. To restore equilibrium the productivity of domestic capital must be further reduced, and this is accomplished by a further increase in leisure. This part of the adjustment is represented by the horizontal movement CD.

3.4.4 Taxes on wages and consumption

These have no effect on either the growth rate or on employment. Their only effect is on the consumption–output ratio, which is reduced. In this respect, the two taxes act very much like lump-sum taxes, as in the fixed-employment AK model of the open economy. But these effects contrast with the closed economy elastic labor supply model, when both the wage tax and the consumption tax operate precisely as does the capital income tax, namely they reduce growth and increase leisure. The difference arises because of the fact that in the open economy (i) the equilibrium growth rate, and (ii) the equilibrium relationship between the rate of return to capital and bonds are both independent of these two tax rates.

The fact that the growth rate is independent of most income taxes (except τ_b) offers an interesting perspective to the following issue. As we observed at the outset, one of the implications of the basic endogenous growth model, a feature that distinguishes it from the traditional neoclassical model, is that its equilibrium growth rate varies inversely with distortionary income taxes. The fact that empirical evidence by Easterly and Rebelo (1993), Jones (1995b), and Stokey and Rebelo (1995) does not support this implication has been used as evidence against these endogenous growth models. Our results suggest some caution might be required in reaching this conclusion. For small economies facing a perfect world capital market, equilibrium growth rates are in fact independent of most tax rates. Instead, such economies respond to changes in tax rates through variations in their equilibrium labor–leisure choice.

3.5 Optimal fiscal policy

Comparing the equilibria of the decentralized and centrally planned economies enables us to characterize the first-best optimal tax policy. First, setting:

$$\hat{\tau}_b = 0 \tag{3.23a}$$

$$1 - \hat{\tau}_k = \frac{1 - g}{1 - \eta}, \quad \text{i.e.} \quad \hat{\tau}_k = \frac{g - \eta}{1 - \eta} \tag{3.23b}$$

the pair of equations (3.10a′, 3.10b′) coincide with (3.10a, 3.10b), thus ensuring that the steady-state growth rate and leisure time in the decentralized economy will replicate those of the centrally planned economy. These optimal tax rates are identical to those obtained for the fixed-employment AK model. They correct for the distortions (if any) induced by government expenditure in financial markets; see Turnovsky (1996a).

From (3.17) and (3.23b) it is seen that the tax on capital income depends upon the deviation in the aggregate share of government expenditure from its optimum. The intuition for this result is as in Turnovsky (1996a), involving the deviation between the social and private returns to capital accumulation. The social return to accumulating a marginal unit of capital is:

$$r_s = (1 - g)\frac{Y}{K} \qquad (3.24a)$$

This consists of the gross marginal product of capital, less the induced claim by government. This measure takes account of the fact that as capital increases and output expands, the size of the government also expands in accordance with (3.2). The private return to capital in the decentralized economy is the after-tax rate of return:

$$r_p \equiv (1 - \tau_k)\frac{\partial Y_i}{\partial K_i} = (1 - \tau_k)(1 - \eta)\frac{Y_i}{K_i} = (1 - \tau_k)(1 - \eta)\frac{Y}{K} \qquad (3.24b)$$

This expression assumes that the private agent operating in a decentralized economy treats the impact of his own rate of capital accumulation on aggregate government expenditure as negligible. The optimal tax on capital is then determined so as to equate the private and social rates of return; i.e. set $r_p = r_s$.

If aggregate government expenditure exceeds the optimum, the costs of the resources utilized by the government exceed the benefits and it has a net adverse effect on the return to capital. The private agent fails to recognize this and overinvests relative to the optimum. This is corrected by imposing a positive tax on private capital income. If government expenditure is below its optimum, the benefits exceed the costs and capital needs to be subsidized. If it is at its optimum, the costs just match the benefits, there are no spillovers from government expenditure to the capital market, and capital income should remain untaxed; i.e. $\hat{\tau}_k = 0$.

The optimal tax on foreign interest income, $\hat{\tau}_b$, is zero, because government expenditure is not tied to interest income. If it were, similar distortions to those involving capital would arise, and when g is away from its optimum, foreign interest income would need to be taxed as well.

Comparing (3.6a) and (3.6a′), and having replicated l through the appropriate tax rates on capital and interest, the consumption–output ratios in the two economies will be replicated if and only if:

$$\left(\frac{1-\hat{\tau}_w}{1+\hat{\tau}_c}\right) = \left(\frac{1-g}{1-\eta}\right) \tag{3.25}$$

The relationship between the optimal tax on wage income and on consumption reflects the effects of externalities on the marginal rate of substitution between consumption and leisure. The marginal rates of substitution (*MRS*) in the centrally planned and in the decentralized economies (subscripted by c and d), obtained by dividing (3.5b) by (3.5a) and the corresponding conditions for the decentralized economy, are:

$$MRS_c = \eta\left(\frac{1-g}{1-\eta}\right)\frac{Y}{1-l}; \quad MRS_d = \eta\left(\frac{1-\tau_w}{1+\tau_c}\right)\frac{Y}{1-l}$$

and the latter will mimic the former if and only if (3.25) holds.

When government expenditure is set optimally, i.e. $g = \eta$, (3.25) reduces to:

$$\hat{\tau}_w = -\hat{\tau}_c \tag{3.25′}$$

That is, the tax on labor income must be equal and opposite to that on consumption. Interpreting the tax on wage income as a negative tax on leisure, (3.25′) says that in the absence of any externality, the optimal tax structure requires that the two utility-enhancing goods, consumption and leisure, be taxed uniformly. This result can be viewed as an intertemporal application of the Ramsey principle of optimal taxation; see Deaton (1981) and Lucas and Stokey (1983). If the utility function is multiplicatively separable in c and l, as we are assuming here, then the uniform taxation of leisure and consumption is optimal.

An alternative interpretation to (3.25′) can be given using a concept due to Prescott (2004), who defines the effective tax on labor income, τ say, by:

$$1 - \tau = \frac{1-\tau_w}{1+\tau_c}, \quad \text{so that } \tau = \frac{\tau_w + \tau_c}{1+\tau_c}$$

which takes account of the fact that to the extent that labor income is being spent on consumption, it is also subject to the consumption tax. Written in this way, (3.25′) requires that the effective tax on labor income be zero.

The first-best optimal integrated fiscal policy is characterized by (3.17), (3.23), and (3.25′). Substituting these conditions into (3.11a) and (3.11b), the corresponding first-best equilibrium growth rate, $\hat{\psi}$, price of capital, $\hat{q}$, and associated time devoted to leisure, $\hat{l}$, are given by

$$\hat{\psi} = \frac{r-\rho}{1-\gamma}; \quad \hat{q} = 1 + h\left(\frac{r-\rho}{1-\gamma}\right)$$

$$(1-\eta)(A\eta^{\eta})^{1/(1-\eta)}(1-\hat{l})^{\eta/(1-\eta)} = r\left[1 + h\left(\frac{r-\rho}{1-\gamma}\right)\right] - \frac{h}{2}\left(\frac{r-\rho}{1-\gamma}\right)^2 \quad (3.26)$$

The optimal tax rates and expenditure shares must also be consistent with the government budget constraint (3.21). Setting $\hat{\tau}_b = \hat{\tau}_k = 0, \hat{\tau}_c = -\hat{\tau}_w$, and evaluating (3.19a), (3.6a) at the optimum yields: $N\hat{w} = \eta\hat{Y}/(1-\hat{l}); \hat{C} = \left(\hat{l}/(1-\hat{l})\right)(\eta/\theta)\hat{Y}$ so that (3.21) may be expressed as:

$$\hat{\tau}_w\left(1 - \left(\frac{\hat{l}}{1-\hat{l}}\right)\frac{1}{\theta}\right)\eta\hat{Y} + T = \eta\hat{Y} \quad (3.21')$$

Any combination of $\hat{\tau}_w$ and T consistent with this equation will satisfy the government budget constraint. This can be feasibly achieved without lump-sum taxation $(T = 0)$, if and only if $(1/\theta)\left(\hat{l}/(1-\hat{l})\right) > 1$.[12] A sufficient condition for this to be met that any plausible economy will satisfy is that the optimal consumption–output ratio (C/Y), exceeds the optimal government production expenditure–output ratio $\hat{g} = \eta$. In this case, (3.21′) will be met by subsidizing the labor–leisure choice and applying an exactly offsetting tax to consumption:[13]

$$\hat{\tau}_w = -\hat{\tau}_c = \frac{1}{\left[1 - (1/\theta)\left(\hat{l}/(1-\hat{l})\right)\right]} < 0 \quad (3.27)$$

Finally, to sustain the first-best optimum, the government will also need to levy an initial one-time lump-sum tax so as to ensure that the initial configuration of assets, consistent with the nation's intertemporal government budget constraint is attained.

---

[12] If $(1/\theta)\left(\hat{l}/(1-\hat{l})\right) < 1$ we would require $\tau_w > 1$, which is clearly infeasible.
[13] In the implausible case where $\eta > (C/Y)$, (3.27) implies that labor income should be taxed and consumption subsidized at more than 100%. Obviously this is infeasible and lump-sum taxation would be required to sustain the optimum.

3.6 Conclusions

Most endogenous growth models assume that labor is supplied inelastically. This is true for the bulk of the literature that deals with closed economies; it is even more true for the sparser literature focusing on the open economy. This assumption is not only unrealistic, but it has strong, and even misleading, policy implications. In this chapter we have extended the AK growth model of Chapter 2 to include an elastic labor supply, determined by the labor–leisure tradeoff. As was the case for the fixed-employment economy, the macroeconomic equilibrium has the characteristic that the economy lies continuously on its balanced growth path, which under plausible conditions always exists. The equilibrium is determined in a very different way from that in the previous analysis. Domestic consumption, capital, and output all grow at a common rate determined by taste parameters, together with the after-tax rate of return on foreign bonds. Given this growth rate and the associated price of capital, the fraction of time devoted to leisure (work) is then determined so as to ensure that the after-tax return to capital equals the after-tax return to foreign bonds.

Our main focus has been on the implications of the elastic labor supply for fiscal policy. We find that the long-run growth rate is independent of almost all domestic fiscal instruments, except the tax on foreign bonds. The essential exogeneity of this growth rate is thus consistent with the empirical evidence on this issue cited by a number of authors. It does, however, contrast sharply with the fixed-employment small open economy AK model in which consumption grows as in this model, but output and capital grow at an independent rate that depends not only upon technological parameters, but also upon both the tax on capital and productive government expenditure.

The other interesting contrast is with the closed economy. In the basic fixed-employment AK model due to Barro (1990), for example, taxes on wages and consumption have no effect; they operate like lump-sum taxes. Endogenizing labor supply in that model ensures that these tax rates have real distortionary effects, operating in a qualitatively similar way as the capital income tax. Introducing elastic labor supply in the small open economy has quite the opposite effect. Not only do the taxes on wages and consumption remain nondistortionary, but now the tax on capital income has no effect on the growth rate. It does affect leisure, although now in precisely the opposite way to how it does so in the closed economy. The bottom line is that how fiscal policy impacts on the equilibrium growth rate of an endogenous growth model depends upon the nature of the economy.

Finally, the optimal tax structure in the decentralized economy has been characterized. In general, the optimal distortionary tax rates will depend upon the chosen levels of government expenditure relative to its optimum. These rates are set in response to externalities that this expenditure generates in (i) financial markets, and (ii) the consumption–leisure choice. If government expenditure is chosen optimally the first externality vanishes. In that case, the optimal tax rate on capital income is zero and leisure and consumption should be taxed uniformly, in accordance with established principles of public finance. Under the assumption we have made that the level of government expenditure is set independently of foreign interest income, the latter should remain untaxed. However, if government expenditure were tied to domestic GNP, rather than GDP, this would cease to be the case, and foreign interest income would have to be taxed in much the same way as domestic capital income.

PART TWO

Transitional dynamics and long-run growth

4

Transitional dynamics and endogenous growth in one-sector models

The models discussed thus far all have the characteristic that consumption and output (capital) are always on their respective balanced growth paths; there are no transitional dynamics. Instead, the economy adjusts with infinite speed to any exogenous shock, thus contradicting the empirical evidence pertaining to the speed of convergence. One of the main conclusions of this literature is that the economy in fact adjusts relatively slowly, with the benchmark estimate of the speed of adjustment being around 2–3% per annum.[1] While the original estimates have been challenged on various empirical and methodological grounds, the consensus remains that the speed of convergence may be somewhat higher than originally suggested, but probably less than 6% per annum.[2] In any event, this implies that the economy is mostly off its balanced growth path, on some dynamic path that converges only gradually to a steady state. It is therefore important to modify the model to allow for such transitional dynamics, and this can be achieved in several ways, all of which assign a central role to a second state variable in determining the equilibrium dynamics.

In this chapter we consider two important modifications to the basic one-sector model that accomplishes this objective. These include: (i) limited access to the world financial market; and (ii) the introduction of public capital. In Chapter 5 we shall show that extending the model to two sectors, having traded and nontraded capital, will also introduce transitional dynamics, the nature of which will depend in part upon the relative sectoral capital intensities. One additional way to introduce transitional dynamics is to modify the technology and allow it to have non-scale growth, along the

---

[1] This benchmark value was originally established by Mankiw, Romer, and Weil (1992), Barro and Sala-i-Martin (1992b), and others.
[2] See e.g. Islam (1995), Caselli, Esquivel and Lefort (1996), and Evans (1998).

lines initially proposed by Jones (1995a, 1995b). This model will be pursued in detail in Chapter 6.[3]

4.1 Upward-sloping supply curve of debt[4]

The assumption that the economy is free to borrow or lend as much as it wants at the given world interest rate in a perfect world capital market is a strong one. While it is convenient, and may serve as a reasonable approximation for small developed economies having access to highly developed and integrated capital markets, it is less plausible for developing economies. But even a small developed country, if it trades international bonds too intensively, will eventually reach a point where it is no longer sufficiently small that it can take the world interest rate as given. In any event, the equilibrium structure changes dramatically when the economy faces restricted access to the world capital market. Not only does this generate transitional dynamics, but it also provides a mechanism linking the equilibrium growth rates of consumption and output, albeit a very different one from the endogeneity of labor supply, discussed in Chapter 3.

The importance of restricted access to international capital markets can be most conveniently addressed in the case of a debtor nation by postulating that the rate of interest at which it may borrow is an increasing function of its debt. This type of constraint was originally proposed by Bardhan (1967) and has been introduced by many authors since then; see Obstfeld (1982), Bhandari, Haque, and Turnovsky (1990), Fisher (1995), Fisher and Terrell (2000). While these specifications are essentially arbitrary, more formal justification of this type of relationship, in terms of default risk and financial intermediation, has been provided by Eaton and Gersovitz (1989) and more recently by Chung and Turnovsky (2007), who also provide some empirical support.[5]

One issue that arises is whether the specification of debt cost should be expressed in terms of its *absolute* level, as originally proposed by Bardhan, or *relative* to some earnings capacity to service the debt, as initially argued by Sachs (1984) and others. In a stationary economy the choice may be

---

[3] Transitional dynamics can be achieved in still other ways by (i) introducing Uzawa (1968) preferences, (ii) adopting the Blanchard (1985)–Weil (1989) overlapping-generations model, and (iii) introducing other state variables such as human capital, education, and health.

[4] The material in Section 4.1 is adapted from Turnovsky (1997d).

[5] A rigorous derivation of (4.1) presumes the existence of risk. Since we do not wish to model a full stochastic economy, we should view (4.1) as representing a convenient reduced form. Some early empirical support is provided by Edwards (1984) who finds a significant positive relationship between the spread over LIBOR (e.g. r^*) and the debt–GNP ratio.

unimportant. However, the latter formulation is appropriate if an equilibrium of ongoing growth is to be sustained, and indeed, this formulation has been adopted in previous models of growing open economies; see e.g. van der Ploeg (1996) and Turnovsky (1997b).[6]

To illustrate the impact of endogenizing the borrowing rate, we focus on a debtor economy and assume that the cost of borrowing from abroad is:

$$r(Z/K) = r^* + \delta \upsilon(Z/K); \quad \upsilon' > 0. \tag{4.1}$$

where $Z \equiv -B$ denotes the aggregate stock of debt, r^* denotes the given world interest rate, and $\delta \upsilon(.)$ is the borrowing premium over the world rate. For simplicity, we return to the specification of Chapter 2, where we consider the impact of distortionary taxes (including now a tax on debt), the revenues of which are rebated. It is important to emphasize that in performing his optimization, the representative agent takes the interest rate as given. This is because the interest rate facing the debtor nation is an increasing function of the economy's *aggregate* debt, which the representative agent, in making his decisions, assumes he is unable to influence. We should point out, however, that the equilibrium and implications are fairly insensitive to variations in this specification that replace Z/K with expressions such as Z/Y or Z/W where W denotes wealth. The important thing is that the borrowing costs be homogeneous of degree one.

In order to focus on the new dimension being introduced, we shall return to the initial assumption of inelastic labor supply so that the objective function and technology revert to:

$$\Omega \equiv \int_0^\infty \frac{1}{\gamma} C_i^\gamma e^{-\rho t} dt \tag{4.2a}$$

$$Y_i = AK^{1-\sigma} K_i^\sigma \tag{4.2b}$$

The key change is in the specification of the agent's instantaneous budget constraint, which we specify as:

$$\dot{Z}_i = (1 + \tau_c)C_i + I_i[1 + (h/2)(I_i/K_i)] - (1 - \tau_y)AK^{1-\sigma} K_i^\sigma \\ + (1 + \tau_z)r(Z/K)Z_i + T_i \tag{4.3a}$$

---

[6] Senhadji (2003) uses a measure of export earning to debt as his measure of ability to service the debt.

This equation, expressed from the standpoint of a debtor, asserts that to the extent the agent's consumption, investment expenses (inclusive of adjustment costs), and interest payments plus all taxes exceed his output he will increase his stock of debt. As before, the (capital) income tax rate is τ_y, while consumption is taxed at τ_c, but in addition, we now assume that debt is taxed at τ_z.[7]

The agent's optimization problem thus becomes to choose his consumption level C_i, his rate of investment I_i, and his rates of capital and debt accumulation, K_i and Z_i, to maximize utility (4.2a), subject to flow budget constraint (4.3a), and the capital accumulation equation:

$$\dot{K}_i = I_i \tag{4.3b}$$

Since all agents are identical, in equilibrium $K_i = K$ (where we normalize the number of agents to be unity) and subscripts will henceforth be dropped.

With this in mind, the optimality conditions with respect to C and I are now

$$C^{\gamma-1} = \lambda(1 + \tau_c) \tag{4.4a}$$

$$1 + h(I/K) = q \tag{4.4b}$$

while optimizing with respect to z and k yields with the arbitrage conditions:

$$\rho - \frac{\dot{\lambda}}{\lambda} = (1 + \tau_z)r\left(\frac{Z}{K}\right) \tag{4.5a}$$

$$(1 - \tau_y)\frac{A\sigma}{q} + \frac{\dot{q}}{q} + \frac{(q-1)^2}{2hq} = (1 + \tau_z)r\left(\frac{Z}{K}\right) \tag{4.5b}$$

These four equations are analogous to (2.2a), (2.2c), (2.4a),and (2.4b), obtained previously; the only difference is that the rates of return on consumption and capital should now be equated to the costs of borrowing, inclusive of tax. In addition, to ensure that the agent's intertemporal budget constraint is met, the usual transversality conditions must apply, and analogously to our previous results this requires:

$$\frac{q-1}{h} < r(1 + \tau_z) \tag{4.6}$$

---

[7] It is possible for $\tau_z < 0$, in which case debt is being subsidized, rather than taxed.

The dynamics of asset accumulation are as follows. First, combining (4.3b) and (4.4b) capital accumulation is given by:

$$\frac{\dot{K}}{K} = \frac{q-1}{h} \tag{4.7a}$$

Second, assuming that the government maintains a balanced budget, now expressed as:

$$\tau_y Y + \tau_z rZ + \tau_c C = T \tag{4.7b}$$

the current account relationship (the national resource constraint) becomes:

$$\dot{Z} = C + I\left[1 + \frac{h}{2}\frac{I}{K}\right] - AK + r\left(\frac{Z}{K}\right)Z \tag{4.7c}$$

which corresponds to (2.6) in the basic model. The difference is that now the interest rate is endogenously determined as a function of the nation's debt–capital ratio, Z/K, and this changes the dynamics fundamentally.

To derive the macrodynamic equilibrium, we need to transform it into stationary variables. For this purpose, it is convenient to express it in terms of $c \equiv C/K$, $z \equiv Z/K$, and q. Differentiating c and z with respect to time yields:

$$\frac{\dot{c}}{c} = \frac{\dot{C}}{C} - \frac{\dot{K}}{K}; \quad \frac{\dot{z}}{z} = \frac{\dot{Z}}{Z} - \frac{\dot{K}}{K} \tag{4.8}$$

Taking the time derivative of (4.4a) and combining with (4.5a) and (4.7a) we obtain:

$$\dot{c} = c\left(\frac{1}{1-\gamma}((1+\tau_z)r(z) - \rho) - \frac{q-1}{h}\right) \tag{4.9a}$$

Next, dividing the current account relationship by Z, and using (4.7a), yields:

$$\dot{z} = c + \left(\frac{q^2-1}{2h}\right) - \left(\frac{q-1}{h}\right)z - A + r(z)z \tag{4.9b}$$

Finally, we may rewrite (4.5b) in the form:

$$\dot{q} = (1+\tau_z)r(z)q - (1-\tau_y)A\sigma - \frac{(q-1)^2}{2h} \tag{4.9c}$$

These three equations determine the evolution of c, z, and q. In contrast to the case of a perfect capital market discussed in earlier chapters, any policy or structural shock to the system will generate transitional dynamics, before the system (if stable) will ultimately converge to its new steady-state equilibrium.

To consider the transitional dynamics we linearize the dynamic system (4.9a)–(4.9c) around its steady-state equilibrium, denoted by $\tilde{c}$, $\tilde{z}$, and $\tilde{q}$, to obtain:

$$
\begin{pmatrix} \dot{c} \\ \dot{z} \\ \dot{q} \end{pmatrix} = \begin{pmatrix} 0 & \frac{\tilde{c}}{1-\gamma} r'(\tilde{z})(1+\tau_z) & -\frac{\tilde{c}}{h} \\ 1 & [r(\tilde{z})+r'(\tilde{z})\tilde{z}] - \left(\frac{\tilde{q}-1}{h}\right) & \left(\frac{\tilde{q}-\tilde{z}}{h}\right) \\ 0 & r'(\tilde{z})(1+\tau_z)\tilde{q} & r(\tilde{z})(1+\tau_z) - \left(\frac{\tilde{q}-1}{h}\right) \end{pmatrix} \begin{pmatrix} c-\tilde{c} \\ z-\tilde{z} \\ q-\tilde{q} \end{pmatrix}
$$

$$(4.10)$$

Recalling the condition (4.6), implied by the transversality condition, the determinant of the matrix of coefficients in (4.10) is negative, while the trace is positive. This implies that this system has two positive (unstable) and one negative (stable) eigenvalue.[8] Since consumption, c, and the price of capital, q, can jump instantaneously, while the ratio of debt to capital, z, is constrained to adjust continuously, the number of unstable roots to this equation equals the number of jump variables, so that starting from an initial debt–capital ratio, z_0, the economy follows the unique stable transitional adjustment path:

$$z(t) = \tilde{z} + (z_0 - \tilde{z})e^{\mu t} \qquad (4.11a)$$

$$q(t) - \tilde{q} = -\frac{(1+\tau_z)r'(\tilde{z})\tilde{q}}{(1+\tau_z)r(\tilde{z}) - ((\tilde{q}-1)/h) - \mu}(z(t) - \tilde{z}) \qquad (4.11b)$$

$$c(t) - \tilde{c} = \frac{\tilde{c}(1+\tau_z)r'(\tilde{z})}{\mu}\left[\frac{1}{1-\gamma} + \frac{\tilde{q}/h}{(1+\tau_z)r(\tilde{z}) - ((\tilde{q}-1)/h) - \mu}\right](z(t) - \tilde{z}) \qquad (4.11c)$$

where $\mu < 0$ denotes the stable eigenvalue. The relationships (4.11b) and (4.11c) describe stable saddlepaths for the price of capital, q, and consumption, c, both of which are negatively sloped. As the debt to capital ratio increases, the cost of borrowing rises, requiring an increase in the equilibrium rate of return

---

[8] This pattern of eigenvalues can be established as follows. The negative determinant implies that the product of the three eigenvalues is negative, implying that the number of negative eigenvalues is either one or three. However, the positive trace, being the sum of the three eigenvalues, rules out the latter case, thus implying one negative eigenvalue.

on capital, which is achieved by a reduction in its price. In addition, the higher interest payments reduce the amount of consumption.

4.1.1 Steady-state equilibrium and long-run adjustments

Steady-state equilibrium is reached when $\dot{c} = \dot{z} = \dot{q} = 0$, so that the corresponding steady-state values of $\tilde{c}, \tilde{z}$, and $\tilde{q}$, and the corresponding growth rate, $\tilde{\phi}$, are determined by:

$$\frac{1}{1-\gamma}\left((1+\tau_z)r(\tilde{z}) - \rho\right) = \frac{\tilde{q}-1}{h} \equiv \tilde{\phi} \tag{4.12a}$$

$$\tilde{c} + \left(\frac{\tilde{q}^2 - 1}{2h}\right) - \left(\frac{\tilde{q}-1}{h}\right)\tilde{z} - A + r(\tilde{z})\tilde{z} = 0 \tag{4.12b}$$

$$(1-\tau_y)A\sigma + \frac{(\tilde{q}-1)^2}{2h} - r(\tilde{z})\tilde{q}(1+\tau_z) = 0 \tag{4.12c}$$

The constant consumption to capital and debt to capital ratios imply that in the long run, consumption, debt, capital, and output all grow at the same rate, $\tilde{\phi}$. This is in sharp contrast to the basic fixed-employment model of Chapter 2, where the small economy had unrestricted access to a perfect world capital market. That opportunity leads to an equilibrium in which both consumption and wealth grow at one steady rate, determined by tastes and borrowing costs, while capital and output grow at another rate, determined by production conditions, with the difference between them being accommodated by appropriate borrowing or lending. With increasing borrowing costs, the economy is forced to incur an equilibrium level of debt such that the consumption and output growth rates are brought into equality. This equilibrating mechanism also contrasts sharply with the equilibrating mechanism in the elastic labor supply model of Chapter 3; see (3.10a) and (3.10b). In that case, it was the allocation of time devoted to leisure that adjusted to ensure that the productivity of capital and its equilibrium growth rate of capital were consistent with the exogenously determined growth rate of consumption.

Being nonlinear, (4.12) raises potential problems of nonuniqueness and nonexistence of a balanced growth equilibrium. This can be seen most directly by combining (4.12a) and (4.12c) to obtain

$$(1-2\gamma)\tilde{q}^2 + 2(h\rho + \gamma)\tilde{q} - \left(1 + 2hA\sigma(1-\tau_y)\right) = 0 \tag{4.13}$$

This is a quadratic equation in $\tilde{q}$ and the economy will ultimately follow a balanced growth path if and only if (4.13) has (at least) one real solution. As long as $\gamma < 1/2$, the existence of real roots to this equation is assured. Given the preponderance of empirical evidence favoring the intertemporal elasticity of substitution being less than unity (i.e. $\gamma < 0$) this condition is almost certain to prevail in practice. However, in the extreme case that $\gamma > 1/2$, it is possible for the returns to capital to dominate sufficiently the costs of debt so that no long-run balanced growth equilibrium exists, where the returns on these two activities are brought to equality.[9]

Provided that the roots are real, (4.13) admits two solutions for $\tilde{q}$, say $\tilde{q}_1, \tilde{q}_2$ corresponding to the negative and positive roots respectively, suggesting the potential existence of two steady-state equilibrium growth paths. In order to be viable, these roots must be (i) nonnegative, and (ii) consistent with the transversality conditions. It is straightforward to show that if $\gamma < 1/2$, the smaller of the two roots, $\tilde{q}_1$, violates (i), while it violates (ii) if $\gamma > 1/2$. By contrast, the larger root, $\tilde{q}_2$, always satisfies both conditions, implying that in fact that there is only one viable solution.

Table 4.1 summarizes the long-run effects of changes in debt costs and fiscal shocks. The intuition behind these results is as follows. The long-run domestic growth rate, $\tilde{\phi} \equiv ((\tilde{q} - 1)/h)$, is determined by (4.13). It is determined entirely by *internal* conditions, such as the production parameters, A, σ, and h, fiscal instruments, τ_y, and the rate of time preference, ρ, but is independent of factors determining *external* borrowing costs, r^*, δ, including the tax on debt, and τ_z. Indeed, the determinants of the long-run growth rate are much closer to those of a closed economy than those determining the growth of capital in an open economy under perfect capital markets. This can be seen by comparing (4.13) with Turnovsky (1996a, eq. 8) and Turnovsky (1996b, eq. 10). The steady-state equilibrium requires that the level of external debt must be such that the tax-adjusted rate at which the country may borrow must equate the growth rate of consumption to that of capital. This variable therefore plays the same role in the adjustment process as does the endogenous interest rate in a closed economy.

Given that $\tilde{q}$ is independent of r^*, it then follows from (4.12a) that the equilibrium net borrowing rate, $\tilde{r}(1 + \tau_z)$, must be independent of r^*. Thus, while the direct effect of a higher world interest rate, r^*, is to raise borrowing costs, this leads to a long-run reduction in the debt–capital ratio that exactly offsets this higher cost and leaves the overall equilibrium cost of debt unchanged. The effect of a lower long-run debt with the borrowing rate

---

[9] We may note the parallels here with the existence problem in the basic model discussed in Chapter 2, although the nature of the tradeoff is very different in the two cases.

Table 4.1. *Effects on long-run equilibrium: decentralized economy*

(a) Debt costs

	r^*	δ
$\tilde{z}$	$-\dfrac{1}{r'}$	$-\dfrac{v}{r'}$
$r(\tilde{z})$	0	0
$\tilde{q}$	0	0
$\tilde{c}$	$\dfrac{r-\left(\frac{\tilde{q}-1}{h}\right)}{r'}>0$	$\dfrac{v\left[r-\left(\frac{\tilde{q}-1}{h}\right)\right]}{r'}>0$

(b) Fiscal shocks

	τ_z	τ_y
$\tilde{z}$	$-\dfrac{r}{(1+\tau_z)r'}<0$	$-\dfrac{A\sigma}{hr'(1+\tau_z)\Delta}>0$
$r(\tilde{z})$	$-\dfrac{r}{1+\tau_z}<0$	$-\dfrac{A\sigma}{h(1+\tau_z)\Delta}<0$
$\tilde{q}$	0	$-\dfrac{A\sigma}{(1-\gamma)\Delta}<0$
$\tilde{c}$	$\dfrac{\left[r+r'\tilde{z}-\left(\frac{\tilde{q}-1}{h}\right)\right]r}{(1+\tau_z)r'}>0$	$\dfrac{A\sigma}{h\Delta}\left\{\dfrac{1}{r'(1+\tau_z)}\left(r+r'\tilde{z}-(\tilde{q}-1)\right)+\left(\dfrac{\tilde{q}-\tilde{z}}{1-\gamma}\right)\right\}<0$

where $\Delta \equiv \left(r(1+\tau_z)-\left(\frac{\tilde{q}-1}{h}\right)\right)\dfrac{1}{1-\gamma}+\dfrac{\tilde{q}}{h}>0$

remaining unchanged is to reduce the long-run debt burden, leaving more resources available for consumption and thus raising the consumption to capital (or equivalently consumption to output) ratio. The responses are qualitatively identical (and indeed proportional) for an increase in the country-specific borrowing premium, δ.

The responses to fiscal shocks summarized in Table 4.1b assume that each change is financed by lump-sum taxation. Since the borrowing costs (inclusive of tax) are determined by $\tilde{q}$, it follows that an increase in the tax on borrowing, τ_z, must lead to a corresponding decrease in the before-tax borrowing rate and this requires a decrease in the debt–capital ratio. This lowers borrowing costs, thus raising the equilibrium consumption–capital ratio. A higher tax on capital income, τ_y, decreases the net return to capital, thus reducing the price of capital, $\tilde{q}$, and the equilibrium growth rate. This requires the equilibrium consumption growth rate to fall and this is accomplished by a reduction in the domestic borrowing costs, brought about by a reduction in the debt–capital ratio. This in turn leads to an increase in the long-run consumption–capital ratio.

4.1.2 Transitional dynamics

The transitional dynamics in response to the two shocks, r^* and τ_y are illustrated in Figures 4.1 and 4.2, respectively. In each case, part (a) illustrates the stable saddlepath dynamics of the debt–capital ratio, z, and the shadow value of capital, q.[10] Part (b) illustrates the transitional growth paths of capital, $\dot{K}/K$, debt, $\dot{Z}/Z$, and consumption, $\dot{C}/C$. These three growth rates always converge to the common long-run growth rate, $\tilde{\phi}$.

An increase in the exogenous world interest rate r^* has been shown to lead to a long-run decline in the debt–capital ratio, with $\tilde{q}$, and the long-run growth rate unchanged. The steady-state equilibrium thus shifts from P to R in Figure 4.1a. With perfect foresight, this anticipated long-run decline in the relative scarcity of capital reduces its shadow value in the short run; in terms of Figure 4.1, q initially drops from P on the original stable saddlepath AA to Q on the new stable locus $A'A'$. This reduction in q induces the economy to begin reducing its rate of capital accumulation, thus increasing its relative scarcity and causing its shadow value to begin to rise. At the same time, the higher borrowing cost causes initial consumption to decline. This reduction in consumption, together with the reduction in investment

---

[10] There is also a stable locus in c-z space, defined by (4.11c), that we have not drawn.

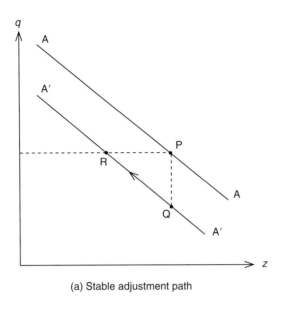

(a) Stable adjustment path

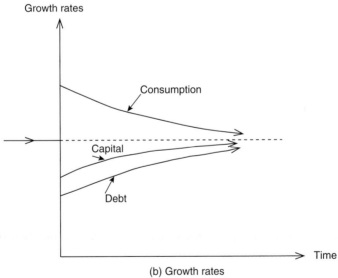

(b) Growth rates

Figure 4.1 Increase in borrowing costs

plus adjustment costs, leads to a reduction in aggregate demand by the
domestic economy. With domestic output fixed instantaneously, there is an
increase in the country's trade balance, the effect of which is to reduce the
initial growth rate of debt. Furthermore, since the decline in aggregate

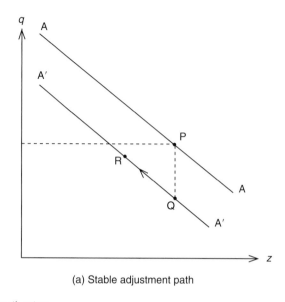

(a) Stable adjustment path

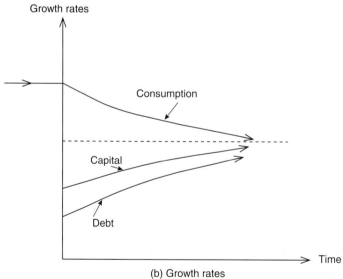

(b) Growth rates

Figure 4.2 Increase in capital income tax

demand reflects more than just the decline in investment, the rate of growth of debt is reduced more than that of capital, so that the debt–capital ratio starts to decline. This gradual reduction in z accompanied by the increase in q is represented by a movement in the direction QR along the new stable saddlepath A′A′. The adjustment ceases when the price of capital is restored to its original value.

The fact that after the initial reduction in q, $\dot{q} > 0$ along the transitional path implies that after its initial decline, the growth rate of capital is in fact increasing along the transitional path. In addition, the fact that $\dot{z} < 0$ along this path implies that $(\dot{Z}/Z) < (\dot{K}/K)$, although it too is rising over time. This is because the increase in the growth of capital and installation costs increases the demand for resources relative to output, thus increasing the need for the country to borrow abroad. Finally, combining (4.4a) and (4.5a) to yield:

$$\frac{\dot{C}}{C} = \frac{(1 + \tau_z)r(z) - \rho}{1 - \gamma}$$

we may infer the following time path for consumption. After the initial decline in C, the increase in the world interest rate causes a corresponding initial increase in borrowing costs, thus raising the initial growth rate in consumption. As the debt–capital ratio declines during the transition, the borrowing rate declines and the growth rate of domestic consumption falls correspondingly. The time paths for the growth rates of consumption, capital, and debt thus follow the convergent paths illustrated in Figure 4.1b.

Figure 4.2 illustrates the dynamics in response to a higher tax on capital income. This is similar to that resulting from a higher foreign interest rate, but with two differences. First, in contrast to the latter, a higher tax on capital income leads to a reduction in the long-run growth rate. The short-run responses in the growth rates of both debt and capital exceed their long-run responses, implying an overshooting in growth rates. Second, the growth rate of consumption does not respond on impact. Instead, it adjusts over time to the gradual reduction in the debt–capital ratio.

An important question facing developing economies concerns the extent to which restricted access to world financial markets affects their growth rates and the ability of their governments' policies to influence the economy. Within this model, access to the world financial markets may be proxied by δ in (4.1), with a decrease in access being reflected by a higher value of this parameter. As we have seen, the long-run growth rate is determined by internal conditions and is therefore unaffected by borrowing conditions. In the short run, less favorable access to the world borrowing market will have an adverse effect on the growth of output, but this is only temporary. Over time the economy adjusts by reducing its foreign debt, thereby reducing the costs of servicing the debt and the drain this imposes on the economy.

The fact that the borrowing premium has a relatively limited effect on the long-run equilibrium is a consequence of the fact that we are dealing with individual representative agents, each of whom has a negligible effect on the borrowing rate. If the agent is sufficiently large so as to take account of his actions on the borrowing rate then it turns out the borrowing premium is much more important in determining the long-run equilibrium of the economy. This is the case, for example, if the economy is operated by a central planner.

4.1.3 Centrally planned economy

As a benchmark, it is useful to compare the adjustments we have discussed in Sections 4.1.1 and 4.1.2 with those that would obtain in a centrally planned economy, in which the planner controls quantities directly. In this case, the decision maker chooses consumption and investment, C and I, and the rates of accumulation of capital and debt, $\dot{K}$ and $\dot{Z}$, directly so as to maximize the utility function (4.2a), subject to the resource constraint of the economy (4.7c). In making these decisions the planner recognizes the effect of his decisions on the cost of borrowing, $r(Z/K)$. He also internalizes the externalities due to the aggregate capital stock in the individual production function, thereby focusing on the social rather than the private rate of return on capital.

Corresponding to (4.4a), (4.7a), (4.5a), and (4.5b), the relevant optimality conditions are now:

$$C^{\gamma-1} = \lambda \tag{4.4a$'$}$$

$$\frac{I}{K} = \frac{\dot{K}}{K} = \frac{q-1}{h} \equiv \phi \tag{4.7a}$$

$$\rho - \frac{\dot{\lambda}}{\lambda} = r\left(\frac{Z}{K}\right) + r'\left(\frac{Z}{K}\right)\cdot\left(\frac{Z}{K}\right) \tag{4.5a$'$}$$

$$\frac{A}{q} + \frac{\dot{q}}{q} + \frac{(q-1)^2}{2hq} + \frac{r'(Z/K)}{q}\cdot\left(\frac{Z}{K}\right)^2 = r\left(\frac{Z}{K}\right) + r'\left(\frac{Z}{K}\right)\cdot\left(\frac{Z}{K}\right) \tag{4.5b$'$}$$

The following modifications to the previous conditions may be observed. First, tax rates are obviously no longer relevant in a centrally planned economy. Second, the interest rate appearing on the right-hand side of (4.5a) and (4.5b) is now replaced by the marginal cost of debt, where the central planner recognizes that increasing his stock of debt and therefore the debt–capital ratio, raises the cost of borrowing. Analogously, increasing the capital stock lowers the debt–capital ratio, thus reducing the cost of further borrowing. This is reflected by the term $[r'(Z/K)/q].(Z/K)^2$ and is an additional component of the rate of return on capital. Finally, the optimality condition for investment (4.7a), remains unchanged.

Repeating the analysis of Section 4.2, the macrodynamic equilibrium is now given by:

$$\dot{c}^* = c^* \left(\frac{1}{1-\gamma}(r(z^*) + r'(z^*)z^* - p) - \frac{q^*-1}{h} \right) \tag{4.9a'}$$

$$\dot{z}^* = c^* + \left(\frac{q^{*2}-1}{2h} \right) - \left(\frac{q^*-1}{h} \right) z^* - A + r(z^*)z^* \tag{4.9b'}$$

$$\dot{q}^* = [r(z^*) + r'(z^*)z^*]q^* - r'(z^*)z^{*2} - A - \frac{(q^*-1)^2}{2h} \tag{4.9c'}$$

where * denotes equilibrium in the centrally planned economy. Linearizing this system of equations yields:

$$\begin{pmatrix} \dot{c}^* \\ \dot{z}^* \\ \dot{q}^* \end{pmatrix} = \begin{pmatrix} 0 & \frac{\tilde{c}^*}{1-\gamma}[2r' + r''\tilde{z}^*] & -\frac{\tilde{c}^*}{h} \\ 1 & [r(\tilde{z}^*) + r'(\tilde{z}^*)\tilde{z}^*] - (\frac{\tilde{q}^*-1}{h}) & (\frac{\tilde{q}^*-\tilde{z}^*}{h}) \\ 0 & [2r' + r''\tilde{z}^*](\tilde{q}^* - \tilde{z}^*) & r(\tilde{z}^*) + r'\tilde{z}^* - (\frac{\tilde{q}^*-1}{h}) \end{pmatrix} \begin{pmatrix} c^* - \tilde{c}^* \\ z^* - \tilde{z}^* \\ q^* - \tilde{q}^* \end{pmatrix}$$
$$\tag{4.10'}$$

As in Section 4.2 the transversality condition, together with the condition that the net asset position of the economy be positive, $\tilde{q}^* - \tilde{z}^* \equiv \tilde{q}^*\tilde{K}^* - \tilde{Z}^* > 0$, ensures that the system (4.10') has one stable and two unstable roots. Starting from the initial debt–capital ratio, z_0^*, the stable transitional adjustment path is

$$z^*(t) = \tilde{z}^* + \left(z_0^* - \tilde{z}^*\right)e^{\mu t} \tag{4.11a'}$$

$$q^*(t) - \tilde{q}^* = -\frac{(2r' + r''\tilde{z}^*)(\tilde{q}^* - \tilde{z}^*)}{r^*(\tilde{z}) + r'\tilde{z}^* - ((\tilde{q}^* - 1)/h) - \mu^*}(z^*(t) - \tilde{z}^*) \tag{4.11b'}$$

$$c^*(t) - \tilde{c}^* = \frac{\tilde{c}^*(2r' + r''\tilde{z}^*)}{\mu^*}\left[\frac{1}{1-\gamma} + \frac{(\tilde{q}^* - z^*)/h}{r^*(\tilde{z}) + r'\tilde{z}^* - ((\tilde{q}^* - 1)/h) - \mu^*}\right](z^*(t) - \tilde{z}^*)$$

$$(4.11c')$$

Equations (4.11b′), (4.11c′) are stable saddlepaths for the price of capital and the consumption–debt ratio and are negatively sloped, as before.

Steady-state equilibrium in the centrally planned system is described by:

$$\frac{1}{1-\gamma}(r(\tilde{z}^*) + r'\tilde{z}^* - \rho) = \frac{\tilde{q}^* - 1}{h} \equiv \tilde{\phi}^* \qquad (4.12a')$$

$$\tilde{c}^* + \left(\frac{\tilde{q}^{*2} - 1}{2h}\right) - \left(\frac{\tilde{q}^* - 1}{h}\right)\tilde{z}^* - A + r(\tilde{z}^*)\tilde{z}^* = 0 \qquad (4.12b')$$

$$A + \frac{(\tilde{q}^* - 1)^2}{2h} + r'\tilde{z}^{*2} - (r(\tilde{z}^*) + r'\tilde{z}^*)\tilde{q}^* = 0 \qquad (4.12c')$$

Equations (4.12a′) and (4.12c′) now determine $\tilde{q}^*$ and $\tilde{z}^*$ jointly, rather than sequentially as in the decentralized economy (cf. (4.13)). Potential problems of nonuniqueness and nonexistence of equilibrium remain as before, and may be compounded depending upon the nature of the debt function $r(z)$.[11]

4.1.4 Replication of first-best optimum steady state

The equilibrium corresponding to that of the centrally planned economy, derived in Section 4.1.3, represents the first-best outcome. In this section we turn to the determination of the tax structure that will enable this to be replicated by the decentralized economy. Two general requirements must be met. The first is that the decentralized economy must ultimately attain the steady state of the centralized economy. Second, having replicated the steady state, the transitional dynamic adjustment paths in the two economies must also coincide. In general, to achieve these twin objectives, the optimal tax must be time-varying.

---

[11] It is straightforward to analyze the effects of increases in the cost of borrowing on the long-run stock of debt and the equilibrium growth rate in the planned economy. Several differences from the corresponding responses noted in Table 4.1 for the decentralized economy arise. The most important difference is that an increase in the cost of borrowing, whether in the form of a higher foreign interest rate or a higher risk premium, will have an adverse effect on the long-run growth rate. It is also apparent by comparing the steady-state equilibrium (4.12′) with (4.12) that the marginal costs of borrowing, as reflected by terms involving r' are more important in the centralized equilibrium.

Consider first the steady state. In order for the steady states in the two equilibria to coincide, the price of capital and the ratio of debt to capital in the two economies must be equal; i.e. $\tilde{q} = \tilde{q}^*, \tilde{z} = \tilde{z}^*$. This will be so if and only if (i) the two stationarity conditions of consumption/capital growth conditions in the two economies, (4.12a) and (4.12a′) coincide and (ii) the rates of return in the two economies, (4.12c) and (4.12c′) coincide. These two conditions will be met if and only if (i) the subsidy to debt, $\hat{\tau}_z$, and (ii) the tax on capital, $\hat{\tau}_y$, in the decentralized economy are chosen to satisfy:

$$(1 + \hat{\tau}_z)\tilde{r}(\tilde{z}^*) = r(\tilde{z}^*) + r'(\tilde{z}^*)\tilde{z}^* \tag{4.14a}$$

$$A + r'(\tilde{z}^*)\tilde{z}^{*2} = (1 - \hat{\tau}_y)A\sigma \tag{4.14b}$$

Provided (4.14a) and (4.14b) hold, $\tilde{q} = \tilde{q}^*, \tilde{z} = \tilde{z}^*$, in which case the equilibrium goods market conditions (4.12b) and (4.12b′) will automatically be satisfied as well.

Solving (4.14a) and (4.14b) for $\hat{\tau}_z$ and $\hat{\tau}_y$, the decentralized steady state will coincide with that in the centrally planned economy if and only if:

$$\hat{\tau}_z = \frac{r'(\tilde{z}^*)\tilde{z}^*}{r(\tilde{z}^*)} \tag{4.15a}$$

$$\hat{\tau}_y = \left(\frac{\sigma - 1}{\sigma}\right) - \frac{r'(\tilde{z}^*)\tilde{z}^{*2}}{A\sigma} \tag{4.15b}$$

Having set the income tax rates in this manner, in order for the government budget to be balanced, the consumption tax, $\hat{\tau}_c$, must be set to satisfy the government budget constraint:

$$\hat{\tau}_c\tilde{c}^* = -\hat{\tau}_z r(\tilde{z}^*)\tilde{z}^* - \hat{\tau}_y A$$

Substituting for (4.15a) and (4.15b) into this relationship we find that the optimal tax on consumption raises revenue of the amount:

$$\hat{\tau}_c\tilde{c}^* = \frac{(1 - \sigma)}{\sigma}A \tag{4.15c}$$

This optimal tax structure reflects the two externalities facing the economy. The first is the production externality, generated by the impact of the aggregate capital stock on the productivity of private capital. The decision by the private sector to accumulate capital leads to an increase in the aggregate capital stock, raising the productivity of private capital. Since the private sector treats the aggregate capital stock as being independent of its investment decision, when in fact it is not, an externality is introduced, requiring a tax on the returns to capital to correct for this distortion and replicate the first-best equilibrium.

In the absence of a country-specific premium associated with borrowing ($r' = 0$), there should be no tax or subsidy on debt. In such an economy, consumption and wealth will grow at one rate, while output and capital will grow at some other rate. Leaving debt untaxed will ensure that the consumption growth rate in the decentralized economy will track the consumption growth rate in the centrally planned economy. A tax on capital income, however, is in general required to correct for the production externality and to ensure that the growth rate of the centrally planned economy is replicated. Given this tax rate, a consumption tax must be residually set to ensure that the government's budget is balanced. The amount of the externality and the required corrective capital income tax depends upon the production externality $(1 - \sigma)$. If $\sigma = 1$, there is no externality, the capital income tax should be set to zero, and there is no need for a consumption tax either.

The upward-sloping supply curve of debt introduces a second externality, internalized by the central planner, but not taken into account by the representative agent in the decentralized economy. This leads to a further modification of the optimal tax policy. Specifically, agents in the decentralized economy fail to take account of the fact that as they collectively increase their amount of borrowing, they raise the aggregate debt–capital ratio, thus raising the cost of debt. Similarly, as they invest in capital and increase the productivity capacity of the economy and its ability to finance debt capital, they lower the aggregate debt–capital ratio, and reduce the cost of debt. Accordingly, by underestimating the true cost of borrowing and underestimating the true benefits to accumulating capital the agents in the decentralized economy under-invest in capital and over-borrow, relative to the first-best optimum. To correct for this misallocation, the cost of debt should be taxed, while the return to capital should be partially subsidized, thus reducing $\hat{\tau}_y < (\sigma - 1)/\sigma$. Indeed, in the absence of any externality from capital, there should be net subsidy on capital income; i.e. $\hat{\tau}_y < 0$.

4.1.5 Replication of first-best optimum transition path

To replicate the entire first-best optimum, we need to track its complete transitional path. In general, if the tax rates in the decentralized economy are set as in (4.15a)–(4.15c) during the transition, the adjustment path followed by the decentralized economy will fail to mimic that of the first-best optimum. To see this we consider the respective eigenvalues and show that in this circumstance $\mu = \mu^*$. For notational convenience we denote the elements of the matrix of coefficients in the linearized centrally planned economy by (a_{ij}). These elements can be immediately identified by referring to (4.10′). The equilibrium eigenvalue in the centrally planned economy is the negative solution to the cubic equation:

$$F(\mu^*) \equiv \mu^*(a_{22} - \mu^*)(a_{33} - \mu^*) - a_{32}[a_{13} + a_{23}\mu^*] \\ + a_{12}(a_{33} - \mu^*) = 0 \tag{4.16}$$

Using this notation, if the tax rates in the decentralized economy are set in accordance with (4.15), thereby replicating the steady state, then the corresponding eigenvalue, μ, in the decentralized economy is determined where

$$G(\mu) \equiv \mu(a_{22} - \mu)(a_{33} - \mu) - r'(1 + \hat{\tau}_z)q[a_{13} + a_{23}\mu] \\ + \frac{c}{1 - \gamma}r'(1 + \hat{\tau}_z)(a_{33} - \mu) = 0 \tag{4.16′}$$

Combining (4.16) and (4.16′) we find that

$$F(\mu) \equiv (r'(1 + \hat{\tau}_z)q - [2r' + r''\tilde{z}][\tilde{q} - \tilde{z}])[a_{13} + a_{23}\mu] \\ - \frac{c}{1 - \gamma}(r'(1 + \hat{\tau}_z) - [2r' + r''\tilde{z}])(a_{33} - \mu)$$

Under weak conditions, $F(\mu) < 0$.[12] It then follows from the fact that the function $F(.)$ is cubic in μ and that μ and μ^* are unique stable eigenvalues that the relationship $\mu^* < \mu < 0$ must hold. In other words, if the tax rates are fixed over time as in (4.15), then the ratio of debt to capital in the decentralized economy, z, determined by (4.14a), will converge too slowly, relative to the optimal rate of adjustment as described by (4.11a′). The intuition for this result is a consequence of the fact that each individual agent treats the cost of borrowing as given and does not take account of their collective impact on the net borrowing costs.

---

[12] A simple sufficient, but not necessary, condition to ensure that this is so includes $\tilde{q} > (2r' + r''\tilde{z})/(2r' + r''\tilde{z}) - r'(1 + \tau_z)$. If the equilibrium is one of positive growth ($\tilde{q} > 1$), this condition will be met certainly as long as the debt–capital ratio is not too large. Weaker conditions can also be obtained.

The speed of adjustment can be modified by introducing a time-varying component to the tax rate. One possibility is to modify the tax (subsidy) rate on debt to:

$$\tau_z(t) = \hat{\tau}_z + \theta[z^*(t) - \tilde{z}^*] \qquad (4.17)$$

where $\hat{\tau}_z$ is given by (4.15a) and θ is a constant, to be determined. The tax rate as specified by (4.17) is time-varying, responding to the changing deviation in the aggregate debt to capital ratio from its steady-state value as the economy evolves. Since $\tau_z(t)$ is a function of aggregate variables, the representative agent takes it as given, and since θ is relevant only along the transitional path (when $z^* \neq \tilde{z}^*$) it has no impact on the steady-state equilibrium. Consequently, setting $\hat{\tau}_z$ in accordance with (4.15) will still replicate the steady state of the first-best optimum. But by varying the tax rate in accordance with (4.17), θ will affect the eigenvalue μ in the decentralized economy and therefore the speed of adjustment along the transitional path. By appropriate choice of θ, the government is able to induce the decentralized economy to track the debt–capital ratio of the centrally planned economy, and thereby track the adjustment paths followed by other variables as well.

Thus the time-varying tax rate on debt (4.17), is able to replicate the entire first-best optimum in the sense that both the steady state and the transitional path will be attained. Having set the distortionary (income) taxes optimally, any combination of lump-sum taxes or consumption tax, satisfying the flow government budget constraint will replicate the first-best optimal path. Note further that with the availability of a full set of tax instruments the problem of time inconsistency of optimal policy does not arise. With the target value for the tax rate on debt at each instant of time being determined by the time path followed by the first-best optimum, the government will always want to choose the tax rate on debt to attain that given and unchanging target path.

4.2 Comparison with basic model

Limitations on foreign borrowing are important constraints on developing economies. Thus far in this chapter we have developed a growth model of such an economy facing an upward-sloping supply curve of debt. The behavior of such a model is in marked contrast to that associated with a small open economy having unlimited access to a perfect world capital market, developed in Chapter 2. In such an economy, consumption is always on a steady growth path, growing at a rate determined by tastes and the fixed world interest rate; capital is also always on its steady growth path, growing at a fixed rate determined by the production conditions in the economy. Differences between these rates are supported by the country's ability to borrow or lend indefinitely at the world interest rate.

In the economy we have been discussing, growth is characterized by transitional dynamics in which consumption and capital converge to a common long-run growth rate. The key adjustment is through the debt–capital ratio, which drives the borrowing rate to a level at which the growth rates are equalized. This structure leads to very different policy implications from those obtained with perfect capital mobility. For example, we have shown that an increase in the tax on capital income will reduce the (common) equilibrium growth rate in the economy, while an increase in the tax (or subsidy) on debt will leave the equilibrium growth rate unaffected. Instead, a tax on debt will discourage the accumulation of debt to the point that the net borrowing cost just equals the (unchanged) equilibrium rate of return on capital. This response contrasts with that obtained with a perfect world bond market when a higher tax on interest income would raise the equilibrium growth rate of capital, but reduce the growth rate of consumption and wealth.

4.3 Public and private capital

We now turn to the second model to be discussed in this chapter, namely one with public, as well as private, capital. Most models analyzing productive government expenditure treat the current *flows* of government expenditure as the sources of contributions to productive capacity. This is true of Aschauer (1988) and Lee (1995) within the context of the stationary Ramsey model, and also of Barro (1990) and Turnovsky (1996b) in the context of the AK model, discussed in Chapter 2. While the flow specification has the virtue of tractability, it is open to the criticism that insofar as productive government expenditures are intended to represent public infrastructure, such as roads and education, it is the accumulated *stock*, rather than the current flow, that is the more appropriate influence on the economy's productive capacity.

Despite this, within the Ramsey framework, relatively few authors have adopted the alternative approach of modeling productive government expenditure as a stock. Arrow and Kurz (1970) were first to model government expenditure as a form of investment, although much of the recent theoretical and empirical interest in the impact of public capital on private capital accumulation and economic growth originated with the work of Aschauer (1989a, 1989b).[13] Subsequently, Baxter and King (1993) studied the macroeconomic implications of increases in the stocks of public goods. They derive the transitional dynamic response of output, investment, consumption, employment, and interest rates to such policies by calibrating a real business cycle model. Fisher and Turnovsky (1998) address similar issues from a more analytical perspective, and this work is further extended by Turnovsky (2004).

The literature introducing both private and public capital into growth models is sparse. Futagami, Morita, and Shibata (1993), Glomm and Ravikumar (1994), and Turnovsky (1997b) do so in a closed economy, while an open economy version is developed by Turnovsky (1997c). Private capital in the Glomm–Ravikumar model fully depreciates each period, rather than being subject to at most gradual (or possibly zero) depreciation. This enables the dynamics of the system to be represented by a single state variable alone, so that the system behaves much more like the Barro model in which government expenditure is introduced as a flow. In particular, under constant returns to scale in the reproducible factors, there are no transitional dynamics and the economy is always on a balanced growth path. Devarajan, Xie, and Zou (1998) address the issue of whether public capital should be provided through taxation or through granting subsidies to private providers. This is extended to an open economy by Chatterjee (2007).

In order not to overly complicate things we shall revert to the case of a small developed economy that has unrestricted access to a perfect world capital market. In this case, the introduction of public capital leads to an equilibrium in which the transitional dynamics can be specified in terms of (i) the ratio of public to private capital, (ii) the consumption to capital ratio, and (iii) the shadow value of private capital. As in the basic model of Chapter 2, consumption and capital may converge to different equilibrium growth rates, with the discrepancy being accommodated by the country's accumulation of traded bonds.

4.3.1 The analytical framework[14]

We shall focus our discussion on the decentralized economy that produces a single traded good. Output of this good, Y_i, produced by the typical domestic

---

[13] See Gramlich (1994) for a comprehensive survey of the subsequent empirical literature.
[14] The following analysis is adapted from Turnovsky (1997c).

representative agent is determined by his privately owned capital stock, K_i, and the services, K_G^s, derived by the firm from its use of public (government) capital stock, in accordance with the constant returns to scale technology:

$$Y_i = F(K_i, K_G^s) \equiv f\left(\frac{K_G^s}{K_i}\right)K_i; \quad f' > 0,\ f'' < 0 \qquad (4.18a)$$

The production function (4.18a) is analogous to (2.29), of the basic Barro (1990) model, although there are two differences. First, and most importantly, we have replaced the flow of public expenditure with the stock of public capital. Thus, (4.18a) embodies the assumption that the services of the public capital stock enhance the productivity of private capital, though at a diminishing rate. Second, we have generalized the Cobb–Douglas production function to any general homogeneous production function of degree one in the two accumulating productive factors, K_i, K_G^s, as suggested in section 2.5. In addition, we continue to abstract from labor so that private capital may be interpreted broadly to include human as well as physical capital; see Rebelo (1991).

The productive services derived by the agent from government capital are analogous to those of section 2.4, namely:

$$K_G^s = K_G(K_i/K)^{1-\varepsilon} \quad 0 \le \varepsilon \le 1 \qquad (4.18b)$$

where K_G denotes the aggregate stock of public capital and K denotes the aggregate stock of private stock, thereby incorporating a specific form of congestion. Just as in equation (2.30), the specification of government services by (4.18b) implies that the use of public capital is congested only by the use of private capital. Other formulations are also possible. For example, public services might be congested by output or employment. But with labor fixed inelastically, (4.18b) is an appropriate specification, especially since our focus is on the interaction of public and private capital accumulation.

Substituting (4.18b) into (4.18a), the individual firm's production function can be expressed as:

$$Y_i = f\left(\frac{K_G}{K_i}\left(\frac{K_i}{K}\right)^{1-\varepsilon}\right)K_i = f\left(\frac{K_G}{K}\left(\frac{K}{K_i}\right)^{\varepsilon}\right)K_i \qquad (4.18a')$$

As long as $\varepsilon \ne 1$, so that the public good is associated with some congestion, aggregate capital is introduced into the production function of the individual firm in an analogous way to Romer (1986). With all agents being identical, the aggregate and individual capital stocks are related by $K = NK_i$, where N is the number of representative agents. Thus, in equilibrium, the individual output Y_i and aggregate output $Y = NY_i$ may be expressed as:

$$Y_i = f\left(\frac{K_G}{K}N^\varepsilon\right)K_i; \quad Y = f\left(\frac{K_G}{K}N^\varepsilon\right)K \qquad (4.18a'')$$

As encountered previously, the production function embodies the potential "scale effect" associated with the population size. For expositional convenience we shall abstract from this and set the number of agents $N = 1$, again enabling us to drop the distinction between aggregate and individual quantities in equilibrium.

The introduction of the constant rate of depreciation of capital introduces little complication and since it becomes important for the calibration of the model that we shall undertake in later chapters, we will allow for the depreciation of both types of capital. Thus, private capital, K, depreciates at the constant rate δ_K, so that, letting I denote the rate of gross private investment, net private capital accumulates at the rate

$$\dot{K} = I - \delta_K K \qquad (4.19a)$$

Likewise, public capital, K_G, depreciates at the constant rate δ_G, so that, letting G denote the rate of gross public investment, the rate of net public capital accumulation follows:

$$\dot{K}_G = G - \delta_G K_G \qquad (4.19b)$$

New output may be transformed to either type of capital. In both cases this process involves adjustment costs (installation costs) that we incorporate in the quadratic (convex) functions:

$$\Phi(I, K) \equiv I\left(1 + \frac{h_1}{2}\frac{I}{K}\right) \qquad (4.20a)$$

$$\Psi(G, K_G) \equiv G\left(1 + \frac{h_2}{2}\frac{G}{K_G}\right) \qquad (4.20b)$$

The specification (4.20a) is familiar from previous models, while (4.20b) assumes an analogous form of installation costs for public capital. The reason for the proportional specification of installation costs and its necessity to sustain ongoing growth has been discussed in earlier chapters. The only point to be added at this stage is that there is no compelling reason to assume that the installation costs for the two types of capital are the same.

As in the basic model of Chapter 2, in order for an equilibrium with steady ongoing growth to be sustained, the current flow of government expenditure, G, must be linked to the size of the economy. Thus analogously to (2.32), we specify the current flow of government spending by:[15]

$$G = gY = gf\left(\frac{K_G}{K}\right)K \qquad (4.21)$$

As long as g remains fixed, the government is claiming a fixed share of the growing output for gross investment, so that an increase in the share, g, parameterizes an expansionary expenditure policy in a growing economy.[16] In Section 4.3.7 below, we also discuss the case where government expenditure is set optimally along with private expenditures. As will be seen, the optimal expenditure policy will require the fraction g to be *time-varying*, continuously adapting to the changing aggregate stocks of public and private capital. This optimum serves as an important benchmark in explaining the effects of changes in government expenditure away from the optimum.

We now turn to the representative agent operating in a decentralized economy. The objective of the agent is to choose his consumption, investment, and rates of accumulation of traded bonds and private capital to maximize his constant elasticity utility function (4.2a), subject to his accumulation of private capital (4.19a) and his own budget constraint, represented by:

$$\dot{B}_i = r(1 - \tau_b)B_i + (1 - \tau_y)f\left(\frac{K_G}{K}\left(\frac{K}{K_i}\right)^\varepsilon\right)K_i$$

$$- C(1 + \tau_c) - I\left(1 + \frac{h_1}{2}\frac{I}{K}\right) - T \qquad (4.22)$$

where: τ_y = rate of taxation on capital income; τ_b = rate of taxation on foreign bond income; τ_c = rate of taxation on consumption; T = time-varying rate of lump-sum taxation (or rebate).

Two points concerning this specification merit comment. First, we assume that the distortionary tax rates τ_b, τ_y, and τ_c are constant through time, being subject to at most once-and-for-all policy changes at discrete times. Second, in performing this optimization, the agent is assumed to treat the stock of public capital, K_G, and the aggregate stock of private capital, K, as given and

---

[15] Other rules determining government expenditure are also possible. For example, (4.21′) below postulates expenditure to be related to total GNP, rather than to current output.

[16] Barro (1990) and Rebelo (1991) in effect parameterize government expenditure in this fashion by assuming that all income tax revenues are spent, i.e. $G = \tau Y$.

independent of his own decisions. With the population size being normalized at unity, the condition $K_i = K$ holds as an equilibrium relationship.

We abstract from government bonds and assume, instead, that through lump-sum taxation the government maintains a continuously balanced budget which, for the above specification of taxation and with G specified in accordance with (4.21), is:

$$T + \tau_y f(K_G/K)K + r\tau_b b + \tau_c C = gf(K_G/K)K\left[1 + \frac{h_2}{2}\frac{gf(K_G/K)}{K_G/K}\right] \quad (4.23)$$

Aggregating (4.22) over the agents and combining with (4.23) yields the national resource constraint:

$$\dot{B} = rB + f\left(\frac{K_G}{K}\right)K - C - I\left(1 + \frac{h_1}{2}\frac{I}{K}\right) - G\left(1 + \frac{h_2}{2}\frac{G}{K_G}\right) \quad (4.24)$$

4.3.2 Equilibrium growth

The representative agent's optimality conditions with respect to consumption and private investment remain unchanged:

$$C^{\gamma-1} = \lambda(1 + \tau_c) \quad (4.4a)$$

$$1 + h_1\left(\frac{I}{K}\right) = q \quad (4.4b')$$

where λ denotes the shadow value of wealth and for simplicity the subscript i is dropped, and q is the market value of private capital. Thus, as before, we may solve (4.4b') for the rate of growth of private capital, ϕ_k:

$$\left(\frac{I}{K}\right) = \frac{q-1}{h_1}; \quad \left(\frac{\dot{K}}{K}\right) = \frac{q-1}{h_1} - \delta_K \equiv \phi_k \quad (4.7a')$$

The optimality condition with respect to traded bonds is given by:

$$\rho - \frac{\dot{\lambda}}{\lambda} = r(1 - \tau_b) \quad (4.5a')$$

so that the equilibrium rate of growth of consumption becomes:

$$\left(\frac{\dot{C}}{C}\right) = \frac{r(1 - \tau_b) - \rho}{1 - \gamma} \equiv \psi \quad (4.25)$$

implying that the level of consumption at time t is:

$$C(t) = C(0)e^{\psi t} \qquad (4.26)$$

It will be apparent that (4.25) and (4.26) are identical to the corresponding expressions, (2.10) and (2.11), in the basic model. The consumption growth rate will be precisely the same, although the level will be different due to the fact that the determinants of $C(0)$ are no longer the same.

The optimality condition with respect to private capital is now modified to:

$$(1 - \tau_y)\frac{[f(k_g) - \varepsilon f'(k_g)k_g]}{q} + \frac{\dot{q}}{q} + \frac{(q-1)^2}{2h_1 q} - \delta_K = r(1 - \tau_b) \qquad (4.5b')$$

where $k_g \equiv K_G/K$ denotes the ratio of public to private capital. The interpretation of this is analogous to that of (2.4b'), the only difference being the inclusion of the depreciation rate. Finally, the following transversality conditions apply:

$$\lim_{t \to \infty} \lambda B e^{-pt} = 0; \quad \lim_{t \to \infty} \lambda q e^{-pt} = 0$$

4.3.3 Dynamics of production

Access to the perfect world capital market, together with the assumption of fixed labor supply, implies that the equilibrium dynamics of the economy dichotomizes, as it did in Chapter 2. Consumption always grows at the constant rate specified by equation (4.25), which is determined entirely by taste parameters and rates of return.

To determine the dynamics of the production side we need to consider the evolution of the two capital stocks, together with the market price of private capital. Because of the homogeneity, what is relevant is the evolution of the relative capital stock, $k_g \equiv K_G/K$. We can thus reduce the dynamics of the production side to a pair of dynamic equations in k_g and q as follows.

First, we may rewrite (4.5b') in the form

$$\dot{q} = [r(1 - \tau_b) + \delta_K]q - \frac{(q-1)^2}{2h_1} - (1 - \tau_y)[f(k_g) - \varepsilon f'(k_g)k_g] \qquad (4.27a)$$

Next, taking the time derivative of k_g yields:

$$\frac{\dot{k}_g}{k_g} = \frac{\dot{K}_G}{K_G} - \frac{\dot{K}}{K} \qquad (4.28)$$

Next, substituting (4.21) into (4.19b) and dividing by K_g yields the growth rate of public capital:

$$\frac{\dot{K}_G}{K_G} = g\frac{f(k_g)}{k_g} - \delta_G \equiv \phi_g \qquad (4.29)$$

and substituting (4.29) and (4.7a′) into (4.28) implies:

$$\frac{\dot{k}_g}{k_g} = \left[g\frac{f(k_g)}{k_g} - \delta_G\right] - \left[\frac{(q-1)}{h_1} - \delta_K\right] \quad (\equiv \phi_g - \phi_k) \qquad (4.27b)$$

Equations (4.27a) and (4.27b) provide a pair of differential equations in q and k_g. Because of the nonlinearity of the system, there are potential problems of nonexistence and nonuniqueness of equilibrium, just as has been encountered in previous models. However, we do not pursue this issue here; for further discussion in this specific instance see Turnovsky (1997c).

Since the equilibrium system (4.27) is nonlinear, we proceed by considering its linearized dynamics about the steady-state equilibrium $(\tilde{q}, \tilde{k}_g)$, namely:[17]

$$\begin{pmatrix} \dot{q} \\ \dot{k}_g \end{pmatrix} = \begin{pmatrix} r(1-\tau_b) + \delta_K - \left(\frac{\tilde{q}-1}{h_1}\right) & (1-\tau_y)\left[\varepsilon f''\tilde{k}_g - (1-\varepsilon)f'\right] \\ -\frac{\tilde{k}_g}{h_1} & gf' - \delta_G - \tilde{\phi}_k \end{pmatrix} \begin{pmatrix} q - \tilde{q} \\ k_g - \tilde{k}_g \end{pmatrix}$$

$$(4.30)$$

The transversality condition will be met if and only if:

$$r(1-\tau_b) + \delta_K > \frac{\tilde{q}-1}{h_1} \qquad (4.31)$$

Under this condition, which is equivalent to $r(1-\tau_b) > \tilde{\phi}_k$, the system is a saddlepoint, the stable eigenvalue of which is denoted by $\mu < 0$.

Because of adjustment costs, the stocks of both public and private capital are assumed to evolve gradually from their initial values, thus implying the same for their ratio. In contrast, we assume that the shadow value of private capital, q, can respond instantaneously to new information as it comes available. The equilibrium dynamics of the linearized system are as follows. The ratio of public to private capital evolves as follows:

$$k_g(t) - \tilde{k}_g = (k_{g,0} - \tilde{k}_g)e^{\mu t} \qquad (4.32a)$$

[17] Note that $f - k_g f'' = \partial Y / \partial K > 0$.

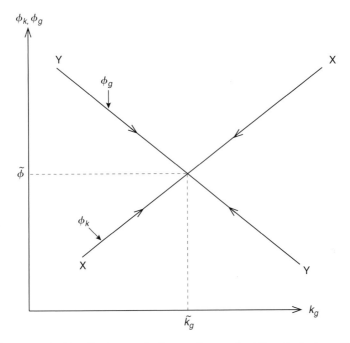

Figure 4.3 Stable adjustment paths for growth rates of public and private capital

while the shadow value of private capital is given by:

$$(q - \tilde{q}) = -\frac{(1 - \tau_y)[\varepsilon f'' \tilde{k}_g - (1 - \varepsilon)f']}{\left\{ r(1 - \tau_b) + \delta_K - \left(\frac{\tilde{q}-1}{h_1}\right) - \mu \right\}} (k_g - \tilde{k}_g) \tag{4.32b}$$

which is negatively sloped, reflecting the fact that the shadow value of private capital varies inversely with its relative scarcity.

It is straightforward, and more to the point of the present discussion, to express the transitional dynamics in terms of growth rates rather than shadow values. In steady-state equilibrium the ratio of public to private capital remains constant, so that both types of capital grow asymptotically at the common rate, denoted by $\tilde{\phi}_k = \tilde{\phi}_g \equiv \tilde{\phi}$. The growth rates of the two capital goods along the economy's transitional path are obtained by linearizing:

$$\phi_k \equiv \frac{q - 1}{h_1} - \delta_K, \quad \phi_g \equiv g\frac{f(k_g)}{k_g} - \delta_G$$

about their common steady state:

$$\tilde{\phi} \equiv \frac{\tilde{q} - 1}{h_1} - \delta_K = g\frac{f(\tilde{k}_g)}{\tilde{k}_g} - \delta_G$$

as k_g and q evolve along (4.32a) and (4.32b). Performing the approximation, the linearized transitional paths followed by the respective growth rates are:

$$\phi_k - \tilde{\phi} = \frac{-(1 - \tau_y)[\varepsilon f''\tilde{k}_g - (1 - \varepsilon)f']/h_1}{\left\{\left[r(1 - \tau_b) - \tilde{\phi}\right] - \mu\right\}}(k_g - \tilde{k}_g) \qquad (4.33a)$$

$$\phi_g - \tilde{\phi} = -\frac{g}{(\tilde{k}_g)^2}\left[f - \tilde{k}_g f'\right](k_g - \tilde{k}_g) \qquad (4.33b)$$

These are illustrated in Figure 4.3, where the upward-sloping locus XX corresponds to the stable transitional adjustment path in the growth rate of private capital and the downward-sloping locus YY corresponds to the stable adjustment in the growth rate of public capital. The striking feature of the adjustment is that during any transition the growth rates of the two forms of capital are moving in opposite directions. This figure forms the basis for the analysis of the dynamic effects of a fiscal expansion.

4.3.4 Equilibrium dynamics: current account

To obtain the time path for the current account we proceed as follows. First, linearize the production function appearing in (4.24). Next, substitute the solutions from (4.7a'), (4.29) and (4.26) into (4.24). This leads to the following linear approximation describing the rate of accumulation of traded bonds:

$$\dot{B} = rB + \Gamma_{P,0}e^{\int_0^t \phi_k(s)ds} + \Gamma_{G,0}e^{\int_0^t \phi_g(s)ds} - C(0)e^{\psi t}$$

where $\Gamma_{P,0}$ and $\Gamma_{G,0}$ reflect the initial impacts of the private and public capital stocks on the economy's net output.[18] Solving this equation and invoking the transversality condition on the traded bond, we can show that:

---

[18] The constants $\Gamma_{P,0}$ and $\Gamma_{G,0}$ are not of any particular interest and hence we do not need to specify them explicitly.

$$C(0) = (r - \psi) \left\{ B_0 + \Gamma_{P,0} \int_0^\infty e^{\int_0^s \phi_k(\tau)d\tau - rs} ds + \Gamma_{G,0} \int_0^\infty e^{\int_0^s \phi_g(\tau)d\tau - rs} ds \right\}$$

$$(4.34a)$$

This equation determines the initial level of consumption $C(0)$, consistent with the intertemporal solvency of the small open economy. The term in parentheses can be interpreted as the present discounted value of wealth, allowing for the fact that both types of capital grow at the respective net rates $\phi_k(t)$ and $\phi_g(t)$. Substituting this initial condition into the general solution for $B(t)$, we find that the stock of traded bonds follows the stable transitional growth path:

$$B(t) = -e^{rt} \left[\Gamma_{P,0} \int_t^\infty e^{\int_0^s \phi_k(\tau)d\tau - rs} ds + \Gamma_{G,0} \int_t^\infty e^{\int_0^s \phi_g(\tau)d\tau - rs} ds - \frac{C(0)}{r - \psi} e^{(\psi - r)t} \right]$$

$$(4.34b)$$

which is analogous to (2.21).

4.3.5 Steady-state fiscal effects

The steady-state shadow value of private capital and the ratio of the two types of capital, $\tilde{q}$ and $\tilde{k}_g$, are determined by setting $\dot{q} = \dot{k}_g = 0$ in (4.27a) and (4.27b), from which the corresponding value of the equilibrium growth rate $\tilde{\phi}$ immediately follows. This forms the basis for the long-run effects of various types of fiscal policy. Here we shall discuss the effects of changes in the tax rates and in the share of government expenditure, on the assumption that the government budget constraint is met through appropriate adjustments in lump-sum taxes. Note that this aspect of the equilibrium is independent of the consumption tax, τ_c, which therefore operates as a lump-sum tax; see also Rebelo (1991). Omitting details, the following results can be established:

$$\frac{\partial \tilde{\phi}}{\partial \tau_b} = \frac{r\tilde{q}g \left[f - \tilde{k}_g f' \right] / h_1 (\tilde{k}_g)^2}{A} > 0;$$

$$(4.35a)$$

$$\frac{\partial \tilde{k}_g}{\partial \tau_b} = \frac{-r\tilde{q}/h_1}{A} < 0; \qquad \frac{\partial \psi}{\partial \tau_b} = \frac{-r}{1 - \gamma} < 0$$

$$\frac{\partial \tilde{\phi}}{\partial \tau_y} = \frac{-g \left[f - \tilde{k}_g f' \right] \left[f - \varepsilon \tilde{k}_g f' \right] / h_1 (\tilde{k}_g)^2}{A} < 0;$$

$$(4.35b)$$

$$\frac{\partial \tilde{k}_g}{\partial \tau_y} = \frac{(f - \varepsilon \tilde{k}_g f') / h_1}{A} > 0; \qquad \frac{\partial \psi}{\partial \tau_y} = 0$$

$$\frac{\partial \tilde{\phi}}{\partial g} = \frac{-(1 - \tau_y)(f/\tilde{k}_g)ff''/h_1}{A} > 0;$$

$$\frac{\partial \tilde{k}_g}{\partial g} = \frac{\left[r(1 - \tau_b) - \tilde{\phi}\right](f/\tilde{k}_g)}{A} > 0; \qquad \frac{\partial \psi}{\partial g} = 0 \qquad (4.35c)$$

where

$$A \equiv \left(g/(\tilde{k}_g)^2\right)[f - \tilde{k}_g f']\left[r(1 - \tau_b) - \tilde{\phi}\right] + (1/h_1)(1 - \tau_y)[(1 - \varepsilon)f' - \varepsilon f''\tilde{k}_g] > 0$$

Intuitively, an increase in the tax on interest income lowers the net rate of return on traded bonds, thereby inducing investors to increase the proportion of private capital in their portfolios, raising the price of capital, and inducing long-run growth in private capital. This growth in private capital reduces the equilibrium ratio of public to private capital. In addition, this tax induces agents to switch from savings to consumption, increasing the amount of initial consumption, but slowing down its growth rate.

An increase in the tax on private capital income has the opposite portfolio effect, lowering the growth of private capital and public capital and increasing the ratio of public to private capital. It leaves the growth rate of consumption unaffected.

In contrast to a centrally planned economy, an increase in the share of output claimed by the government, financed by a lump-sum tax, raises the equilibrium growth rate of capital unambiguously. This is because lump-sum taxation avoids the excess burden of taxation associated with distortionary taxes. At the same time, the transversality conditions prevent the growth rate from being increased indefinitely through an ever-increasing share of government expenditure.

4.3.6 Transitional dynamics

Figure 4.4 illustrates the transitional dynamics in capital following the three types of fiscal disturbance. Part (a) illustrates the effects of higher income tax rates, while part (b) traces out the dynamic adjustment in response to a higher proportion of government expenditure. In each case, the economy is initially in steady-state equilibrium at the point P.

The immediate effect of an increase in the tax rate on interest income, τ_b, is to induce agents to begin switching their portfolios from bonds to capital. The rate of growth of private capital increases, reducing the ratio of public to private capital in the economy. As k_g declines (i.e. the relative abundance

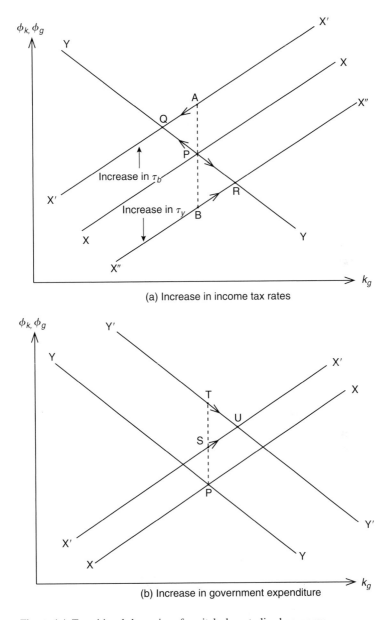

(a) Increase in income tax rates

(b) Increase in government expenditure

Figure 4.4 Transitional dynamics of capital: decentralized economy

of private capital increases), its shadow value declines, causing the growth
rate of private capital to decline. The transitional adjustment in the growth
rate of private capital is illustrated by the initial jump from P to A, on the

new stable arm X'X', followed by the continuous decline, AQ, to the new steady state at Q. With the growth of public capital being tied through aggregate output to the capital stocks in accordance with (4.21), the growth rate of public capital does not respond instantaneously to the higher tax rate τ_b. Instead, as k_g declines, the average productivity of public capital, f/k_g, rises, causing the growth rate of public capital to rise gradually over time. The stable arm YY remains fixed and the growth rate of public capital occurs gradually along the path PQ.

The transitional response to a higher tax on capital, τ_y, is the mirror image of what we have just been discussing. The higher tax on capital generates an initial decline in the rate of growth of private investment, followed by a gradual, but only partial, increase. This is represented by the initial jump from P to B, to the new stable path X''X'', followed by the continuous increase along BR, to the new equilibrium at R. The growth of public capital does not respond immediately, but declines gradually, as its average productivity f/k_g falls. This is represented by the continuous movement along PR in Figure 4.4a.

The transitional adjustment of the two types of capital to an increase in government expenditure is illustrated in Figure 4.4b. In this case, the long-run increase in the equilibrium growth rate is sufficiently large to generate a corresponding partial increase in the short-run growth rate of private capital, followed by a further continuous increase along SU. In contrast, the direct impact of the increase in government expenditure is to cause the growth rate of public capital to overshoot on impact and decline thereafter to its new (higher) growth rate as the ratio of public to private capital declines during the transition.

4.3.7 Optimal fiscal policy

The presence of public capital in production, the stock of which grows endogenously with the economy, but which agents take as given, has two important consequences for policy. First, it raises the question of the optimal stock of government capital. Since government capital is subject to declining marginal productivity, at some point the marginal resources devoted to public investment may be utilized more productively elsewhere in the economy, thus limiting the size of public capital. Second, the fact the stock of government capital grows endogenously with the size of the economy, a link that private agents ignore, implies the presence of an externality, the size of which depends upon the degree of congestion. This implies that the time path of the decentralized economy that we have been discussing deviates from the socially optimal time path, thus creating the potential for taxation to correct for the distortion. The analysis of this is discussed in detail elsewhere; see Turnovsky (1997c). Here we simply summarize the main issues, pointing out that the analytical procedure is similar to that discussed earlier in the chapter to deal with the externality associated with debt.

To determine the optimal rate of government expenditure it is most convenient to focus on the problem from the viewpoint of the central planner. The procedure is essentially as set out in Section 4.1, where the central planner internalizes the externalities, in this case arising from the fact that public capital increases with the size of the economy. Analytically, the central planner includes the accumulation of public capital in his optimization, a consequence of which is that the macroeconomic equilibrium involves the time path of the shadow of public capital, as well as private capital. This means that the order of the macrodynamic equilibrium on the output side increases from two (as in (4.28) for the decentralized economy) to three, requiring one "sluggish" (the relative stocks of capital) and now two "jump" variables (the two shadow values) for a unique stable adjustment path to prevail.

Using this framework one can establish that the long-run growth-maximizing level of g, $\bar{g}$ say, *exceeds* the long-run welfare-maximizing level, $\hat{g}$. This is in contrast to Barro (1990), who, introducing government expenditure as a flow in the production function, finds that the welfare-maximizing and growth-maximizing shares of government expenditure coincide, as we observed in Section 2.4. The difference is accounted for by the fact that when government expenditure influences production as a flow, maximizing the marginal product of government expenditure net of its resource cost maximizes the growth rate of capital. But it also maximizes the social return to public expenditure, thereby maximizing overall intertemporal welfare. By contrast, when government expenditure affects output as a stock, public capital needs to be accumulated to attain the growth-maximizing level. This involves forgoing consumption, leading to welfare losses relative to the social optimum. Intertemporal welfare is raised by reducing the growth rate, thereby enabling the agent to enjoy more consumption.

The optimal tax structure is characterized as the one that will enable the decentralized economy to replicate the first-best outcome of the centrally planned economy. There are two general requirements to be met. The first is that the decentralized economy must ultimately attain the steady state of the centralized economy. Second, having replicated the steady state, the transitional dynamic adjustment paths in the two economies must also coincide.

Omitting details, the optimal tax rates in the steady state are:

$$\hat{\tau}_b = 0 \qquad (4.36a)$$

$$\hat{\tau}_y = -\tilde{v}g + \frac{(1 - \varepsilon)f'\tilde{k}_g(1 + \tilde{v}g)}{f - \varepsilon\tilde{k}_g f'} \qquad (4.36b)$$

where v denotes the shadow value of allocating a marginal unit of output to the government, measured in terms of the unitary price of foreign bonds. It reflects the deviation of government spending from its optimum. These expressions can be given the following intuitive interpretation. Since there is no distortion in the bond market, the tax rate on foreign bond income should be zero, and indeed (4.36a) will replicate the growth rate of consumption.

The intuition behind the optimal (capital) income tax rate, $\hat{\tau}_y$, given in (4.36b) can be understood by comparing the *private* and *social* returns to private capital accumulation in the presence of public capital. Recalling (4.5b$'$), the steady-state private return to accumulating a marginal unit of private capital is:

$$r_p \equiv (1 - \tau_y)\frac{[f(\tilde{k}_g) - \varepsilon f'(\tilde{k}_g)\tilde{k}_g]}{\tilde{q}} + \frac{(\tilde{q} - 1)^2}{2h_1\tilde{q}} - \delta_K$$

In contrast, the steady-state social return to accumulating a marginal unit of private capital is:

$$r_s \equiv (1 + \tilde{v}g)\frac{[f - \tilde{k}_g f']}{\tilde{q}} + \frac{(\tilde{q} - 1)^2}{2h_1\tilde{q}} - \delta_K$$

This takes account of the fact that, since the government maintains a fixed expenditure ratio, gY, the accumulation of private capital indirectly causes the government to increase its rate of investment, the social value of which is $\tilde{v}$, while, in addition, the central planner internalizes the congestion. The optimal tax rate, $\hat{\tau}_y$, is set so as to equate r_p to r_s. The income tax rate thus corrects for two potential sources of externality: (i) the size of the government relative to its social optimum, and (ii) the degree of congestion.

Suppose that there is no congestion, so that $\varepsilon = 1$, and that $\tilde{v} > 0$, so that the relative stock of government capital is less than optimal. In this case, the optimal tax on private capital income is $\hat{\tau}_y < 0$; see (4.36b). Since private investment increases output and therefore has the desirable effect of increasing the size of public capital, it generates a positive externality and therefore should be encouraged through a subsidy. On the other hand, if $\tilde{v} < 0$ and the government is too large relative to the optimum, capital income should be taxed positively. This is because the induced expansion of the government through private investment now generates a negative externality and should be discouraged through taxation. Finally, if $\tilde{v} = 0$, so that the size of the government sector is optimal, the induced change in government expenditure is just worth its cost. There is no externality and so private capital income should be untaxed. The first-best optimum can be reached either through lump-sum taxation alone, or equivalently through a consumption tax. At the other extreme, suppose that $\varepsilon = 0$, so that congestion is proportional. If the stock of public capital is at its social optimum, $\tilde{v} = 0$, the income from private capital should now be taxed at the rate, $\hat{\tau}_y = \tilde{k}_g f'/f$, the share of public capital in the overall social optimum.

The idea that the presence of congestion favors an income tax over lump-sum taxation or a consumption tax has been shown previously by Barro and Sala-i-Martin (1992a) and Turnovsky (1996a). In these models, in which government expenditure appears as a flow, there are no adjustment costs and if congestion is proportional ($\varepsilon = 0$), the optimal tax rate turns out to be $\hat{\tau}_y = \hat{g}$ so that the expenditure is fully financed by the capital income tax. In the present case, $\hat{\tau}_y \gtrless \hat{g}$, reflecting the fact that while congestion in public capital enhances the return to private capital, thus providing an incentive for private investment, this needs to be weighed against the adjustment costs associated with the latter.

The result that the optimal tax rate does depend upon the degree of congestion contrasts with that of Glomm and Ravikumar (1994), who reach the opposite conclusion. The difference is due to the formulation of congestion and the fact that we are imposing constant returns to scale in the two forms of capital in the absence of labor. If we adopt the Glomm–Ravikumar specification of congestion, the only assumption consistent with ongoing growth is for $\varepsilon = 0$, in which case our expression (4.34b) with $\tilde{v} = 0$ also reduces to the Barro expression $\hat{\tau}_k = f' \tilde{k}_g / f.$[19]

The other aspect of the optimal tax structure – the differential taxation of capital and interest income when g is not at its optimum – is due to the form of the government expenditure rule (4.21), where gross public investment is assumed to be a fixed proportion of output. It is through this relationship that the accumulation of private capital generates the externality that needs to be corrected by a tax on capital income. Since government expenditure is unrelated to interest income, the accumulation of bonds by the agent generates no such externality.

---

[19] Glomm and Ravikumar (1994) specify congestion (using the present notation) in the form $K_G^s = K_G / K^\zeta$ where $\zeta \geq 0$, rather than in the form (4.18b) adopted here.

While the expenditure rule (4.21) is plausible, it is arbitrary, and we therefore briefly consider the implications of modifying (4.21) to:

$$G = g\left[f\left(\frac{K_G}{K}\right)K + rB\right] \tag{4.21$'$}$$

so that government expenditure is proportional to GNP. In this case the accumulation of bonds generates an externality completely analogous to that generated by private capital. To replicate the first-best optimum will therefore require the taxation of both forms of income and, with G being proportional to the sum of the income sources, both sources of income will have to be taxed equally in order to replicate the first-best equilibrium.[20]

To replicate the growth rates of the capital stocks in the two economies is more involved. Basically we need to equate the stable eigenvalues in the decentralized and centrally planned economies and this requires the optimal capital income tax rate, τ_y, to be time-varying. Essentially the method is similar to that which we applied in the previous model.

4.4 Role of public capital: conclusions

As noted previously, virtually all of the analytical work addressing the role of public expenditure in determining the productive performance of the economy has introduced government expenditure as a flow in the production function. It is therefore subject to the criticism that, insofar as it is intended to represent the infrastructure of the economy, it is an inadequate measure of what is really relevant, namely the accumulated stock of publicly provided capital. In the latter part of this chapter, we have introduced both public and private capital into an endogenous growth model of a small open economy. Apart from its intrinsic importance, the small open economy has the advantage of enabling us to focus on the dynamic interaction of the adjustments of the two types of capital in the most transparent way.

We conclude by drawing the parallels and highlighting the differences between considering productive government expenditure in the form of capital and the more standard practice of introducing it as a flow. The first difference is that the introduction of public capital together with private capital generates transitional dynamics in the growth of both types of

---

[20] If $G = gfK + g'rb$ then the two forms of income will be taxed at differential rates. The specifications in (4.21) and (4.21$'$) correspond to polar cases. When government spending is optimally determined then the specifics of any underlying rule cease to matter.

capital. This is in contrast to the case where government expenditure appears as a flow, when the private capital stock is always on its balanced growth path; see Section 2.4. Second, not only do the two types of capital evolve at different time-varying rates during the transition, but they also approach their common equilibrium growth rate from opposite directions. In response to an increase in the size of the government, say, the growth of public capital initially overshoots, before gradually declining to the new equilibrium growth rate. The growth rate of private capital always under- shoots on impact – and indeed may initially respond perversely – before gradually increasing to its new equilibrium. This pattern of adjustment is reversed in response to tax changes. Now the growth rate of private capital initially overshoots its long-run response – positively in the case of a tax on interest, negatively in the case of a tax on capital – while the growth of public capital adjusts gradually to the new equilibrium.

Third, as in the case where productive government expenditure impacts as a flow, there is a growth-maximizing size of productive government expenditure. However, in contrast to that case, maximizing the equilibrium growth rate does not coincide with welfare maximization. The process of accumulating the public capital necessary to maximize the equilibrium growth rate of capital may involve consumption losses, which more than outweigh the benefits to future production. The economy may be better off with a slightly lower growth rate and higher consumption.

Finally, as in the more conventional formulation, the introduction of government capital introduces an externality in production. As in the sim- pler model this can be corrected by a combination of income taxes and/or lump-sum taxes, enabling the decentralized economy to replicate the first- best equilibrium of the centrally planned economy. But in contrast to the simple model, the income tax necessary to achieve this varies along the transitional path. The steady-state component has a simple structure aimed at correcting for potential externalities due to (i) the deviation in govern- ment expenditure from its social optimum, and (ii) the effects of congestion associated with public capital. The transitional component is aimed at inducing the representative agent to take proper account of the fact that the shadow value of public capital varies inversely with the changing ratio of public to private capital along the adjustment path.[21]

---

[21] We may note that with the consumption tax essentially operating as a lump-sum tax, the issue of time inconsistency, often identified with optimal capital taxation, does not arise. Given an unchanging time path characterizing the first-best optimum, the policy maker will have no incentive to deviate from it.

5

Two-sector growth models

5.1 Introduction[1]

The one-sector production model, while an essential analytical tool of aggregate economics, is inevitably limited as a framework for analyzing the full economy-wide impacts of policy shocks and structural changes. This is particularly problematic in an international economy, one of the key characteristics of which is the fact that international trading activities affect different parts of the economy to varying degrees. Some parts of the economy are specialized in exports or export-related activities, others in imports or import-related activities, while other sectors, notably service industries, operate more or less independently of the international environment. The differential impacts on these various sectors were a central issue in the debate over the Dutch disease and the discovery of oil in Northern Europe, as well as in assessing the effects of mineral discoveries in Australia. In both cases the discovery of the resource led to a change in the country's terms of trade, and this in turn had an effect on the country's traditional export sectors, as well as on its import-competing sectors. Or, to take another example, a tariff imposed on a country's imports, by changing the country's terms of trade, will also have consequences elsewhere in the economy. To capture these relative price effects one needs to augment the basic model to introduce a second, or perhaps even more, sectors.

Two-sector models of economic growth were pioneered by Uzawa (1961), Takayama (1963), and others in the context of a closed economy. In this early literature, the two sectors corresponded to the production of the consumption good and the production of the investment good, respectively. The key result in that early literature focused on the uniqueness and stability of equilibrium, which was shown to depend critically upon the capital intensity of the investment good sector relative to the consumption sector.

[1] This chapter draws on material presented in Turnovsky (1996d).

104

In a seminal paper, Lucas (1988) introduced the two-sector endogenous growth model. The Lucas model includes two capital goods, physical capital and human capital. The former is produced, together with consumption goods, in the final output sector, using both human and physical capital. Human capital is produced in the education sector, also using both physical capital and human capital. The agent's decisions at any instant of time are (i) how much to consume, (ii) how to allocate his physical and human capital across the two sectors, and (iii) at what rates to accumulate total physical and human capital over time. Having two capital goods, this model is characterized by transitional dynamics. However, because two-sector endogenous growth models initially proved to be intractable, much of the early analysis was restricted to balanced growth paths (see e.g. Lucas, 1988; Devereux and Love, 1994) or to analyzing the transitional dynamics using numerical simulation methods (see e.g. Mulligan and Sala-i-Martin, 1993; Pecorino, 1993; and Devereux and Love, 1994). One important exception to this is Bond, Wang, and Yip (1996), who using the methods of the standard two-sector trade model, provided an effective analysis of the dynamic structure of the two-sector endogenous growth model. In fact, if one identifies physical capital with traded capital and human capital with nontraded capital, it becomes natural to interpret the Lucas model within an international context, as being an endogenous growth version of the so-called "dependent economy" model.

5.1.1 The dependent economy model: a brief background

The dependent economy model has a long history and has become an essential workhorse of international macroeconomics. By distinguishing between traded and nontraded goods, it provides a convenient general equilibrium framework for analyzing the behavior of the real exchange rate both in a static context, as in the early models of the 1960s, as well as in a dynamic framework.[2] Modern analytical treatments of nontraded goods in a macroeconomic setting can be traced to the Australian school of Salter (1959), Corden (1960), Swan (1960), Pearce (1961), and McDougall (1965), to which should be added the important work of Diaz-Alejandro (1965) from a Latin American perspective. In the United States, Balassa (1964) and

---

[2] The first published use of the term "dependent economy" was by Salter (1959) to describe an economy that was a price taker on world markets, but also produced nontraded goods for domestic use. The term is still very much in use even though nontraded goods account for a substantial share of the GDP of large OECD countries, which can hardly be described as being dependent.

Samuelson (1964) singled out the role of productivity differences in the traded good industries across countries as the primary long-run reason for differences in the relative prices of nontraded goods. Balassa and Samuelson focused on the *supply-side* determinants of the relative price of nontraded goods, in contrast to the Australian school's emphasis on the *demand-side* determinants of the relative price of nontradables, taking the supply side of the economy as given.

During the 1970s the incorporation of investment into this framework by Fischer and Frenkel (1972, 1974), Bruno (1976), and others began a process of extending the short-run character of the model to a longer-run treatment of the determination of the relative price of nontradables, the capital stock, and the current account in a small open economy. These early dynamic models were open economy extensions of the standard portfolio balance macro-dynamic models of that period. Moreover, a decade or so later several authors had begun to incorporate capital formation into an intertemporal optimizing framework; see e.g. Razin (1984), Murphy (1986), Brock (1988), and Obstfeld (1989).

Once the distinction between traded and nontraded goods is introduced, the way investment is classified becomes important. Intuitively, investment can reasonably be placed into either category. Capital goods, taking the form of infrastructure and construction, are presumably nontraded; investment goods in the form of machinery or inventories are obviously potentially tradable. Different treatments of investment, reflecting these different possibilities, can be found in the literature.[3] For analytical reasons most of the earlier literature assumes that investment falls entirely into one category or another, and on balance, the treatment of capital as nontraded is more prevalent.

Brock and Turnovsky (1994) develop an intertemporal two-sector dependent economy model that includes both traded and nontraded capital goods. Their model, which employs a Ramsey-type technology, shows that a general analysis, incorporating both types of capital simultaneously, is in fact tractable, and their analysis provides a characterization of the roles of the two capital goods in the adjustment process. The analysis to be presented below can also be viewed as an adaptation of their framework to an endogenous growth context.

Finally, one of the most interesting aspects of the dynamics is that they depend critically upon the relative capital intensities of the two sectors. If the

---

[3] A summary of some of the approaches adopted, as well as the applications of the model is provided by Turnovsky (1997a).

traded good is the more capital intensive, the adjustment of the real exchange rate to any unanticipated permanent shock occurs immediately. The subsequent accumulation or decumulation of capital in response to such a shock occurs with no concurrent change in the real exchange rate. By contrast, if the nontraded sector is the more capital intensive, the transitional adjustment in the capital stock will be accompanied by an appropriate change in the real exchange rate.[4]

The next section lays out the theoretical framework, while Section 5.3 derives and characterizes the macroeconomic equilibrium. Section 5.4 illustrates the model by analyzing the steady-state growth effects of three types of disturbance: (i) a demand disturbance in the form of an increase in the rate of time preference; (ii) productivity shocks in the two sectors; and (iii) foreign price shocks in the form of a higher world interest rate, and a higher price of imported investment goods. Whether prices have transitional dynamics will be shown to depend critically upon the relative intensities of the two sectors in the two capital goods. Section 5.5 discusses the nature of the transitional dynamics in two examples where it occurs.

5.2 The model

The economy is inhabited by a single infinitely lived representative agent. The agent accumulates two types of capital for rental at the competitively determined rental rate. The first is traded capital, K (say machinery), and the second is nontraded capital, H (say structures). Neither capital good is subject to depreciation. For expositional simplicity there is no government, but that can be easily added as in previous chapters.

These two forms of capital are employed by the agent to produce a tradable good, Y_T, taken to be the numeraire, using a linearly homogeneous production function:

$$Y_T = aK_T^a H_T^{(1-a)}; \quad 0 < a < 1 \tag{5.1a}$$

where K_T and H_T denote the respective allocations of the capital goods to the production of the traded good. The agent also produces a nontraded good, Y_N,

---

[4] Two-sector models that include sectoral externalities are often associated with indeterminate solutions. By excluding such externalities we avoid this issue. Examples of two-sector growth models in an open economy which allow for externalities that generate indeterminacy include Weder (2001) and Meng (2003). The latter is particularly close in its general structure to the present framework.

by means of an analogous production function

$$Y_N = bK_N^\beta H_N^{(1-\beta)}; \quad 0 < \beta < 1 . \tag{5.1b}$$

The fact that the two production functions are linearly homogeneous in the two reproducible factors, K and H, is critical for an equilibrium with steady endogenous growth to exist. The relative price of nontraded goods, p, is taken as parametrically given by the agent, and is determined by market-clearing conditions in the economy. Both forms of capital are costlessly and instant-aneously mobile across the two sectors, with the sectoral allocations being constrained by:

$$K_T + K_N = K \tag{5.2a}$$

$$H_T + H_N = H \tag{5.2b}$$

The accumulation of traded capital involves adjustment costs.[5] With both production functions having constant returns to scale, and the small economy having access to a perfect world bond market, these adjustment costs are necessary in order to avoid imposing constraints on the technological par-ameters to ensure that the arbitrage conditions equating rates of return are met.[6] Thus we assume that in order to accumulate traded capital at the rate:

$$\dot{K} = I \tag{5.3}$$

involves costs represented by the quadratic (convex) function:

$$\Phi(I,K) = I(p^* + hI/2K) \tag{5.4}$$

where p^* represents the exogenous world price of new traded capital. This equation is analogous to (2.1c), the only minor difference is that we allow the price of new traded capital to deviate from that of other traded commodities.

---

[5] It would be straightforward to introduce adjustment costs on nontraded capital. There is no need to do so, as their rate of adjustment is constrained by the endogenous adjustment in the relative price of nontraded goods; see also Brock and Turnovsky (1994). The assumption that sectoral allocation factor movements occur both costlessly and instantaneously, while standard in this Heckscher–Ohlin-type production framework, is also strong. The structure changes dramatically if one introduces retrofit costs associated with intrasectoral factor movements. Various formulations of this in a non-growth model are provided by Mussa (1978), Gavin (1990), and, more recently, Morshed and Turnovsky (2004).

[6] In the analysis of Brock and Turnovsky (1994) this is unnecessary since their production functions are linearly homogeneous in the three factors of production: traded capital, nontraded capital, and the nonreproducible factor, labor.

In addition to accumulating the two types of capital, the agent accumulates traded bonds, B, that pay an exogenously given world interest rate, r. Thus the agent's instantaneous budget constraint is specified by:

$$\dot{B} = aK_T^a H_T^{1-a} + pbK_N^\beta H_N^{1-\beta} + rB - C_T - pC_N$$
$$\qquad -I(p^* + hI/2K) - p\dot{H} \qquad\qquad (5.5)$$

where C_T and C_N are the agent's consumption of the traded and nontraded goods.

The agent's optimization decision is to choose the rate of consumption (C_T, C_N), capital allocation decisions (K_T, K_N, H_T, H_N), and rates of capital accumulation, I and $\dot{H}$, to maximize the intertemporal isoelastic utility function:

$$\Omega \equiv \int_o^\infty (1/\gamma)\left(C_T^\theta C_N^{1-\theta}\right)^\gamma e^{-\rho t} dt \qquad\qquad (5.6)$$

subject to the constraints (5.2)–(5.4) and the initial stocks of assets, K_0, H_0, and B_0.

The following optimality conditions with respect to C_T, C_N, K_T, K_N, H_T, H_N, and I obtain:

$$\theta C_T^{\theta\gamma-1} C_N^{\gamma(1-\theta)} = \lambda \qquad\qquad (5.7a)$$

$$(1-\theta) C_T^{\theta\gamma} C_N^{\gamma(1-\theta)-1} = \lambda p \qquad\qquad (5.7b)$$

$$a a K_T^{a-1} H_T^{1-a} = pb\beta K_N^{\beta-1} H_N^{1-\beta} \equiv r_k \qquad\qquad (5.7c)$$

$$a(1-a) K_T^a H_T^{-a} = pb(1-\beta) K_N^\beta H_N^{-\beta} \equiv r_h \qquad\qquad (5.7d)$$

$$p^* + h(I/K) = q \qquad\qquad (5.7e)$$

where, as in previous chapters, λ is the marginal utility of wealth held in the form of traded bonds, and q reflects the market price of installed traded capital in terms of the price of foreign bonds. The first pair of equations are the usual intertemporal envelope conditions relating the marginal utility of the two consumption goods to the shadow value of wealth. Equations (5.7c) and (5.7d) equate the marginal returns to traded and nontraded capital across the two sectors. The quantities r_k and r_h define the marginal physical products of traded and nontraded capital, respectively, measured in terms of traded output (the numeraire). Equation (5.7e) equates the marginal cost of an additional unit of investment, inclusive of the marginal installation cost hI/K, to the market value of capital. Equation (5.7e) may be immediately solved to yield the following expression for the rate of accumulation of traded capital:

$$\frac{I}{K} = \frac{\dot{K}}{K} = \frac{(q - p^*)}{h} \equiv \phi(t) \tag{5.8}$$

so that starting from an initial level of K_0, the stock of capital at time t is
$K(t) = K_0 e^{\int_0^t \phi(s)ds}$.

Applying the standard optimality conditions with respect to the traded bond, B, and the two forms of capital, K and H, leads to the arbitrage conditions:

$$\rho - \frac{\dot{\lambda}}{\lambda} = r \tag{5.9a}$$

$$\frac{r_k}{q} + \frac{\dot{q}}{q} + \frac{(q - p^*)^2}{2hq} = r \tag{5.9b}$$

$$\frac{r_h}{p} + \frac{\dot{p}}{p} = r \tag{5.9c}$$

These equations are analogous to (2.4a) and (2.4b) of the basic model. As before, (5.9a) is the standard Keynes–Ramsey consumption rule, equating the marginal return on consumption to the fixed rate of return on holding a foreign bond. With p and r both being constants, it implies a constant growth rate of the marginal utility λ. Likewise (5.9b) equates the rate of return on traded capital to the rate of return on the traded bond. The former has three components. The first is the marginal physical product of traded capital per unit of installed capital (valued at the price q), the second is the rate of capital gain, while the third reflects the contribution of a higher traded capital stock to reducing installation costs. The final equation equates the total rate of return on nontraded capital, which consists of its marginal physical product plus its rate of capital gain, to the rate of return on the traded bond.

Finally, in order to ensure that the agent's intertemporal budget constraint is met, the following transversality conditions must be imposed:

$$\lim_{t \to \infty} \lambda B e^{-\rho t} = 0; \quad \lim_{t \to \infty} \lambda q K e^{-\rho t} = 0; \quad \lim_{t \to \infty} \lambda p H e^{-\rho t} = 0 \qquad (5.10)$$

5.3 Determination of macroeconomic equilibrium

We define aggregate consumption C, expressed with the traded good as numeraire, by:

$$C \equiv C_T + p C_N$$

This definition, together with the optimality conditions (5.7a) and (5.7b), implies that consumptions of the two goods are:

$$C_T = \theta C; \quad p C_N = (1 - \theta) C \qquad (5.11)$$

leading to:

$$\frac{\dot{C}_T}{C_T} = \frac{\dot{C}}{C}; \quad \frac{\dot{p}}{p} + \frac{\dot{C}_N}{C_N} = \frac{\dot{C}}{C} \qquad (5.12)$$

Combining the time derivative of (5.7a) with (5.12) implies that aggregate consumption grows at the rate:

$$\frac{\dot{C}}{C} = \frac{r - \rho - \gamma(1 - \theta)(\dot{p}/p)}{1 - \gamma} \equiv \psi(t) \qquad (5.13)$$

where at this point the rate of inflation of the relative price, $\dot{p}/p$, is yet to be determined.

The strategy for deriving the macroeconomic equilibrium involves three stages, the first of which determines the static allocation of existing resources, while the latter two determine the dynamics. In the first stage we express the sectoral capital intensities and marginal physical products of capital in terms of the relative price of nontraded to traded goods and also express the absolute levels of the allocation of capital in terms of the gradually evolving aggregate stocks, K and H. As is characteristic of two-factor two-sector growth models, the dynamics of the system decouple, and in the second stage we solve for the price dynamics. Having determined prices, the third stage then solves for the equilibrium rates of accumulation of the aggregate stocks of assets, K, H, and B.

5.3.1 Static allocation conditions

Let $\omega \equiv K_T/H_T$ denote the traded to nontraded capital ratio in the traded sector. Dividing equation (5.7c) by (5.7d) yields:

$$\frac{K_N}{H_N} = \left(\frac{1-a}{1-\beta}\right)\left(\frac{\beta}{a}\right)\omega \qquad (5.14)$$

implying that the capital intensities in the two sectors move proportionately. Substituting (5.14) into the first equation of (5.7c) implies:

$$\omega = \delta p^{(1/(a-\beta))} \quad \text{where} \quad \delta \equiv \left[\left(\frac{\beta}{a}\right)^{\beta}\left(\frac{1-\beta}{1-a}\right)^{1-\beta}\frac{b}{a}\right]^{(1/(a-\beta))} \qquad (5.15a)$$

This equation, together with (5.14), yields simple relationships between the sectoral capital intensities and the relative price of nontraded to traded output. Combined with (5.7c) and (5.7d) these in turn lead to the following expressions for the marginal physical products of the two types of capital:

$$r_k(p) = aa\omega^{a-1} = aa\delta^{a-1}p^{((a-1)/(a-\beta))} \qquad (5.15b)$$

$$r_h(p) = a(1-a)\omega^{a} = a(1-a)\delta^{a}p^{(a/(a-\beta))} \qquad (5.15c)$$

Equation (5.14), together with the sectoral allocation relationships (5.2a) and (5.2b), leads to the following expressions for the levels of the capital stocks instantaneously employed in the two sectors:

$$H_T = \frac{\beta(1-a)\omega H - a(1-\beta)K}{\omega(\beta-a)} \quad K_T = \frac{\beta(1-a)\omega H - a(1-\beta)K}{(\beta-a)} \qquad (5.16a)$$

$$H_N = \frac{a(1-\beta)[K-\omega H]}{\omega(\beta-a)} \quad K_N = \frac{\beta(1-a)[K-\omega H]}{(\beta-a)} \qquad (5.16b)$$

which in turn can be expressed in terms of the relative price p by substituting for ω from (5.15a). The equilibrium sectoral allocation of capital depends upon the relative sectoral capital intensity $\beta-a$. Intuitively, an increase in K, say, will raise the aggregate K/H ratio, attracting resources toward the sector that is relatively intensive in traded capital. If $a > \beta$ this is the traded sector. Thus K_T and H_T will rise. If H is held fixed, the additional nontraded capital used in the traded sector must be attracted from the nontraded sector, so that H_N declines. This lowers the marginal physical product of traded capital in the nontraded sector and induces a shift in traded capital away from that sector, as well; that is, K_N declines.

In order for the sectoral capital allocations K_i, H_i to be nonnegative, the sectoral and aggregate capital intensities must satisfy the following conditions:

$$
\text{If } \beta > a : \frac{r_h}{r_k}\left(\frac{\beta}{1-\beta}\right) \equiv \frac{K_N}{H_N} > \frac{K}{H} > \frac{K_T}{H_T} \equiv \frac{r_h}{r_k}\left(\frac{a}{1-a}\right)
$$
$$
\text{if } \beta < a : \frac{r_h}{r_k}\left(\frac{\beta}{1-\beta}\right) \equiv \frac{K_N}{H_N} < \frac{K}{H} < \frac{K_T}{H_T} \equiv \frac{r_h}{r_k}\left(\frac{a}{1-a}\right)
$$
(5.17)

These inequalities define a cone within which the aggregate K/H ratio must lie for a feasible equilibrium to obtain.[7]

5.3.2 Price dynamics

By observing the expressions for r_k and r_h given in (5.15b) and (5.15c), in conjunction with the arbitrage conditions on the two types of capital (5.9b) and (5.9c), it is seen that the dynamics of the relative price, p, and of the price of (installed) traded capital, q, proceed independently of the aggregate stocks of capital, being determined by the pair of equations:

$$
\dot{p} = rp - a(1-a)\delta^a p^{a/(a-\beta)}
$$
(5.18a)

$$
\dot{q} = rq - \frac{(q-p^*)^2}{2h} - aa\delta^{a-1}p^{((a-1)/(a-\beta))}
$$
(5.18b)

These equations are recursive; the relative price of the two goods evolves autonomously in accordance with (5.18a), and in turn determines the evolution of the market price of installed traded capital.

Equations (5.18a) and (5.18b) emphasize the importance of adjustment costs and the associated price of capital in equilibrating the rates of return. In the absence of such costs ($h \to 0, q \to p^*$) and (5.18b) reduces to a static equation determining p. This will be consistent with (5.18a) if and only if

[7] These inequalities are sometimes referred to as the Lerner–Pearce conditions; they ensure that incomplete specialization prevails.

the technological parameters are appropriately tied to the foreign rate of interest.[8]

The critical determinant of the growth of traded capital is the market price of installed capital, q, the price of which is determined by the solution to the pair of differential equations (5.18a) and (5.18b). In order for the traded capital stock domiciled in the economy ultimately to follow a path of steady growth or decline, the stationary solution to this pair of equations, attained when $\dot{p} = \dot{q} = 0$, must have (at least) one *real* solution. Thus, the steady-state relative price of nontraded goods $\tilde{p}$ must be either zero, which we shall rule out, or:

$$\tilde{p} = \left[\frac{r}{(a(1-a)\delta^a)} \right]^{((a-\beta)/\beta)} \tag{5.19a}$$

so that the steady-state real rate of return on nontraded capital $r_h(\tilde{p})/\tilde{p}$ just matches the return on traded bonds, r.

The corresponding steady-state value of q, $\tilde{q}$, is the solution to the quadratic equation:

$$r_k(\tilde{p}) + \frac{(\tilde{q} - p^*)^2}{2h} = r\tilde{q} \tag{5.19b}$$

This equation is analogous to (2.13) of the basic model and, as in that case, a necessary and sufficient condition for the stock of traded capital ultimately to converge to a steady growth path is that this equation have real roots, and this will be so if and only if:

$$r_k(\tilde{p}) \le r \left[p^* + \frac{hr}{2} \right] \tag{5.20}$$

a condition that we shall henceforth assume is met.

Figures 5.1 and 5.2 illustrate the phase diagrams for the price dynamics (5.18a) and (5.18b) in the case that (5.20) holds, so that a steady-state growth path for traded capital exists. Figure 5.1 assumes $\beta > a$, so that the nontraded sector is relatively intensive in traded capital, while Figure 5.2 corresponds to $a > \beta$, so that the relative sectoral intensities in the two types of capital are

---

[8] The specific constraints can be written most conveniently as
$a(1-a)\delta^a p^{(\beta/(a-\beta))} p^* = rp^* = aa\delta^{a-1} p^{((a-1)/(a-\beta))}$. Eliminating p from these equalities imposes a constraint on the exogenously given technological coefficients, which is the analogue of the requirement that $a = r$ in the one-sector model.

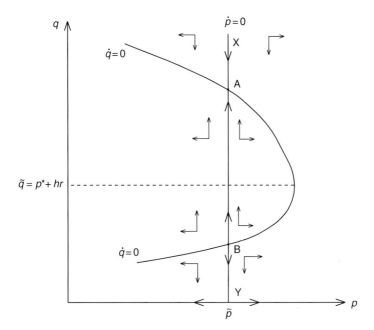

Figure 5.1 Phase diagram: $\beta > \alpha$

reversed.[9] If the roots of (5.19b) are real, the potential arises for two steady-state equilibrium growth rates for traded capital to exist. Denoting the two roots by q_1 (smaller) and q_2 (larger), for both capital intensities two cases can be identified:

Case I: $r > r_k(\tilde{p})$, which implies $q_2 > p^* > q_1 > 0$
Case II: $r < r_k(\tilde{p})$, which implies $q_2 > q_1 > p^*$

Consider first Figure 5.1, which corresponds to $\beta > \alpha$. From the phase diagram it is seen that the equilibrium point B, which corresponds to the smaller equilibrium value, q_1, is an unstable node, while A, which corresponds to the larger equilibrium value, q_2, is a saddlepoint, with the vertical locus XY being the stable saddlepath. Thus, if the system starts out from any point other than B on XY it will converge to A; otherwise it will diverge and there will be no steady growth path. But, any time path for q which converges to A violates the transversality condition for traded capital (5.10), which

---

[9] Since there are only two factors of production, the statement that the traded sector is relatively intensive in traded (nontraded) capital is equivalent to the statement that the nontraded sector is relatively intensive in nontraded (traded) capital.

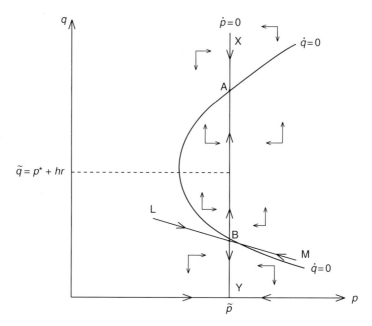

Figure 5.2 Phase diagram: $a > \beta$

needs to be met.[10] The only solution for q which is consistent with the transversality condition and the attainment of a steady growth path for traded capital is the unstable equilibrium point B.

Figure 5.2, which corresponds to $a > \beta$, is analogous. In this case, the equilibrium point B, which corresponds to the smaller equilibrium, q_1, is a saddlepoint, with the stable saddlepath being the negatively sloped locus LM. The equilibrium A, which corresponds to the larger equilibrium value, q_2, is now a locally stable node. But as in Figure 5.1, any time path for q which converges to A violates the transversality condition for traded capital.[11] Thus, in this case the only solutions for p and q which are consistent with both the

---

[10] To see this, observe that $\lim_{t \to \infty} q'Ke^{-\rho t} = \lim_{t \to \infty} q\lambda Ke^{-\rho t}$. Solving equations (5.8) and (5.9a), implies $K(t) = K_0 e^{((q-p^*)/h)t}$; $\lambda(t) = \lambda(0)e^{(\rho-r)t}$, where K_0 is the given initial stock of domestic capital and $\lambda(0)$ is the endogenously determined initial marginal utility of wealth. Combining these expressions implies $\lim_{t \to \infty} q'Ke^{-\rho t} = q\lambda(0)K_0 \lim_{t \to \infty} e^{\int_0^t [(q(s)-p^*)/h]ds - rt}$.
Substituting the solution for the larger root q_2 into this expression, it is clearly seen that this limit diverges, thereby violating the transversality condition on the capital stock. Similarly, the smaller root q_1 ensures that the required transversality condition holds.
[11] The argument is as in note 10.

transversality condition and the attainment of a steady growth path for traded capital lie on the stable saddlepath LM.

The behavior of prices can thus be summarized by:

Proposition 5.1: (i) If $\beta > a$ so that the nontraded sector is relatively intensive in traded capital, the only solutions for p and q which are consistent with the transversality condition on traded capital are $p = \tilde{p}$ given by (5.19a), and $q = q_1$, the (unstable) steady-state solution given by the smaller root to (5.19b). In this case there are *no transitional dynamics in either the relative price of nontraded to traded goods or the market price of capital.* In response to any shock, these prices immediately jump to their respective new steady-state values.

(ii) If $a > \beta$ so that the traded sector is relatively intensive in traded capital, the only solutions for p and q which are consistent with the transversality condition on traded capital are that p and q lie on the stable saddlepath *LM*, ultimately converging to $p = \tilde{p}$ given by (5.19a), and $q = q_1$, the (unstable) steady-state solution given by the smaller root to (5.19b). In this case, a shock to the economy *will generate transitional adjustment paths in both p and q.*

The significant feature of Proposition 5.1 is that it indicates that the dynamic behavior of asset prices, $p(t)$ and $q(t)$, is intimately tied to the production structure of the economy, as reflected by the relative sectoral capital intensities. Many would argue that (ii) is the more plausible of these two cases; that is, the tradable sector, manufacturing goods say, is relatively intensive in tradable capital – for example, equipment.[12] In this case, one would expect a shock to the economy to lead to a jump in asset prices, followed by a smooth transition. The stable eigenvalue to the linearized approximation to the dynamic system represented by (5.18a) and (5.18b) is $\beta r/(\beta-a) < 0$, in which case the formal solution to the local dynamics is as follows:[13]

$$p(t) - \tilde{p} = [p(0) - \tilde{p}]e^{(\beta r/(\beta-a))t} \tag{5.21a}$$

$$q(t) - \tilde{q} = \left[\frac{((1-a)/(\beta-a))(r_k(\tilde{p})/\tilde{p})}{([(p^* + hr) - \tilde{q}]/h) - (\beta r/(\beta-a))} \right](p(t) - \tilde{p}) \tag{5.21b}$$

The equilibrium market price of traded capital, $\tilde{q}$, appearing in (5.21b) is the smaller root q_1 to (5.19b), though for convenience, the subscript 1 is

---

[12] See e.g. Fischer and Frenkel (1974) and Brock (1988).
[13] In fact equations (5.18a) and (5.18b) are of a form which permit exact solutions to be obtained.

omitted.[14] From the solution we see that $p^* + hr > \tilde{q}$, so that with $a > \beta$, (5.21b) is a negatively sloped locus (being a linear approximation to LM in Figure 5.2). Accordingly, the two asset prices move in opposite directions during this phase of the transition. Both prices are forward-looking variables so that their respective initial values, $p(0)$ and $q(0)$, will be determined to satisfy the transversality condition on nontraded (human) wealth; see (5.33) below.

The behavior of the sectoral capital intensities ω, K_N/H_N, and the real marginal physical products $r_k(p)$, $r_h(p)$ will mirror that of p. Thus if $\beta > a$ they too will remain constant throughout at their respective steady-state values, $\tilde{\omega}, \tilde{r}_k$, and $\tilde{r}_h$, while if the sectoral intensity is reversed they will vary through time in response to the evolution of the relative price p.

As is standard in the two-good, two-sector, two-factor model, the steady-state relative price and all factors which depend upon it are determined solely by production conditions; they are therefore independent of any source of demand shock. The latter, however, will generate transitional responses in these variables in the case where $a > \beta$.[15]

5.3.3 Asset dynamics

In order to derive the dynamics of asset accumulation, it is useful to begin with the following relationships, expressing the equilibrium sectoral outputs in terms of the aggregate stocks of capital, K and H. These are derived from the production functions by utilizing the optimality conditions (5.7c) and (5.7d), together with (5.15b) and (5.15c), and reflect the equilibrium sectoral adjustments in K_T, H_T, etc. as determined in (5.16a) and (5.16b):

$$Y_T = \frac{-r_k(1 - \beta)K + r_h\beta H}{(\beta - a)}; \quad Y_N = \frac{r_k(1 - a)K - r_h aH}{p(\beta - a)} \tag{5.22}$$

An increase in the aggregate stock of traded capital, K, will attract resources to the sector that is relatively intensive in traded capital. If $a > \beta$ that sector is the traded sector, the output of which increases at the expense of the nontraded sector.

Define aggregate wealth, with the traded good as numeraire, as:

$$W = qK + pH + B \tag{5.23}$$

---

[14] The formal solution is $q_1 = [p^* + hr] - \left([p^* + hr]^2 - \left[(p^*)^2 + 2hr_k(\tilde{p}) \right] \right)^{1/2}$

[15] We can observe that the relative sectoral capital intensity plays precisely the same role in determining the nature of the price dynamics as it does in the Brock–Turnovsky (1994) Ramsey-type analysis.

Differentiating this expression with respect to t and noting: (i) the accumulation equations (5.3) and (5.4); (ii) the production functions (5.1a) and (5.1b), in conjunction with (5.22); (iii) the definition of aggregate consumption C; (iv) the optimality condition for investment (5.8); and (v) the arbitrage conditions (5.9b) and (5.9c), leads to the following relationship describing the rate of aggregate wealth accumulation:

$$\dot{W}(t) = rW(t) - C(t) \tag{5.24}$$

The form of this wealth accumulation relationship is standard. The only difference here is that C evolves in accordance with (5.13), which depends upon $\dot{p}/p$, which in turn depends upon the relative sectoral capital intensities. Indeed the entire profile of asset accumulation depends upon whether $\beta \gtrless a$ and the two cases will be discussed in turn.

(i) $\beta > a$: nontraded sector relatively intensive in traded capital
In this case p remains at its steady-state level $\tilde{p}$; $\dot{p} \equiv 0$ so that consumption grows at the steady rate (see (5.13)):

$$\frac{\dot{C}}{C} = \frac{r - \rho}{1 - \gamma} \equiv \tilde{\psi}, \text{ i.e. } C(t) = C(0)e^{\tilde{\psi}t} \tag{5.25}$$

Substituting this into (5.24) and solving, while invoking the transversality conditions (5.10), imposes the restriction $r > \tilde{\psi}$ and implies the constant equilibrium consumption–wealth ratio:

$$\frac{C}{W} = r - \tilde{\psi} = \frac{\rho - \gamma r}{1 - \gamma} \tag{5.26}$$

Aggregate wealth therefore grows at the same rate as consumption, with both variables being on their respective equilibrium steady-state growth paths; i.e. $\dot{W}/W = \dot{C}/C = \tilde{\psi}$.

We turn now to the components of W, and in particular to the two types of capital. With p constant over time, q is also constant, so that traded capital grows at the steady rate:

$$\frac{\dot{K}}{K} = \tilde{\phi} = \frac{(\tilde{q} - p^*)}{h} \tag{5.27}$$

where $\tilde{q}$ is the solution to (5.19b).

Comparing (5.25) and (5.27) we see that consumption and wealth on the one hand, and traded capital on the other, are always on their respective steady-state growth paths, growing at the rates $\tilde{\psi}$ and $\tilde{\phi}$. The former is driven by the difference between the rate of return on foreign bonds and the domestic rate of time preference. The latter is determined by $\tilde{q}$, which is determined by the technological conditions in the domestic economy, the adjustment costs h, the cost of imported investment goods p^*, and the return on foreign assets.[16]

The market clearing condition for nontraded capital is specified by $\dot{H} = Y_N - C_N$, which using (5.22) and (5.11) can be written as:

$$\dot{H} = \frac{(\tilde{r}_k(1-a)K - \tilde{r}_h aH)}{\tilde{p}(\beta - a)} - (1 - \theta)\frac{C}{\tilde{p}} \qquad (5.28)$$

Substituting $K(t) = K_0 e^{\tilde{\phi}t}$ and $C(t) = C(0)e^{\tilde{\psi}t}$ into this equation, the solution for H, starting from the initial stock of nontraded capital H_0, is:

$$
\begin{aligned}
H(t) = {} & \left[H_0 - \frac{(1-a)\tilde{r}_k}{(\beta - a)\tilde{p}\left[\tilde{\phi} + ar/(\beta - a)\right]}K_0 + \frac{(1-\theta)}{\tilde{p}[\tilde{\psi} + ar/(\beta - a)]}C(0) \right] e^{-(ar/(\beta - a))t} \\
& + \frac{(1-a)\tilde{r}_k}{(\beta - a)\tilde{p}\left[\tilde{\phi} + ar/(\beta - a)\right]}K_0 e^{\tilde{\phi}t} - \frac{(1-\theta)}{\tilde{p}[\tilde{\psi} + ar/(\beta - a)]}C(0)e^{\tilde{\psi}t}
\end{aligned}
$$

$$(5.29)$$

The transversality condition $\lim_{t\to\infty} \lambda pHe^{-\rho t} = 0$ in (5.10) now reduces to $\lim_{t\to\infty} He^{-rt} = 0$. Applying this to the three exponential terms in (5.29), the following conditions must hold: (i) $(ar/(\beta - a)) + r > 0$; (ii) $r > \tilde{\phi}$; (iii) $r > \tilde{\psi}$. Condition (i) is assured under the capital intensity assumption $\beta > a$; condition (ii) is satisfied by the smaller root q_1 (see note 10); condition (iii) has been imposed by the transversality conditions upon aggregate wealth and is necessary and sufficient for the consumption–wealth ratio to be nonnegative; see (5.25) and (5.26).

The important observation is that the evolution of nontraded capital, $H(t)$, involves a transitional adjustment path. It is restricted, however, by the requirement that the steady-state K/H ratio must lie within the cone defined in (5.17), and for this to occur the growth rate of H must converge to that of K. If

---

[16] We shall assume that the country is sufficiently small that it can maintain a growth rate which is unrelated to that in the rest of the world. Ultimately, this requirement imposes a constraint on the growth rate of the economy. If it grows faster than the rest of the world, at some point it will cease to be small.

$\theta = 1$ so that the agent does not consume the nontraded good – a natural assumption if H is interpreted as being human capital – the convergence of the growth rate of nontraded capital, $H(t)$, to the growth rate, ϕ, of traded capital is assured. However, if $\theta < 1$ so that the agent consumes some of the nontraded good, the additional restriction $\phi > \psi$ must be imposed. This is because if $\psi > \phi$, so that consumption were to grow faster than traded capital, nontraded capital would ultimately need to grow at the rate of consumption in order to generate the nontraded output to satisfy the faster-growing nontraded consumption demand. The K/H ratio would therefore converge to zero, violating (5.17).

Thus assuming that either $\theta = 1$ or $\phi > \psi$, (5.29) implies that the ratio of traded to nontraded capital will converge to a balanced growth path along which:[17]

$$\frac{\tilde{K}}{\tilde{H}} = \frac{[\phi(\beta - a) + ar]}{(1 - a)} \frac{\tilde{p}}{r_k(\tilde{p})} \qquad (5.30)$$

Using the fact that in steady-state $\tilde{r}_h = \tilde{p}r$, the steady-state K/H ratio (5.30) can be shown to satisfy the inequalities in (5.17) as long as the (common) equilibrium growth rate of capital $\phi \geq 0$.[18] If the growth rate is strictly positive then $\tilde{K}/\tilde{H}$ lies within the feasible cone. However, if $\phi = 0$, so that the economy is in fact stationary, then $\tilde{K}/\tilde{H} \to \tilde{K}_T/\tilde{H}_T$ and the equilibrium output of the nontraded good, Y_N, reduces to zero; see (5.22). The economy therefore is fully specialized in the production of the traded commodity. This is because with either no nontraded consumption ($\theta = 1$), or declining consumption ($\phi = 0 > \psi$) and a fixed stock of nontraded capital, asymptotically, there is no demand for additional output of the nontraded good. All production needs can be met by allocating the existing fixed stocks of the two capital goods between the two sectors. The case where $\phi < 0$, so that the economy is declining, drives $\tilde{K}/H$ beyond the boundary of the cone defined by $\tilde{K}_T/\tilde{H}_T$. This is because in a contracting economy $Y_N < 0$ in order for market clearance of the nontraded good, $\dot{H} = Y_N - C_N$, to hold. While this is unsatisfactory, it can be easily remedied, and a declining economy accommodated, by allowing nontraded capital to depreciate.

From these solutions for W, K, and H, we can derive the long-run implications for traded bonds. Rewriting (5.23) in the form:

---

[17] Using the expressions for $\tilde{\phi}$ and $\tilde{\psi}$ the restriction $\tilde{\phi} > \tilde{\psi}$ can be expressed in terms of underlying taste and technology parameters.

[18] In showing that the solution for K/H given in (5.30) satisfies (5.17), use is also made of the transversality condition $r > \phi$.

$$B = W - \tilde{q}K - \tilde{p}H$$

it is evident that holdings of traded bonds are also subject to transitional dynamics, and their growth rate may converge either to that of wealth accumulation or that of capital accumulation. Which it will be will depend in part upon whether or not the agent consumes nontraded output. In the event that he does not ($\theta = 1$), there is no restriction on the relative growth rates ϕ and ψ. In that case it is possible for $\tilde{\psi} > \tilde{\phi}$ so that K and H both grow asymptotically slower than W; eventually the country will become a net creditor and continue to accumulate further foreign assets. This condition characterizes a relatively patient country in which the agents choose to consume a small fraction of their wealth. This enables them to accumulate foreign assets, running up a current account surplus, and generating a positively growing stock of foreign assets. It is the income from these assets that permits the small economy to sustain long-run growth rates of consumption and total wealth in excess of the growth rate of capital and productive capacity. However, as long as the agent consumes *some* nontraded output, the restriction $\tilde{\phi} > \tilde{\psi}$ must be imposed. In this case the country is relatively impatient. In the long run, the country consumes beyond its productive capacity and accumulates an increasing foreign debt.

(ii) $a > \beta$: traded sector relatively intensive in traded capital

Recall equation (5.13), the solution to which is $C(t) = C(0)e^{\int_0^t \psi(s)ds}$. Substituting this into the wealth accumulation equation (5.24), solving the equation, and invoking the transversality condition implies the aggregate consumption to wealth ratio:

$$\frac{C}{W} = \frac{1}{\int_t^\infty e^{\int_t^\tau [r-\psi(s)]ds} d\tau} \tag{5.31}$$

where $\psi(t)$ is given in (5.13). In general, the consumption–wealth ratio is now time-varying. To the extent that the domestic agent consumes the foreign good ($\theta < 1$), movements in the relative price of the two consumption goods give rise to income and substitution effects, which are exactly offsetting when the utility function is logarithmic ($\gamma = 0$).[19] Using (5.23) and the solution for $C(t)$, the equilibrium rate of growth of aggregate wealth may be expressed as:

---

[19] See e.g. Sandmo (1970) for a discussion of the income and substitution effects for the isoelastic utility function.

$$\frac{\dot{W}}{W} = \frac{\dot{C}}{C} + \left\{ (r - \psi) - \frac{C}{W} \right\} \tag{5.32}$$

Thus both aggregate wealth and consumption have transitional dynamic time paths, reflecting the differential impacts of the relative price movements. As the price level converges to its steady-state level (i.e. as $\dot{p} \to 0$), C/W converges to its steady-state ratio (5.26), while $\dot{C}/C$ and $\dot{W}/W$ converge to their common constant growth rate (5.25).

The growth rate of traded capital is given by (5.8) and is also time-varying, reflecting the evolution of q along the stable locus. However, as q approaches its steady state, the growth rate of traded capital approaches the steady-state rate given in (5.27).

With the relative price of nontraded capital, $p(t)$, being time-varying, it is convenient to focus on the rate of accumulation of nontraded capital in value terms, which is given by:

$$\frac{d(pH)}{dt} = \left[r + \frac{r_h(p)}{p} \left(\frac{\beta}{a - \beta} \right) \right] (pH) - r_k(p) \left(\frac{1 - a}{a - \beta} \right) K - (1 - \theta)C$$

In the neighborhood of steady-state equilibrium, this equation can be approximated by:

$$\frac{d(pH)}{dt} = \tilde{r} \left(\frac{a}{a - \beta} \right) (pH) - \tilde{r}_k \left(\frac{1 - a}{a - \beta} \right) K - (1 - \theta)C$$

A linear approximation to the solution for the time path of $p(t)H(t)$, valid in the neighborhood of the steady-state growth path, when the solutions for asset prices are near their respective steady-state levels, $\tilde{p}$, and $\tilde{q}$, is thus given by:

$$
p(t)\,H(t) = \left[p(0)H_0 - \frac{(1 - a)\tilde{r}_k}{(\beta - a)\left[\tilde{\phi} + ar/(\beta - a)\right]} K_0 + \frac{(1 - \theta)}{\left[\tilde{\psi} + ar/(\beta - a)\right]} C(0) \right]
$$
$$
\times e^{-(ar/(\beta - a))t} + \frac{(1 - a)\tilde{r}_k}{(\beta - a)\left[\tilde{\phi} + ar/(\beta - a)\right]} K_0 e^{\tilde{\phi}t}
$$
$$
- \frac{(1 - \theta)}{\left[\tilde{\psi} + ar/(\beta - a)\right]} C(0) e^{\tilde{\psi}t}
$$

$$\tag{5.28$'$}$$

However, with the reversal of sectoral relative capital intensities (i.e. $a > \beta$), condition (i), necessary for the transversality condition to hold, is no longer automatically met. This is because the partial effect of a higher pH is to increase its flow at the nonsustainable rate $ar/(a - \beta) > r$. Indeed, in order for the transversality condition to hold, we now require the term in the first parentheses in (5.28′) to be zero. Noting that in the neighborhood of steady state:

$$C(0) = (r - \tilde{\psi})W(0) = (r - \tilde{\psi})[q(0)K_0 + p(0)H_0 + B_0]$$

in order for the transversality condition to hold we require:

$$p(0)H_0 - \frac{(1 - a)\tilde{r}_k}{(\beta - a)\left[\tilde{\phi} + ar/(\beta - a)\right]} K_0$$
$$+ \frac{(1 - \theta)(r - \tilde{\psi})}{[\tilde{\psi} + ar/(\beta - a)]}[q(0)K_0 + p(0)H_0 + B_0] = 0 \qquad (5.33)$$

While this transversality condition has been derived in terms of non-traded capital, it is in fact a recasting of the conventional national inter-temporal budget constraint. This can be seen as follows.

Conditions we have imposed have ensured that $\lim_{t \to \infty} \lambda W e^{-\rho t} = \lim_{t \to \infty} q\lambda K e^{-\rho t} = 0$ are met. It then follows from the definition of W in (5.22) that this implies $\lim_{t \to \infty} \lambda[pH + B]e^{-\rho t} = 0$. Thus the transversality condition on nontraded capital in (5.10), together with the solution for $\lambda(t) = \lambda(0)e^{(\rho - r)t}$, implies $\lim_{t \to \infty} Be^{-rt} = 0$ and this latter condition is equivalent to the national intertemporal budget constraint. As a result, (5.33) imposes conditions on the initial relative price of the two goods, $p(0)$, and on the initial price of installed capital, $q(0)$, that ensure that the resulting path of net exports so generated is consistent with the intertemporal solvency of the economy. This equation, taken in conjunction with the stable saddlepath (5.20b), determines the initial values of the two price levels, $p(0)$ and $q(0)$ – both of which may respond instantaneously to new information – consistent with stable adjustment. The previous comments with respect to convergence of the aggregate K/H ratio and the behavior of traded bonds B continue to hold, at least locally.

5.4 Structural changes

We turn now to analyzing the effects of alternative types of disturbance on the equilibrium. Three types of shock will be considered:

(i) domestic demand shock, taking the form of an increase in the rate of time preference;
(ii) domestic supply shocks, taking the form of proportional shifts in the production functions of the two sectors;
(iii) foreign price shocks, taking the form of (a) an increase in the foreign interest rate; (b) an increase in the price of imported investment.

The effects of these disturbances upon the steady-state equilibria of key domestic variables are summarized in Table 5.1. Since the balanced growth equilibrium is characterized by only two growth rates, $\tilde{\psi}$ and $\tilde{\phi}$, these are the only two growth rates reported. We shall assume that $\theta < 1$ so that the growth rate of nontraded capital converges to that of traded capital. Thus $\tilde{\phi}$ can simply be referred to as the growth rate of capital. In the case where $\beta > a$, the adjustments described in the table occur instantaneously; however, if $a > \beta$ they represent long-run responses, following a transitional adjustment, to be discussed in Section 5.5 below.

5.4.1 Increase in rate of time preference

As noted, the steady-state relative price, the marginal physical products of capital, and sectoral capital intensities are all determined by supply conditions and are independent of any domestic demand shock. Thus, $\tilde{p}, \tilde{\omega}, \tilde{r}_h, \tilde{r}_k$, and $\tilde{q}$ are all independent of ρ. The equilibrium growth rate of traded capital, being determined by $\tilde{q}$, is therefore also independent of ρ. The same applies to nontraded capital. The only response to an increase in the rate of time preference is to induce domestic residents to increase the fraction of wealth that is consumed, leading to a reduction in the growth rate of consumption and wealth; see Table 5.1, col. 1.

5.4.2 Increase in productivity

Column 2 of Table 5.1 summarizes the effects of a specified percentage increase in productivity in producing the traded commodity, as represented by the Hicks-neutral technical change da/a. The key to understanding these relationships (as well as those in column 3) is provided by the static efficiency conditions (5.7c), (5.7d), and the steady-state version of (5.9c), together with (5.18b).

First, the increased efficiency in producing the traded good raises the relative price of the nontraded good; i.e. $\tilde{p}$ must rise. In steady-state equilibrium, the real rate of return on nontraded capital measured in terms of the numeraire, $\tilde{r}_h/\tilde{p}$, must equal the foreign interest rate. With the latter remaining fixed, $\tilde{r}_h$

Table 5.1. *Balanced growth effects*

	Domestic demand shock	Domestic supply shocks		Foreign price shocks	
	dp	$\frac{da}{a}$	$\frac{db}{b}$	$\frac{dr}{r}$	dp^*
	(1)	(2)	(3)	(4)	(5)
$\frac{d\tilde{p}}{\tilde{p}}$	0	1	$-\frac{a}{\beta}$	$\frac{a-\beta}{\beta}$	0
$\frac{d\tilde{\omega}}{\tilde{\omega}}$	0	0	$-\frac{1}{\beta}$	$\frac{1}{\beta}$	0
$\frac{d\tilde{r}_h}{\tilde{r}_h}$	0	1	$-\frac{a}{\beta}$	$\frac{a}{\beta}$	0
$\frac{d\tilde{r}_k}{\tilde{r}_k}$	0	1	$\frac{1-a}{\beta}$	$-\frac{1-a}{\beta}$	0
$d\tilde{q}$	0	$\frac{h(\tilde{r}_k/a)}{(p^*+hr)-\tilde{q}}$	$\frac{h\left(\frac{1-a}{\beta}\right)\left(\frac{\tilde{r}_k}{b}\right)}{(p^*+hr)-\tilde{q}}$	$\frac{-h\left(\frac{1-a}{\beta}\right)\left(\frac{\tilde{r}_k}{r}\right)}{(p^*+hr)-\tilde{q}}$	$\frac{p^*-\tilde{q}}{(p^*+hr)-\tilde{q}}$
$d\left(\frac{\tilde{c}}{\tilde{w}}\right)$	$\frac{1}{1-\gamma}$	0	0	$-\frac{\gamma}{1-\gamma}$	0
$d\tilde{\psi}$	$-\frac{1}{1-\gamma}$	0	0	$\frac{1}{1-\gamma}$	0
$d\tilde{\phi}$	0	$\frac{(\tilde{r}_k/a)}{(p^*+hr)-\tilde{q}}$	$\frac{\left(\frac{1-a}{\beta}\right)\left(\frac{\tilde{r}_k}{b}\right)}{(p^*+hr)-\tilde{q}}$	$-\frac{\left(\frac{1-a}{\beta}\right)\left(\frac{\tilde{r}_k}{r}\right)}{(p^*+hr)-\tilde{q}}$	$-\frac{hr}{(p^*+hr)-\tilde{q}}$

Note: $p^* + hr - q > 0$

must therefore rise in proportion to the relative price $\tilde{p}$. But in order for the value of the marginal physical product of nontraded capital in terms of the numeraire (i.e. $\tilde{r}_h/\tilde{p}$) to remain constant, the relative capital intensity ratio in the nontraded sector K_N/H_N must remain constant. And since, further, capital is freely mobile across sectors, the relative capital intensity in the traded sector, K_T/H_T, remains constant as well; i.e. ω remains unchanged. It then immediately follows that the marginal physical product of traded capital in the traded sector, $\tilde{r}_k$, increases in proportion to the productivity increase, implying that the increase in the relative price of the nontraded good is similarly proportionate. The higher marginal physical product of traded capital implies a higher rate of return to traded capital, thereby increasing the market price of installed capital, $\tilde{q}$. This in turn raises the growth rate of traded capital and therefore that of nontraded capital as well. By contrast, the higher productivity of traded output has no effect either on the steady-state consumption–wealth ratio, or on the equilibrium growth rates of consumption or wealth, all of which are determined by the difference between the rate of return on foreign bonds and the domestic rate of time preference.

From the results reported in Table 5.1 it is straightforward to determine the effect of the increase in da/a on the equilibrium aggregate traded–nontraded capital ratio, K/H, reported in (5.30). With $\tilde{r}_k/\tilde{p}$ remaining constant, the only effect is through the growth rate, with this depending upon the relative sectoral capital intensities. Thus, the increase in the growth rate, $\tilde{\phi}$, stemming from the productivity increase, will raise the ratio K/H if $\beta > a$ and lower it otherwise. This is because during the transition K grows faster than H, so that relatively more traded than nontraded capital is accumulated. If $a > \beta$ the decline in p during the transition implies that H must grow at a faster rate than K, so that over time the K/H ratio will fall.

Column 3 summarizes the analogous effects of a specified percentage increase in the productivity of producing the nontraded good, as represented by the change db/b. Here the choice of numeraire plays a role, leading to differences from the previous productivity shock. First, the increase in efficiency of producing the nontraded good will reduce its relative price; i.e. $\tilde{p}$ will fall. With the world interest rate fixed, equilibrium in the world bond market requires that $\tilde{r}_h$ now declines in proportion to the decline in relative price $\tilde{p}$. Now in order for $\tilde{r}_h/\tilde{p}$ to remain constant in the face of an increase in the efficiency of the production of the nontraded good (i.e. larger b), the relative capital intensity ratio in the nontraded sector K_N/H_N must decline, with an identical decline occurring in the traded sector. In other words, $\tilde{\omega}$ falls. The decline in K_T/H_T raises the marginal physical product of traded capital in terms of the numeraire; i.e. $\tilde{r}_k$ rises. Thus in contrast to the case of the productivity shock da, the two marginal physical products, $\tilde{r}_k$ and $\tilde{r}_h$, move in opposite directions. The higher marginal physical product of traded capital raises its installed price and the equilibrium growth rate of capital. The consumption–wealth ratio, as well as the equilibrium growth rates of consumption and total wealth, remain unaffected. The effect on the ratio of traded to nontraded capital is similar to that discussed in connection with the change in da/a, although in addition to the growth effect, which remains precisely as before, the increase in $\tilde{r}_k/\tilde{p}$ causes a decline in the K/H ratio.

5.4.3 Foreign price shocks

An increase in the foreign interest rate raises $\tilde{r}_h/\tilde{p}$. With the production function for the nontraded sector remaining constant, this raises the relative sectoral capital intensity in the nontraded sector, K_N/H_N (see [5.7d]), raising K_T/H_T proportionately; i.e. $\tilde{\omega}$ rises. The rise in K_T/H_T reduces the marginal physical product of traded capital in the traded sector, so that $\tilde{r}_k$ falls. In order for the value of the marginal physical product of the two types of capital to be equated across the two sectors, the relative price of the nontraded good must move to offset the impact of the higher sectoral capital intensity $\tilde{\omega}$ on the marginal physical product of capital in that sector. Thus $\tilde{p}$ must rise or fall according to whether $a \gtrless \beta$. Whatever the response of the relative price, it is dominated by the direct effect of the foreign interest and $\tilde{r}_h$ rises unambiguously. The decline in the marginal physical product of traded capital reduces the market price of installed capital, thereby reducing the equilibrium growth rate of capital. Thus in all these respects, the foreign interest rate operates like a negative shock to the productivity of nontraded output. Its effect on the equilibrium ratio of traded to nontraded capital is therefore the reverse of that in section 5.4.2.

But it also has consumption effects. The higher interest rate has a positive income effect dr and a negative substitution effect $-dr/(1-\gamma)$, with the net effect being $-\gamma dr/(1-\gamma)$. Whatever the net effect on consumption, the higher income is more than offsetting, so that the net effect is to raise the growth rate of consumption and wealth.

Finally, an increase in the import price of investment, p^*, has neither a production effect nor a demand effect. It therefore has no effect on the relative price, the sectoral relative capital intensities, the marginal physical products, all of which are determined by production conditions, or on consumption, or the growth rates of consumption and wealth. The only impact is on the price of installed capital and the growth rate of the two capital goods. A higher cost of new investment reduces $\tilde{q}$ if $\tilde{q} > p^*$, so that there is positive growth, and raises it otherwise. This is because, in a positively growing economy, a higher import price of investment reduces the rate of return on traded capital resulting from valuation effects (the third term in [5.9b]). This needs to be offset by a reduction in the price of installed capital, q, in order to restore the rate of return on traded capital to the fixed rate of return on traded bonds. Consequently, the rate of growth of capital in a positively growing economy declines, while the rate of decline in a stagnating economy – one having negative growth – increases. These growth rates translate immediately to impacts on the equilibrium K/H ratio, as for previous shocks.

5.5 Transitional dynamics

We now consider the case where the traded sector is relatively more capital-intensive in traded capital (i.e. $a > \beta$) so that the adjustment to any shock

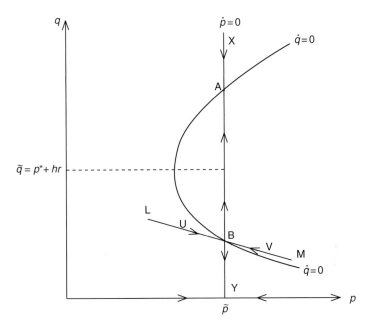

Figure 5.3 Increase in Rate of Time Preference: $a > \beta$

involves a path of transitional dynamics. Two examples are illustrated in Figures 5.3 and 5.4.

Figure 5.3 illustrates the transitional adjustment in the case where the domestic economy becomes more impatient, and increases its rate of time preference. Suppose that the economy is initially in the steady-state equilibrium denoted by B. Since the steady-state values of $\tilde{p}$ and $\tilde{q}$ are independent of the rate of time preference, the stable saddlepath LM remains unchanged following this change in ρ, so that the system ultimately returns to B.

Upon impact, the higher rate of time preference will generate initial changes in both the relative price, $p(0)$, and in the price of installed capital, $q(0)$. These initial jumps are required so as to: (i) keep the economy on the stable saddlepath, in this case LM; (ii) ensure that the transversality condition (5.33) for nontraded capital is satisfied. The movement is thus represented by a discrete jump from B to U or from B to V, at which point the economy reverses itself and proceeds continuously back to the equilibrium B.

The increase in the rate of time preference, ρ, raises the C/W ratio, thereby increasing the initial consumption demand for both goods. In order for (5.33) to be maintained, this must be offset by a decline in initial wealth

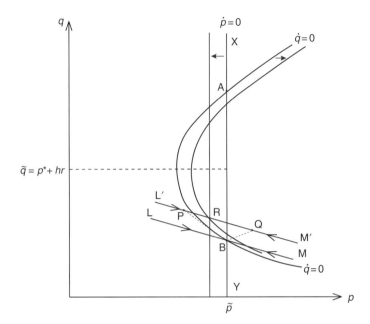

Figure 5.4 Increase in Rate of Productivity: $a > \beta$

and this is accomplished by initial jumps in the two prices $dp(0)$, $dq(0)$. At the same time, these initial price changes are constrained by the requirement that they remain on the stable saddlepath LM. Denoting the negative slope of that line by $-\zeta$ (where $\zeta > 0$) we require $dq(0) = -\zeta dp(0)$, so that the two prices move in opposite directions. In general, we can establish a critical value of the ratio of nontraded to traded capital, $\bar{\kappa}$ say, such that the required initial reduction in wealth is accomplished by a reduction in the price of the relatively abundant form of capital, in terms of this critical ratio.

Thus if the initial ratio of nontraded to traded capital $H_0/K_0 > \bar{\kappa}$, the wealth reduction is brought about by a reduction in $p(0)$ together with a smaller increase in $q(0)$. This is represented by a jump from B to U and an initial increase in the growth rate of traded capital. The reduction in the relative price of nontraded output has immediate effects on the sectoral capital intensities and the rates of return on the two forms of capital, in accordance with (5.15). These effects are all transitory as the economy returns to B along UB. If the relative size of the two forms of capital is reversed, so that $H_0/K_0 < \bar{\kappa}$ holds, the reduction in wealth is accomplished by a reduction in $q(0)$, together with an increase in $p(0)$. The adjustment is a jump from B to V and involves a reduction in the growth rate of traded capital, which, however, is only temporary, as the economy eventually returns to B along VB.

Figure 5.4 illustrates the dynamics in response to an increase in the productivity of the nontraded good, as represented by an increase in b. In this case the $\dot{p} = 0$ locus moves to the left and the $\dot{q} = 0$ locus shifts to the right. The new equilibrium is now at the point R, lying to the northwest of B, with the stable saddlepath shifting up from LM to $L'M'$. The transition to the new saddlepath occurs through jumps in $p(0)$ and $q(0)$ and this may take place in the direction BR or along BQ, depending in part upon the initial relative sectoral intensities. But after the initial jump, the economy proceeds continuously along the new stable saddlepath to R.

5.6 Conclusions

This chapter has presented a two-sector endogenous growth model of a small open economy with traded and nontraded capital goods. As such it extends two important bodies of literature. The first is the dependent economy model, which has proved to be a standard workhorse in international economics. Second, identifying traded capital with physical capital, and nontraded capital with human capital, the model is equivalent to the two-sector, two-capital-good, endogenous growth models that have recently been so prominent in the literature. The assumption that the economy faces a perfect bond market is crucial in enabling a tractable closed-form solution to be obtained.

A key feature of the model is that the accumulation of traded capital takes place by means of a convex cost of adjustment function. This raises a number of issues with respect to the nature of the steady growth equilibrium. First, despite the linear technology, it is possible in the presence of adjustment costs for no steady-state growth path to exist. This will be so if the differences between the valuation of new capital and the resources it utilizes are too large. Second, the rate of growth of traded capital on the one hand, and the rate of growth of domestic consumption and wealth on the other, are determined largely independently. The former is determined by the equilibrium "Tobin q," and depends mainly on production conditions, including the adjustment costs to investment. The latter are determined much more by taste parameters, such as the rate of time preference and the intertemporal elasticity of substitution.

The nature of the economy's growth path depends critically upon the relative sectoral capital intensities of the two domestic production functions. In the case where the *nontraded sector is relatively intensive in traded capital*

($\beta > a$), neither the relative price of nontraded output nor the price of installed capital undergoes transitional dynamics; they are always at their respective steady-state levels. Thus traded capital and aggregate wealth are always on their respective steady-state growth paths, in general growing at different rates. Nontraded capital undergoes transitional dynamics, ultimately converging to the growth rate of traded capital and an equilibrium ratio of traded to nontraded capital.

In the case where it is the *traded sector which is relatively intensive in traded capital* ($a > \beta$), both asset prices will follow transitional paths, before eventually converging to their respective steady-state equilibria, which remain the same as when $\beta > a$. Corresponding to these transitional paths for prices are transitional growth paths for traded capital and wealth, which too converge to the same respective steady-state growth paths as before. Thus an important general implication of our framework is that the qualitative behavior of asset prices in a small economy depends crucially upon its underlying production structure and, specifically, upon the relative intensities of the two sectors in the two types of capital.

6

Non-scale growth models

6.1 Introduction[1]

As we noted briefly in Chapter 2, an important potential difficulty associated with endogenous growth models is that they may exhibit "scale effects," meaning that variations in the *levels* of key variables pertaining to the size of the economy, such as the population, number of people employed in the research sector, or the capital stock, exert *permanent* influences on national growth rates. In addition, they also suggest that policy variables, most notably tax rates, may have a profound effect on the equilibrium growth rate. These theoretical predictions run counter to recent empirical evidence obtained from studies based on the USA and other OECD countries.[2] This has led to the development of a new class of so-called "non-scale" growth models, in which technology and capital accumulation are still endogenous, but long-run growth rates are now independent of changes in policy and other scale variables.[3] Instead, long-run growth rates are determined by the exogenous growth rate of labor in conjunction with production elasticities. In this respect these new models are closer in spirit to the traditional Solow–Swan neo-classical growth model, which in fact emerges as a special case.

The non-scale specification has both advantages and disadvantages. One attractive feature is that a balanced growth equilibrium obtains with few restrictions on returns to scale. This is in contrast to endogenous growth models,

---

[1] This chapter draws on material in Eicher and Turnovsky (1999b).

[2] For example, OECD data support neither the claim of R&D-based growth models that a doubling of the resources devoted to R&D efforts should increase the rate of growth proportionately, nor the proposition of AK models that an increase in investment rates results in higher growth (Jones, 1995b). Tax rates have been shown to be ineffective in influencing long-run growth in the USA; see Backus, Kehoe, and Kehoe (1992) and Stokey and Rebelo (1995).

[3] The term "non-scale" reflects the characteristic that a country's growth rate is independent of the scale of the economy, as measured, for example, by the size of population; see Jones (1995a), Segerstrom (1995), and Young (1998). Eicher and Turnovsky (1999a) provide a general characterization of non-scale growth using a two-sector production technology.

which require constant returns to scale in the accumulated factors of production for balanced growth to prevail.[4] It also contrasts with the traditional neoclassical growth model, for which constant returns to scale in capital and labor must hold. Thus the non-scale growth model has the important advantage of flexibility, in that the relevance of the production elasticities to growth provides a possible explanation for the observed diversity of long-run growth rates. On the other hand, a balanced growth with non-constant returns to scale to be sustained requires the production function to be of Cobb–Douglas form, and is unsustainable for more general technologies.[5]

One other feature of the non-scale model is that the increased flexibility of the technology raises the dimensionality of the adjustment relative to that of the corresponding endogenous growth model. Thus, while the one-sector AK growth models, like those discussed in Part I, always lie on their balanced growth path (and therefore have no transitional dynamics), the corresponding one-sector non-scale growth model is described by a second-order system that is saddlepoint-stable. This implies that the balanced growth equilibrium is approached along a one-dimensional stable locus. If we introduce an upward-sloping supply of debt function into the AK model, this leads to a third-order system having one stable eigenvalue and also a one-dimensional stable locus; see Chapter 4. As we shall show in this chapter, if we introduce increasing borrowing costs into the non-scale model, this leads to a fourth-order dynamic system, with the stable manifold being a two-dimensional locus. The upshot is that the non-scale model introduces flexibility into the transitional characteristics of the economy that can be important in helping explain observed differences in adjustments across sectors; see e.g. Bernard and Jones (1996).

The fact that the transitional dynamics in the presence of international capital market imperfections is of higher order can help provide interesting insights. For example, events in East Asia and Mexico in the 1990s demonstrated that simple *one-time* policy changes can generate inherently nonlinear adjustments in the sense that they can lead to an initial period of excessive capital inflows, followed by substantial capital outflows at some later stage.[6] Conventional dynamic endogenous growth models of open economies, such as those discussed in Chapters 4 and 5, are usually

---

[4] Solow (1994) refers to this as a knife-edge condition. See Jones (1999) for discussion of this issue.
[5] See Eicher and Turnovsky (1999a).
[6] For example, Thailand's recent financial liberalization involved increased subsidies (reduced taxes) on foreign borrowing, leading to (perceived) excessive capital inflows that eventually led to a balance of payments crisis with associated net capital outflows; see Guitan (1998).

characterized by one-dimensional transitional adjustment paths, and therefore require at least two time-separate and offsetting policy shocks in order to account for such reversals in capital flows. By contrast, a simple non-scale model can generate such capital flow reversals as part of the intrinsic transitional dynamics following a one-time policy event.

To keep the analysis tractable we restrict the production technology to only a single sector. Initially we consider a conventional pure small open economy facing a perfect world capital market, and assume that capital accumulation is subject to convex adjustment costs, as in the benchmark model of Chapter 2. Subsequently, we modify the model by introducing a capital market imperfection, in the form of an upward-sloping supply schedule of funds, introduced in Chapter 4.

As in previous models, the presence of a perfect world capital market generates a sharp dichotomy between the behavior and determinants of the equilibrium growth rates of the consumption side and the production side, although differences now emerge. Consumption is always on its balanced growth path and its equilibrium growth rate is determined by domestic preferences and the net-of-tax foreign interest rate. On the other hand, while the long-run growth rate of output (and capital) is now determined by the production and population growth parameters alone they are subject to transitional dynamics.[7]

Also, as in Chapter 4, the introduction of the capital market imperfection fundamentally changes both the dynamic structure and long-run policy effectiveness. The evolution of all variables becomes interrelated and subject to transitional dynamics. Borrowing constraints thus yield an equilibrium in which the equilibrium growth rates of *both* output and consumption are determined by the production and population growth parameters alone, precisely as in a non-scale closed economy; cf. Jones (1995a) and Eicher and Turnovsky (1999a).

To illustrate the dynamics, we consider two alternative policy changes. The first we call "financial liberalization," which takes the form of a reduction in the tax on debt (or debt subsidy), and is often seen as a cause of the events in Thailand and Korea in the 1990s. We show that while the equilibrium levels of capital and output remain unchanged, a subsidy to debt increases the debt–capital ratio permanently, exclusively through an increase in the level of debt. The higher debt and higher cost of borrowing raise the costs of debt service so that long-run consumption per capita must

---

[7] This contrasts with the open economy AK model developed in Chapter 2, for example, in which the production side is also always on its steady balanced growth.

decline, since output remains unchanged. The transitional adjustment followed by capital and debt is especially interesting since it involves a loop consisting of three distinct phases. Initially, a reduction in borrowing costs raises the incentives to accumulate both debt and capital. During the intermediate phase, the increased debt raises debt service costs, leaving less output for investment, so that capital accumulation slows and eventually declines. Finally, during the third stage the reduction in capital and the higher associated debt costs, eventually more than offset the benefits of the initial subsidy, causing debt to decline, along with capital, toward the new long-run equilibrium.

We also examine an increase in a distortionary income tax and find that, in contrast to a reduction in the tax on debt, it leads to proportionate long-run declines in the stocks of capital and debt. While a variety of transitional time paths are possible, monotonic adjustment in both variables is the most plausible.

6.2 Small open economy

We begin with the basic canonical model, discussed in Chapter 2, of a small open economy that consumes and produces a single traded commodity. Initially we assume that each individual is endowed with a fixed quantity of labor, L_i. Labor is fully employed so that total labor supply, equal to population, N, grows exponentially at the steady rate $\dot{N} = nN$. As before, individual domestic output, Y_i, of the traded commodity is determined by the individual's private capital stock, K_i, his labor supply, L_i, and the aggregate capital stock, $K \, (= NK_i)$:

$$Y_i = a'L_i^{1-\sigma}K_i^{\sigma}K^{\eta} \equiv aK_i^{\sigma}K^{\eta} \quad 0 < \sigma < 1, \eta \lessgtr 0 \tag{6.1a}$$

Aggregate consumption in the economy is denoted by C, so that the per capita consumption of the individual agent at time t is $C/N = C_i$, yielding the agent utility over an infinite time horizon represented by the intertemporal isoelastic utility function:

$$\Omega \equiv \int_o^{\infty} \tfrac{1}{\gamma}C_i^{\gamma}e^{-\rho t}dt \quad -\infty < \gamma < 1 \tag{6.1b}$$

Agents accumulate physical capital, subject to the usual adjustment costs:

$$\Phi(I_i, K_i) = I_i + h\tfrac{I_i^2}{2K_i} = I_i\left(1 + \tfrac{h}{2}\tfrac{I_i}{K_i}\right)$$

so that the net rate of capital accumulation is given by:

$$\dot{K}_i = I_i - nK_i \tag{6.1c}$$

Agents also accumulate foreign bonds, B_i, which pay a fixed rate of return, r. We shall assume that income from current production is taxed at the rate τ_y, income from bonds is taxed at the rate τ_b, while, in addition, consumption is taxed at the rate τ_c. Thus the individual agent's instantaneous budget constraint is described by:

$$\begin{aligned} \dot{B}_i =& (1 - \tau_y)Y_i + [r(1 - \tau_b) - n]B_i - (1 + \tau_c)C_i \\ & - I_i[1 + (h/2)(I_i/K_i)] + T_i \end{aligned} \tag{6.1d}$$

As before, the agent's decisions are to choose his rates of consumption, C_i, investment, I_i, and asset accumulation, B_i and K_i, to maximize the intertemporal utility function (6.1a), subject to the accumulation equations (6.1c) and (6.1d). The resulting optimality conditions are:

$$C_i^{\gamma-1} = \lambda(1 + \tau_c) \tag{6.2a}$$

$$1 + h(I_i/K_i) = q \tag{6.2b}$$

$$\rho - \frac{\dot{\lambda}}{\lambda} = r(1 - \tau_b) \tag{6.3a}$$

$$\frac{(1 - \tau_y)\sigma Y_i}{qK_i} + \frac{\dot{q}}{q} + \frac{(q - 1)^2}{2hq} = r(1 - \tau_b) \tag{6.3b}$$

together with the transversality conditions:

$$\lim_{t \to \infty} \lambda B_i e^{-\rho t} = 0; \quad \lim_{t \to \infty} \lambda q K_i e^{-\rho t} = 0 \tag{6.3c}$$

where λ is the shadow value (marginal utility) of wealth in the form of internationally traded bonds and q is the value of capital in terms of the (unitary) price of foreign bonds.[8] Solving equation (6.3b) yields the following expression for the rate of capital accumulation:

---

[8] Since the shadow values λ, and q pertain to individuals they should have subscripts i appended to them. But as agents are identical, their respective shadow values are the same, and for notational simplicity the subscripts are suppressed.

$$\frac{\dot{K}_i}{K_i} = \frac{I_i}{K_i} - n = \frac{q-1}{h} - n \equiv \phi_i \qquad (6.4)$$

so that the growth rate of the aggregate capital stock, is $\phi = \phi_i + n$:

$$\frac{\dot{K}}{K} = \frac{I}{K} = \frac{q-1}{h} \equiv \phi \qquad (6.4')$$

6.3 Aggregate dynamics

Our objective is to analyze the dynamics of the aggregate economy about a stationary growth path. Since the economy comprises one production sector, which produces both output and capital goods, along such an equilibrium path, aggregate output and the aggregate capital stock must grow at the same constant rate, so that the aggregate output–capital ratio remains unchanged. Summing the individual production functions (6.1a) over the N agents, the aggregate production function is:

$$Y = aK^{\eta+\sigma}N^{1-\sigma} \equiv aK^{\sigma_K}N^{\sigma_N} \qquad (6.5)$$

where $\sigma_N \equiv 1 - \sigma$ = share of labor in aggregate output, and $\sigma_K \equiv \sigma + \eta$ = share of capital in aggregate output. Thus $\sigma_K + \sigma_N = 1 + \eta$ measures total returns to scale of the social aggregate production function. Taking percentage changes of (6.5) and imposing the long-run condition of a constant Y/K ratio, the long-run equilibrium growth of capital and output, g, is given by:

$$g \equiv \left(\frac{\sigma_N}{1 - \sigma_K}\right)n > 0 \qquad (6.6)$$

We shall show below that as long as the dynamics of the system are stable, $\sigma_K < 1$, in which case the long-run equilibrium growth is $g > 0$, as indicated. Under constant returns to scale (the neoclassical model), $g = n$, the rate of population growth. Otherwise g exceeds n or is less than n, that is, there is positive or negative per capita growth, according to whether returns to scale are increasing or decreasing, $\eta \gtrless 0$.

To analyze the transitional dynamics of the economy about the long-run stationary growth path, it is convenient to express the system in terms of the relative price of installed capital, q, and the following stationary variables:

$$c \equiv \frac{C}{N^{(\sigma_N/(1-\sigma_K))}}; \quad k \equiv \frac{K}{N^{(\sigma_N/(1-\sigma_K))}}; \quad b \equiv \frac{B}{N^{(\sigma_N/(1-\sigma_K))}} \qquad (6.7)$$

Under standard conditions of constant social returns to scale ($\sigma_N + \sigma_K = 1$), the quantities in (6.7) reduce to standard per capita quantities; i.e. $c = C/N = C_i$, etc. Otherwise they represent "scale-adjusted" per capita quantities.

6.3.1 Consumption dynamics

To determine the growth rate of consumption we take the time derivative of (6.2a) and combine with (6.3a) to find that the individual's consumption grows at the constant rate:

$$\frac{\dot{C_i}}{C_i} = \frac{r(1-\tau_b) - \rho - n}{1-\gamma} \equiv \psi_i \qquad (6.8)$$

With all individuals being identical, the growth rate of aggregate consumption is $\Psi = \Psi_i + n$, so that:

$$\frac{\dot{C}}{C} = \frac{r(1-\tau_b) - \rho - \gamma n}{1-\gamma} \equiv \psi \qquad (6.8')$$

Differentiating c in (6.7) and using (6.8'), the growth rate of the scale-adjusted per capita consumption is:

$$\frac{\dot{C}}{C} = \frac{r(1-\tau_b) - \rho - \gamma n}{1-\gamma} - \left(\frac{\sigma_N}{1-\sigma_K}\right) n \equiv \psi - g \qquad (6.9a)$$

Equations (6.8), (6.8'), and (6.9a) all share the property that with a perfect world capital market, the corresponding consumption growth rates are constant and independent of the production characteristics of the domestic economy. In addition, these equilibrium growth rates vary inversely with the tax on foreign bond income, but are independent of all other tax rates. These aspects of the dynamics of consumption remain unchanged from the basic AK model discussed in Chapter 2.[9]

---

[9] It is important to note that this dependence of the consumption path on exogenous factors would not vanish if we introduced another sector to the non-scale model, as in Jones (1995a) or Eicher and Turnovsky (1999a). The exogeneity of the consumption path is a function of the constant return to foreign bonds and is unrelated to the accumulation of domestic variables. In fact, the rate of return to any domestic factors must adjust to match the foreign return.

6.3.2 Capital and the price of capital

The dynamics of capital accumulation are, however, distinctly different from those of the standard open economy AK model, where like consumption, capital always lies on its balanced growth path. In the present model we find that the scale-adjusted capital–labor ratio, k, and the relative price of capital, q, converge to a long-run steady growth path along a transitional locus. To derive this path we differentiate k in (6.7) with respect to time and combine with (6.4'), to obtain:

$$\frac{\dot{k}}{k} = \left[\frac{q-1}{h} - \left(\frac{\sigma_N}{1-\sigma_K}\right)n\right] = \phi - g \qquad (6.9b)$$

To derive the law of motion for the relative price of the capital good, we substitute the production function (6.1a), the aggregation condition, $K = NK_i$, and (6.7) into the arbitrage condition (6.3b). The latter can then be expressed as:

$$\dot{q} = r(1-\tau_b)q - \frac{(q-1)^2}{2h} - (1-\tau_y)a\sigma k^{\sigma_K-1} \qquad (6.9c)$$

Thus (6.9b) and (6.9c) comprise a pair of equations in q and k, that evolve independently of consumption.

   In order for the domestic capital stock ultimately to follow a path of steady growth (or decline), the stationary solution to (6.9b) and (6.9c), attained when $\dot{q} = \dot{k} = 0$, must have (at least) one *real* solution. Setting $\dot{q} = \dot{k} = 0$ we see that the steady-state values of q and k, $\tilde{q}$ and $\tilde{k}$, are determined recursively as follows. First, the steady-state price of installed capital is:

$$\tilde{q} = 1 + h\left(\frac{\sigma_N}{1-\sigma_K}\right)n = 1 + hg \qquad (6.10a)$$

Having determined $\tilde{q}$ from this equation, the equilibrium scale-adjusted capital–labor ratio, $\tilde{k}$, is determined from the steady-state arbitrage condition:

$$(1-\tau_y)a\sigma\tilde{k}^{\sigma_K-1} + \frac{(\tilde{q}-1)^2}{2h} = r(1-\tau_b)\tilde{q} \qquad (6.10b)$$

In order to be viable, the long-run equilibrium must satisfy the transversality conditions. Substituting (6.3a), (6.4') into (6.3c) and evaluating this requires that:

$$r(1 - \tau_b) > g > 0 \tag{6.11}$$

That is, the after-tax interest rate on foreign bonds must exceed the growth rate of domestic aggregate output. Observe that the condition (6.11) ensures that (6.10a) and (6.10b) imply a unique steady-state equilibrium having (i) a positive equilibrium growth rate of capital (output), $\tilde{\phi} = g$, and (ii) a positive scale-adjusted capital–labor ratio, $\tilde{k}$.[10]

The equilibrium of the production side is thus fundamentally different in the non-scale economy from that of the simple AK technology. First, it is characterized by transitional dynamics (6.9b) and (6.9c), the nature of which will be discussed below. Second, in contrast to the AK technology where the existence of a balanced equilibrium growth rate depends upon the size of the adjustment costs, the condition (6.11) *always* ensures the existence of a unique equilibrium growth rate of capital.[11] Moreover, as is evident from (6.6), provided $\sigma_K < 1$ the steady-state growth rate of aggregate capital (and output) is (i) strictly positive, and (ii) depends upon the returns to scale in the production function. Specifically, the growth rate is greater than or less than that of labor, according to whether there are increasing or decreasing returns to scale in aggregate production, and this provides the channel through which the externality permanently influences the market equilibrium. Finally, the growth rate is independent of the taxes levied upon interest or capital income. This implication contrasts with the corresponding (fixed-employment) AK model of the small open economy in which the growth of output increases with the former tax rate and decreases with the latter.

One further interesting aspect is the response of the relative price of capital, q, to the cost of adjustment h. From equation (2.4b) we see that in the AK model an increase in h reduces the component of the return to capital arising from the favorable impact of capital on installation costs, so that for the total return to capital to remain equal to the fixed return on foreign bonds, q must *decline*. In the non-scale economy, with the equilibrium growth rate determined by production elasticities, an increase in h requires a *higher* q, in

---

[10] This may be shown as follows:

$$(1 - \tau_y) a \sigma \tilde{k}^{\sigma_K - 1} = r(1 - \tau_b)\tilde{q} - (\tilde{q} - 1)^2 / 2h$$

Using (6.10a) and (6.11) the right-hand side of this equation exceeds $g(1 + hg/2) > 0$, thus implying $\tilde{k}^{\sigma_K - 1} > 0$ and hence $\tilde{k} > 0$.

[11] The AK model corresponds to $\sigma + \eta = \sigma_K = 1$ in (6.10b). This yields a quadratic equation in $\tilde{q}$, which may or may not have a real solution. In the case that it does, the smaller root yields the equilibrium growth rate of output $\phi = (\tilde{q} - 1)/h$. Equilibrium growth is thus determined by (6.10b), rather than by (6.10a), as in the non-scale model.

order for the growth rate of capital to equal the equilibrium growth rate of output; see (6.10a).

Linearizing (6.9b) and (6.9c) around (6.10a) and (6.10b), the local transitional dynamics of capital and its shadow price can be represented by the system:

$$\begin{pmatrix} \dot{k} \\ \dot{q} \end{pmatrix} = \begin{pmatrix} 0 & \tilde{k}/h \\ -(1-\tau_y)a\sigma(\sigma_K-1)\tilde{k}^{\sigma_K-2} & r(1-\tau_b)-g \end{pmatrix} \begin{pmatrix} k-\tilde{k} \\ q-\tilde{q} \end{pmatrix} \quad (6.12)$$

From (6.10a) we see that a necessary and sufficient condition for the equilibrium growth rate of output, g, to be positive is that $\sigma_K < 1$. This condition implies $\eta < \sigma_N = 1 - \sigma$, so that the share of external spillover generated by private capital accumulation, and hence the overall social increasing returns to scale, cannot exceed the exogenously growing factor's share (labor) in production. Assuming that this condition is met, the determinant of the matrix appearing in (6.12) is negative, implying that the dynamics are a saddlepoint. As usual, we assume that the capital stock accumulates slowly, so that k evolves gradually from its initial value, K_0, while the shadow value of capital may adjust instantaneously to new information. The stable saddlepath is thus:

$$k(t) = \tilde{k} + (k_0 - \tilde{k})e^{\mu t} \quad (6.13a)$$

$$q(t) - \tilde{q} = \frac{\mu h}{\tilde{k}}\left(k(t) - \tilde{k}\right) \quad (6.13b)$$

where $\mu < 0$ is the stable eigenvalue to (6.12). Thus (6.13b) defines a negatively sloped locus between the scale-adjusted capital–labor ratio and the relative price of capital.

Figure 6.1 illustrates the phase diagram for the linearized dynamic subsystem (6.12). The value $\tilde{q} = 1 + hg$ corresponds to the $\dot{k} = 0$ locus. The value $q^* = 1 + hr(1-\tau_b)$ denotes the value of q at which the slope of the $\dot{q} = 0$ locus becomes vertical. Steady-state equilibrium is at the intersection of the $\dot{k} = 0$ and the $\dot{q} = 0$ loci, with SS being the negatively sloped saddlepath through that point.

6.3.3 Accumulation of foreign debt

As in the simple AK model, an important aspect of this equilibrium is that differential growth rates of consumption and domestic output can be sustained.

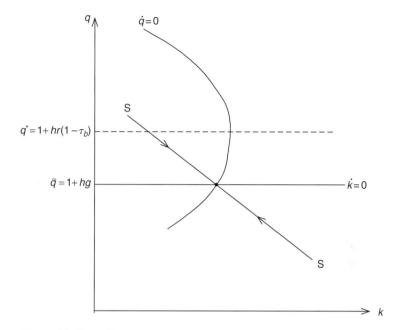

Figure 6.1 Phase diagram

This is a consequence of the economy being small in the world bond market and we now consider the implications for its net asset position.[12]

The domestic government is assumed to maintain a continuously balanced budget. Thus we assume that all tax revenues are rebated to the private sector, in accordance with:

$$T = NT_i = \tau_y aK^{\sigma_K} N^{\sigma_N} + \tau_b rB + \tau_c C \tag{6.14}$$

Aggregating the individual consumer's flow budget constraint (6.1c), and substituting for (6.14) implies that the aggregate net rate of accumulation of traded bonds by the private sector, the nation's current account balance, is described by:

$$\dot{B} = rB + aK^{\sigma_K} N^{\sigma_N} - C - I(1 + (h/2)(I/K)) \tag{6.15}$$

---

[12] We shall assume that the country is sufficiently small that it can maintain a growth rate which is unrelated to that in the rest of the world. Ultimately, this requirement imposes a constraint on the growth rate of the economy. If it grows faster than the rest of the world, at some point it will cease to be small. While we do not pursue the issue here, we should note that the issue of convergence in international growth rates is an important one.

In the appendix to this chapter we show that provided the transversality conditions (6.3c) hold, the linearized solution to the scale-adjusted per capita stock of bonds, starting from the initial stock of bonds, b_0, is given by:

$$b(t) = -\frac{M}{r-g} - \frac{L}{r-g-\mu}e^{\mu t} + \left(b_0 + \frac{M}{r-g} + \frac{L}{r-g-\mu}\right)e^{(\psi-g)t} \quad (6.16)$$

where M and L are constants defined and interpreted in the Appendix.

As we can observe from (6.16), traded bonds are subject to transitional dynamics, in the sense that their growth rate $\dot{b}/b$ varies through time. There are two cases. First, if $\psi < g$, $b \rightarrow -M/(r-g)$, so that asymptotically bonds grow at the same rate as capital, g. Second, if $\psi > g$, the scale-adjusted stock of traded bonds grows at the rate $\psi - g$, with the aggregate stock of traded bonds growing at the rate ψ. Which case is relevant depends critically upon the size of the consumer rate of time preference relative to the rate of return on investment opportunities.

Subtracting (6.8′) from (6.6), yields:

$$g - \psi = \left(\frac{\sigma_N}{1-\sigma_K}\right)n - \left(\frac{r(1-\tau_b) - \rho - \gamma n}{1-\gamma}\right) \quad (6.17)$$

The condition $\psi > g$ is associated with a relatively patient consumer (i.e. ρ is small) and vice versa. In this case, domestic consumption grows faster than does domestic capital stock or output in the long run. Patient agents choose to consume a small fraction of their wealth, which enables them to accumulate foreign assets. The ensuing current account surplus generates a growing stock of foreign assets, the income from which enables the economy to sustain a long-run growth rate of consumption in excess of the growth rate of domestic productive capacity. The opposite applies if $\psi < g$.

6.4 Upward-sloping supply curve of debt

As we have discussed in Chapter 4, the assumption that the economy is free to borrow or lend as much as it wants at a fixed interest rate in a perfect world capital market is strong, particularly for developing economies, which because of risk considerations have restricted access to world financial markets. The key institutional factor that we wish to take into account is that world capital markets assess the risk associated with lending to specific economies in terms of their credit worthiness and their ability to service the associated debt costs. We therefore now examine how the macrodynamic equilibrium is affected if the country confronts an upward-sloping supply curve of debt of the type discussed in Chapter 4, namely:

$$r(Z/K) = r^* + v(Z/K); \quad v' > 0 \tag{6.18}$$

where r^* is the exogenously given world interest rate and $v(Z/K)$ is the country-specific borrowing premium that increases with the nation's debt–capital ratio.

In specifying (6.18) we are viewing the imperfection of the bond market from the standpoint of a borrowing nation. This seems more natural in the sense that it is the debtor nation that in reality is the source of the risk underlying the borrowing premium. But recognizing that $Z = -B$, the stock of net credit, one can formulate the analysis symmetrically in terms of a downward-sloping supply of credit to the world credit market. However, since most developing economies are debtor nations, we shall assume $Z \geq 0$. With this formulation an increase in r^* describes an increase in the world interest rate, while an exogenous shift in the function v represents a change in the country-specific borrowing rate.

As we shall see, the dynamics change dramatically when the economy faces an upward sloping supply curve of debt. As was the case in Chapter 4, the increasing cost of borrowing ties the consumption and production decisions together, in contrast to the case of a perfect world capital market discussed in Section 6.3, which permits a decoupling of these two sets of decisions.

The representative agent's decision remains the maximization of the utility function (6.1b), subject to the capital accumulation equation (6.1c), and the flow budget constraint, now expressed as:

$$
\begin{aligned}
\dot{Z}_i =&(1 + \tau_c)C_i + I_i\left[1 + \frac{h\,I_i}{2\,K_i}\right] - (1 - \tau_y)Y_i \\
&+ \left[(1 + \tau_z)r\left(\frac{Z}{K}\right) - n\right]Z_i - T_i
\end{aligned}
\tag{6.19}
$$

where τ_z is now a tax on debt. The constraint (6.19), expressed from the standpoint of a debtor, asserts that to the extent that the agent's consumption, outstanding interest payments plus investment expenses exceed his net revenue, he will increase his stock of debt. Again we wish to emphasize that in performing his optimization, the representative agent takes the interest rate, which depends upon the economy's aggregate debt, as given.

The optimality conditions with respect to C_i and I_i remain given by (6.2a) and (6.2b), with the latter implying (6.4), as before. The optimality conditions with respect to debt and capital are now modified to incorporate the endogenous interest rate as a function of the nation's debt–capital ratio, Z/K:

$$\rho - \frac{\dot{\lambda}}{\lambda} = (1 + \tau_z)r\left(\frac{Z}{K}\right) \qquad (6.3a')$$

$$\frac{(1 - \tau_y)\sigma Y_i}{qK_i} + \frac{\dot{q}}{q} + \frac{(q-1)^2}{2hq} = (1 + \tau_z)r\left(\frac{Z}{K}\right) \qquad (6.3b')$$

which are essentially identical to (4.5a) and (4.5b).

As in Section 4.3.3, the government rebates all revenues in accordance with (6.14), or, writing the equation in terms of aggregate debt:

$$T = NT_i = \tau_y aK^{\sigma_K} N^{\sigma_N} + \tau_z rZ + \tau_c C \qquad (6.14')$$

Combining (6.19) with (6.14') implies that the economy's net rate of accumulation of debt, its current account deficit, is described by:

$$\dot{Z} = C + I\left[1 + \frac{h}{2}\frac{I}{K}\right] - aK^{\sigma_K} N^{\sigma_N} + r\left(\frac{Z}{K}\right)Z \qquad (6.19')$$

which is virtually identical to (4.7c).

6.4.1 Macrodynamic equilibrium

Transforming the system in terms of the stationary "scale-adjusted" per capita variables defined in (6.7), together with the price of capital, q, the equilibrium dynamics are now expressed by:

$$\frac{\dot{c}}{c} = \frac{r(z/k)(1 + \tau_z) - \rho - \gamma n}{1 - \gamma} - \left(\frac{\sigma_N}{1 - \sigma_K}\right)n \equiv \psi - g \qquad (6.20a)$$

$$\frac{\dot{k}}{k} = \left[\frac{q - 1}{h} - \left(\frac{\sigma_N}{1 - \sigma_K}\right)n\right] = \phi - g \qquad (6.20b)$$

$$\dot{q} = r(z/k)(1 + \tau_z)q - \frac{(q-1)^2}{2h} - (1 - \tau_y)a\sigma k^{\sigma_K - 1} \qquad (6.20\text{c})$$

$$\dot{z} = (r(z/k) - g)z - ak^{\sigma_K} + c + \left(\frac{q^2 - 1}{2h}\right)k \qquad (6.20\text{d})$$

Since the cost of borrowing depends upon the nation's debt–capital ratio, all four dynamic equations are linked in an indecomposable fourth-order system, the variables of which are subject to transitional dynamics, and the properties of which are briefly discussed below. In particular, all variables, including consumption, are now subject to transitional dynamics.

The steady-state growth path is obtained when $\dot{c} = \dot{k} = \dot{z} = \dot{q} = 0$, so that the corresponding steady-state values of c, k, z, q, denoted by tildes, are determined by:

$$\frac{1}{1-\gamma}\left((1 + \tau_z)r(\tilde{z}/\tilde{k}) - \rho - \gamma n\right) = g \qquad (6.21\text{a})$$

$$\tilde{q} = 1 + h\left(\frac{\sigma_N}{1 - \sigma_K}\right)n = 1 + hg \qquad (6.21\text{b})$$

$$(1 - \tau_y)\frac{a\sigma\tilde{k}^{\sigma_K - 1}}{\tilde{q}} + \frac{(\tilde{q} - 1)^2}{2h\tilde{q}} = (1 + \tau_z)r(\tilde{z}/\tilde{k}) \qquad (6.21\text{c})$$

$$\tilde{c} + \left(\frac{\tilde{q}^2 - 1}{2h}\right)\tilde{k} - a\tilde{k}^{\sigma_K} + \left(r(\tilde{z}/\tilde{k}) - g\right)\tilde{z} = 0 \qquad (6.21\text{d})$$

This steady state has a simple recursive structure. First, the steady-state price of installed capital is determined by (6.21b), so that the equilibrium growth rate equals g. Given the non-scale nature of the model, the restricted access to the world financial market has no adverse impact on the country's long-run growth rate of output. Thus the same condition applies in a small economy facing a perfect world capital market. But in contrast to such an economy, long-run domestic consumption grows at the same rate as domestic output. This is achieved through the adjustment in the country's debt to capital ratio $(\tilde{z}/\tilde{k})$, and hence in the cost of borrowing. Having determined both $\tilde{q}$ and $(\tilde{z}/\tilde{k})$, (6.21c) determines the scale-adjusted capital–labor ratio, $\tilde{k}$, such that the after-tax rate of return on capital equals the after-tax equilibrium cost of debt. Finally, given $\tilde{q}$, $(\tilde{z}/\tilde{k})$, and $\tilde{k}$, equation (6.21d) determines the equilibrium scale-adjusted per capita consumption, $\tilde{c}$.

Since the steady-state equilibrium requires that the scale-adjusted quantities all be constant, it follows that consumption, capital, output, and debt, must all grow at the common long-run rate, g, which in addition must be consistent with the transversality condition. By direct calculation, this can be shown to reduce to: $\tilde{r}(1 + \tau_z) > g$. Substituting from (6.21a), this can be expressed in terms of exogenous parameters as:

$$\rho > \frac{\gamma(\sigma_N + \sigma_K - 1)n}{(1 - \sigma_K)}$$

As long as this condition is met, the steady-state equilibrium is unique.

We can now characterize and compare the steady state (6.21) to that of the exogenous interest rate case of Section 6.3. In contrast to the previous case, the endogenous interest rate ties both output and consumption growth to the exogenous production and population growth parameters embodied in g. A reduction in the tax on debt, τ_z, which in a pure small open economy would raise the consumption growth rate permanently, will have only a transitory effect. This is because it will encourage the economy to accumulate debt, raising the debt–capital ratio and the cost of borrowing, and thus offsetting the effects of the subsidy, to the point where the net cost of borrowing is unchanged; see (6.21a). With $\tilde{q}$ being determined independently, and the long-run after-tax cost of debt unchanged, equation (6.21c) implies that the equilibrium stock of capital, $\tilde{k}$, remains unchanged. Thus the increase in the debt–capital ratio is accomplished entirely by an increase in debt, $\tilde{z}$. The higher debt and the higher cost of borrowing raises the costs of debt service, so that with output remaining unchanged, long-run consumption per capita must decline.

Long-run borrowing costs are determined by the debt–capital ratio, $(\tilde{z}/\tilde{k})$, and are therefore independent of the domestic income tax, τ_y. Thus an increase in τ_y must lead to a proportional adjustment in $\tilde{k}$ and $\tilde{z}$. With $\tilde{q}$ fixed, the arbitrage condition (6.21c) implies that an increase in τ_y must lead to a reduction in $\tilde{k}$ and therefore a proportional reduction in $\tilde{z}$. The resulting effect on per capita consumption, $\tilde{c}$, is ambiguous. While the reduction in capital lowers output, the reduced debt costs leave more resources available for consumption. On balance we find that a higher income tax rate will reduce long-run consumption if and only if $C/Y > (1 - \sigma_K)$.

6.4.2 Transitional dynamics

We are interested in characterizing the transitional dynamics of the economy in order to trace out the adjustment paths in response to alternative policy measures pertaining to external indebtedness. Specifically, we will present a more complex and novel adjustment mechanism in response to changes in the domestic income tax rate, and especially in the tax (or subsidy) on foreign debt. The linearized dynamics to this system are expressed by the fourth-order system:

$$
\begin{pmatrix} \dot{k} \\ \dot{z} \\ \dot{q} \\ \dot{c} \end{pmatrix} = \begin{pmatrix} 0 & 0 & \tilde{k}/h & 0 \\ a_{21} & \tilde{r} + \tilde{r}'.(\tilde{z}/\tilde{k}) - g & \tilde{q}\tilde{k}/h & 1 \\ a_{31} & (1+\tau_z)\tilde{r}'.(\tilde{q}/\tilde{k}) & (1+\tau_z)\tilde{r} - g & 0 \\ \dfrac{-(1+\tau_z)\tilde{r}'.(\tilde{z}\tilde{c}/\tilde{k}^2)}{1-\gamma} & \dfrac{(1+\tau_z)\tilde{r}'.(\tilde{c}/\tilde{k})}{1-\gamma} & 0 & 0 \end{pmatrix} \begin{pmatrix} k - \tilde{k} \\ z - \tilde{z} \\ q - \tilde{q} \\ c - \tilde{c} \end{pmatrix}
$$

$$(6.22)$$

where

$$
a_{21} \equiv a(1 - \sigma_K)\tilde{k}^{\sigma_K - 1} - \frac{\tilde{z}}{h}\left[\tilde{r} + \tilde{r}'.\frac{\tilde{z}}{h} - g\right] - \frac{\tilde{c}}{\tilde{k}}
$$

$$
a_{31} \equiv -(1+\tau_z)\tilde{r}'.\frac{\tilde{z}\tilde{q}}{\tilde{k}^2} + \left(1 - \tau_y\right)a\sigma(1 - \sigma_K)\tilde{k}^{\sigma_K - 2}
$$

It is straightforward to show that both the determinant and the trace of the matrix in (6.22) are positive, implying that there are either two or four eigenvalues having positive real parts. Various sufficient conditions can be established to ensure that there are in fact two positive and two negative roots, in which case with capital and debt, k and z, evolving gradually, and c and q allowed to jump instantaneously, the dynamics are represented by a unique stable saddlepath. Being second order, it allows for nonlinear adjustment paths for both capital and debt along which both variables may overshoot their respective long-run equilibria. The simplest sufficient condition to ensure a unique stable saddlepath is $C/Y > (1 - \sigma_K)$. In extensive simulations and sensitivity analysis, Eicher and Turnovsky (1999a) find that this constraint is never violated, and they attain saddlepoint stability in all cases.

Henceforth we assume that the stability properties are ensured so that we can denote the two stable roots by μ_1 and μ_2, with $\mu_2 < \mu_1 < 0$. The stable solution is of the generic form:

$$
k(t) - \tilde{k} = B_1 e^{\mu_1 t} + B_2 e^{\mu_2 t} \tag{6.23a}
$$

$$z(t) - \tilde{z} = B_1 v_{21} e^{\mu_1 t} + B_2 v_{22} e^{\mu_2 t} \tag{6.23b}$$

$$q(t) - \tilde{q} = B_1 v_{31} e^{\mu_1 t} + B_2 v_{32} e^{\mu_2 t} \tag{6.23c}$$

$$c(t) - \tilde{c} = B_1 v_{41} e^{\mu_1 t} + B_2 v_{42} e^{\mu_2 t} \tag{6.23d}$$

where B_1, B_2 are arbitrary constants and the vector $(1 \; v_{2i} \; v_{3i} \; v_{4i})'$ $i = 1, 2$ (where the prime denotes vector transpose) is the normalized eigenvector associated with the stable eigenvalue, μ_i. That is, $(1 \; v_{2i} \; v_{3i} \; v_{4i})'$ satisfies:

$$
\begin{pmatrix}
-\mu_i & 0 & (\tilde{k}/h) & 0 \\
a_{21} & \tilde{r} + \tilde{r}'.(\tilde{z}/\tilde{k}) - g - \mu_i & (\tilde{q}\tilde{k}/h) & 1 \\
a_{31} & (1+\tau_z)\tilde{r}'.(\tilde{q}/\tilde{k}) & (1+\tau_z)\tilde{r} - g - \mu_i & 0 \\
-\dfrac{(1+\tau_z)\tilde{r}'.(\tilde{z}\tilde{c}/\tilde{k}^2)}{1-\gamma} & \dfrac{(1+\tau_z)\tilde{r}'.(\tilde{c}/\tilde{k})}{1-\gamma} & 0 & -\mu_i
\end{pmatrix}
\begin{pmatrix}
1 \\
v_{2i} \\
v_{3i} \\
v_{4i}
\end{pmatrix} = 0
\tag{6.24}
$$

The arbitrary constants B_1, and B_2, appearing in the solution (6.23), are obtained from initial conditions, specifically that the economy starts out with given initial stocks of capital and debt, k_0 and z_0. Setting $t = 0$ in (6.23a) and (6.23b) and letting $d\tilde{k} \equiv \tilde{k} - k_0, d\tilde{z} \equiv \tilde{z} - z_0$, B_1 and B_2 are given by:

$$B_1 = \frac{d\tilde{z} - v_{22}d\tilde{k}}{v_{22} - v_{21}}; \quad B_2 = \frac{v_{21}d\tilde{k} - d\tilde{z}}{v_{22} - v_{21}} \tag{6.25}$$

The constants B_1 and B_2 thus depend upon the specific shocks, and once determined, the complete solution for the equilibrium evolution follows from (6.23).

We shall focus our attention on the dynamics of capital and debt. These depend critically upon v_{2i} and v_{3i}, $i = 1, 2$. From (6.24) we obtain:

$$v_{3i} = \frac{h}{\tilde{k}} \mu_i < 0, \; i = 1, 2 \tag{6.26a}$$

$$v_{2i} = -\frac{(a_{31} + [(1 + \tau_z)\tilde{r} - g - \mu_i](h/\tilde{k})\mu_i)}{\tilde{r}'(1 + \tau_z)(\tilde{q}/\tilde{k})}, \; i = 1, 2 \tag{6.26b}$$

In general, v_{2i} can be positive or negative. A weak condition for $v_{22} > v_{21} > 0$ is that the interest elasticity of the debt supply function exceeds $1 - \sigma_K$.[13] This

---

[13] To establish this, substitute (6.21c) into the expression for a_{31}. This condition suffices to ensure $a_{31} < 0$

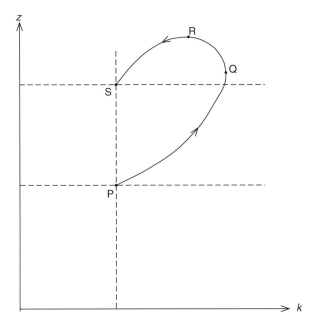

Figure 6.2 Transitional dynamics: decrease in τ_z

condition establishes a relationship between the elasticities of the marginal productivities of foreign debt and capital. In general, the slope along the transitional path in z-k space is given by:

$$\frac{dz}{dk} = \frac{B_1 v_{21}\mu_1 e^{\mu_1 t} + B_2 v_{22}\mu_2 e^{\mu_2 t}}{B_1 \mu_1 e^{\mu_1 t} + B_2 \mu_2 e^{\mu_2 t}} \tag{6.27}$$

where B_1 and B_2 are given by (6.25). Note that since $0 > \mu_1 > \mu_2$ as $t \to \infty$, this converges to the new steady state along the direction $(dz/dk)_{t\to\infty} = v_{21} > 0$.

Decrease in τ_z**:** In our analysis of the steady state we have seen that the endogenously determined interest rate links output and consumption growth to the parameters embodied in g. Financial liberalization, in the form of a reduction in the tax on debt, τ_z, which would raise the consumption growth rate permanently in a pure small open economy, now has only a transitory effect. While the long-run stock of national debt increases, the long-run stock of capital remains unchanged. This is illustrated in Figure 6.2 by a long-run move from P to S. The transitional dynamics are along the path PQRS. With $d\tilde{k} = 0$ for this shock, $B_2 = -B_1$ and the slope along the transitional locus is given by:

$$\frac{dz}{dk} = \frac{v_{21}\mu_1 e^{\mu_1 t} - v_{22}\mu_2 e^{\mu_2 t}}{\mu_1 e^{\mu_1 t} - \mu_2 e^{\mu_2 t}} \tag{6.28}$$

Evaluating this expression at $t = 0$ and for $t \to \infty$, we see that the locus both begins its transition and converges to the new steady state in a positive direction, as drawn. Since the long-run stock of capital is unchanged this must imply a transitional loop.

The intuition for this adjustment path can be broken into three distinct phases. First, the immediate effect of a lower tax on borrowing is to lower the net costs of borrowing. In order for asset market equilibrium to prevail the rate of return on capital must decline and given the instantaneous stock of capital, its shadow value, q, must immediately rise. Thus the reduction in borrowing costs and the rise in the shadow value of capital generates an incentive to accumulate both additional debt and capital. This is represented by the movement in the positive direction PQ in Figure 6.2. The second phase starts as the increased debt raises debt service costs, leaving less output for investment so that capital accumulation slows and eventually declines. This part of the transition is represented by the movement in the negative direction QR. The reduction in capital and accumulating debt raises debt costs even further, eventually more than offsetting the benefits of the initial subsidy. This causes debt to decline along with capital, as represented by the movement along the final segment RS toward the new steady-state equilibrium at S.[14] This adjustment may be summarized in the following proposition:

Proposition 6.1: A decrease in the tax on foreign debt, τ_z, leads to capital flow reversals (an adjustment loop) as both foreign and domestic capital overshoot their respective new steady-state levels during the transition.

Increase in τ_y: To characterize the transitional dynamics in this case, we recall from our analysis of the steady state that a higher income tax reduces the long-run stock of capital and debt proportionately. We have also shown that, irrespective of the shock, both debt and capital will converge asymptotically to the new equilibrium in a positive direction, which in this case means that they will both be reduced together in the direction $(dz/dk)_{t \to \infty} = v_{21} > 0$. The early stages of the transition are somewhat ambiguous, however. It is straightforward to show that:

---

[14] It can be shown from equation (6.23c) that the relative price of capital adjusts according to a similar transition loop.

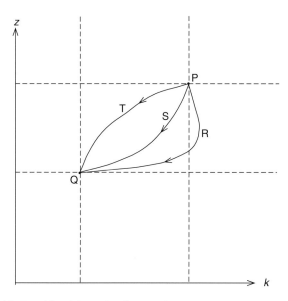

Figure 6.3 Transitional dynamics: increase in τ_y

$$\left(\frac{dz}{dk}\right)_{t=0} = \frac{(v_{21}\mu_1 - v_{22}\mu_2)d\tilde{z} + v_{21}v_{22}(\mu_2 - \mu_1)d\tilde{k}}{(\mu_1 - \mu_2)d\tilde{z} + (v_{21}\mu_2 - v_{22}\mu_1)d\tilde{k}}$$

$$\frac{d\tilde{z}}{\tilde{z}} = \frac{d\tilde{k}}{\tilde{k}} < 0$$

The reduction in long-term debt, $d\tilde{z} < 0$, will tend to generate an immediate reduction in capital and debt, for precisely analogous reasons to those just discussed above in conjunction with the subsidy to debt. At the same time, the reduced after-tax return on capital income must be compensated either by an initial reduction in q, or an initial increase in $\dot{q}$ in order to maintain portfolio balance equilibrium, given the initial unchanging cost of debt; see (6.3b′). It seems most plausible that the long-run reduction in the capital stock, $d\tilde{k} < 0$, will induce a decline in q, thus adding to the incentives to reduce the stock of capital in the short run. However, we are unable to rule out the possibility that the initial response consists of an increase in q accompanied by a large increase in $\dot{q}$, thus generating an initial increase in capital.

Figure 6.3 illustrates a variety of possible time paths whereby the long-run reduction in capital and debt are accomplished. Of these, we view the monotonic paths PSQ and PTQ as most likely. We summarize the transitional dynamics in this case with the proposition:

Proposition 6.2: An increase in the income tax, τ_y, leads to a monotone reduction in debt during transition. Domestic capital may, however, increase during early stages of the transition, before converging to a lower steady-state level.

6.5 Elastic labor supply

Throughout this chapter we have assumed that labor is supplied inelastically. This turns out to be an important condition in the case where the economy has unlimited access to a perfect world capital market supply, since, once this is imposed, all other parameters are unrestricted. However, the combination of (i) perfect capital market and (ii) endogenous labor supply requires a much stronger condition for a consistent equilibrium to obtain. This is because the optimality condition for labor supply must now be taken into account. With the fraction of time allocated to work constant in steady state, this relationship implies that the steady-state consumption–output ratio must be constant, thereby imposing the equality of the long-run growth rates of consumption and output (and capital). Thus equating (6.6) to (6.8) we must have:

$$\psi \equiv \frac{r(1 - \tau_b) - \rho - \gamma n}{1 - \gamma} = \left(\frac{\sigma_N}{1 - \sigma_K}\right) n \equiv g \qquad (6.29)$$

That is, the return on foreign bonds, given the taste parameters, must be such that the implied growth rate of consumption is driven to that of capital, which is determined by the population growth rate in conjunction with the productive elasticities, in accordance with the non-scale growth model.

If all the quantities in (6.29) are constants, then this relationship imposes a constraint between them. In fact, condition (6.29) is the growth analogue to the well-known knife-edge condition in the stationary Ramsey model, $r = \rho$, necessary for an interior equilibrium to exist, and to which it reduces in the absence of growth ($n = 0$); see Turnovsky (1997a). Note, further, that if there are constant returns to scale, (6.29) simplifies to

$$r(1 - \tau_b) = \rho + n \qquad (6.29')$$

which is the familiar long-run viability condition for the standard Ramsey growth model. But now, with the more general productive structure, (6.29) involves both the productive elasticities, σ_K and σ_N, as well as the intertemporal elasticity measure, γ.[15]

6.5.1 Macrodynamic equilibrium

Being a generalization of previous models, the macrodynamic equilibrium of the present model includes elements of the earlier discussion, and here we merely sketch its structure. Following previous procedures, the macrodynamic equilibrium includes the set of equations:

$$\dot{k} = \left(\frac{q-1}{h} - g\right)k \tag{6.30a}$$

$$\dot{q} = r(1-\tau_b)q - \frac{(q-1)^2}{2h} - (1-\tau_y)a(1-l)^{\sigma_N}\sigma k^{\sigma_K-1} \tag{6.30b}$$

$$\dot{l} = \frac{(1-\gamma)\sigma_K}{F(l)}\left(g - \frac{q-1}{h}\right) \tag{6.30c}$$

where, analogously to (3.9b):

$$F(l) \equiv \frac{1-\gamma(1+\theta)}{l} + \frac{(1-\gamma)(1-\sigma_N)}{1-l}$$

And in deriving (6.30c) we have used the condition (6.29). Note that (6.30a) and (6.30c) imply that scale-adjusted capital, k, and leisure, l, move in inverse proportion, and, to a linear approximation, the distances from their respective steady states (denoted by tildes) are related by:

$$l(t) - \tilde{l} = -\frac{(1-\gamma)\sigma_K}{F(\tilde{l})\tilde{k}}\left(k(t) - \tilde{k}\right) \tag{6.31}$$

Intuitively, as capital increases, the return to labor rises and the desirability of leisure declines. Note from (6.31) that employment is now subject to transitional dynamics that mirror the path of capital.

Equation (6.31) introduces a linear dependence into the three dynamic equations, thus implying that the stationary equations corresponding to (6.30a), (6.30b), and (6.30c) do not suffice to determine the steady state.

---

[15] In the case of imperfect capital mobility r is not constant. Now (6.29) no longer imposes a constraint among exogenous coefficients, but rather determines the equilibrium debt to capital ratio.

Setting $\dot{k} = \dot{l} = 0$, we see that both (6.30a) and (6.30c) imply that the steady-state price of installed capital, $\tilde{q}$, remains as determined by (6.30a). Given this value of $\tilde{q}$, the remaining steady-state relationship (obtained by setting $\dot{q} = 0$ in [6.30b]) determines only the equilibrium marginal physical product of capital, which except in polar cases depends upon *both* $\tilde{l}$ and $\tilde{k}$. If employment is fixed, then this determines $\tilde{k}$; if $\sigma_K = 1$, so that we have an AK technology (as in Section 3.3), then this determines $\tilde{l}$.

But in the present case, where both $\tilde{l}$ and $\tilde{k}$ are endogenously determined, further consideration is required to pin each down. The additional relationship is the current account. This requires that $\tilde{l}$ be appropriately chosen to ensure that (6.15) generates a consumption path that is consistent with the nation's intertemporal budget constraint. The argument is basically similar to that of the stationary Ramsey model, as set out in Turnovsky (1997a) and has the characteristic that the long-run equilibrium values of $\tilde{l}$ and $\tilde{k}$ are dependent upon initial conditions.[16]

6.6 Conclusions

In this chapter we developed a one-sector non-scale growth model of an open economy. Initially, the economy was assumed to face a perfect world capital market, and subsequently we examined the economy in the presence of international capital market imperfections.

With the introduction of a perfect world capital market, the non-scale structure of closed economy models is no longer fully retained. Consumption growth is determined by a combination of tastes and the exogenous world return on capital, just as in the endogenous growth model. But in contrast to the AK model, the dynamics of capital and its relative price are subject to transitional dynamics that can be conveniently represented in terms of what we call "scale-adjusted" per capita quantities. The long-run growth rate of domestic output and capital is determined by a combination of the exogenously given growth rate of labor, together with the production elasticities of capital and labor. Most importantly, it is unaffected by either the taxation of foreign interest or domestic income, though both will have transitory effects. The former will generate a short-run increase in the growth rate of output, leading to the accumulation of capital; the latter will have the opposite effect. In the long run both these are reflected in the adjustment of the factor mix chosen by the economy.

---

[16] For further discussion, see Turnovsky (2002a).

The second part of the chapter introduced international capital market imperfections, in the form of an upward-sloping supply curve of debt. As a result of this constraint the dynamics of the consumption, output, and capital growth rates are fully linked, with their common long-run equilibrium growth rate being determined by the interaction between the technological elasticities and the population growth rate. An interesting aspect of this higher-order dynamic model is that it provides an explanation for capital flow reversals that are consistent with one-time policy changes. Effectively the model implies that financial liberalization may generate capital inflow reversals during the transition from one stationary state to another, such as those that occurred in Asia during the 1990s.

Appendix

Utilizing the normalizations in (6.7) and substituting the expressions for aggregate investment and capital (6.4′) into (6.15) enables this equation to be expressed in the scale-adjusted per capita form:

$$\dot{b} = (r - g)b + ak^{\sigma_K} - c - \left[(q^2 - 1)/2h\right]k \qquad (6.A.1)$$

Starting from given initial stock, b_0, and using the stable solution to (6.12) the linearized solution to this equation is:

$$
\begin{aligned}
b(t) = &\left(b_0 + \frac{M}{r-g} + \frac{L}{r-g-\mu} - \frac{c(0)}{r-\mu}\right)e^{(r-g)t} - \frac{M}{r-g} \\
&- \frac{L}{r-g-\psi}e^{\mu t} + \frac{c(0)}{r-\psi}e^{(\psi-g)t}
\end{aligned}
\qquad (6.A.2)
$$

where:

$$M \equiv a\tilde{k}^{\sigma_K} - \left((\tilde{q}^2 - 1)/2h\right)\tilde{k}$$
$$L = \left(k_0 - \tilde{k}\right)\left[a\sigma_K\tilde{k}^{\sigma_K-1} - \left((\tilde{q}^2 - 1)/2h\right) - \mu\tilde{q}\right]$$

In order to ensure national intertemporal solvency, the transversality condition $\lim_{t\to\infty} \lambda B e^{-\rho t} = \lim_{t\to\infty} \lambda(0)N_0 b e^{(g-r(1-\tau_b))t} = 0$ must be satisfied and this will hold if and only if:

$$r(1 - \tau_b) - g > 0 \qquad (6.A.3a)$$

$$r(1 - \tau_b) - \psi > 0 \qquad (6.A.3b)$$

$$c(0) = (r - \psi)\left(b_0 + \frac{M}{r - g} + \frac{L}{r - g - \mu}\right) \qquad \text{(6.A.3c)}$$

Condition (6.A.3a) is ensured by (6.12), while (6.A.3b) imposes an upper bound on the rate of growth of consumption. This latter condition reduces to $\gamma < \rho/[r(1 - \tau_b) - n]$, imposing an upper limit on the intertemporal elasticity of substitution. This is certainly met in the case of a logarithmic utility function and given the empirical evidence indicating small elasticities of substitution $(\gamma < 0)$, will hold under less restrictive conditions as well. The third condition determines the feasible initial level of consumption, and, imposing this condition, (6.A.2) reduces to (6.15) of the text.

PART THREE

Foreign aid, capital accumulation, and economic growth

7

Basic model of foreign aid

7.1 Introduction

Investment in public infrastructure is widely recognized as being an essential component of economic development and growth. Services associated with the use of infrastructure account for roughly 7 to 9 percent of GDP in low- and middle-income countries. Infrastructure in these countries typically represents about 20 percent of total investment and 40 to 60 percent of public investment.[1] The stock of physical infrastructure is thus an important input in the production process of such economies, raising the efficiency and productivity of the private sector, and thereby providing a crucial channel for growth, distribution of output, and ultimately higher living standards.

The significance of infrastructure has assumed a central role in the context of the expansion of the European Union (EU). In several instances, the per capita level of GDP of members acceding to the Union has been below the EU average. For example, in 1988, the per capita GDPs (in purchasing power parity) of Greece, Ireland, and Portugal were only 54.4, 64.6, and 53.8 percent, respectively, of the EU average. Moreover, these countries were also experiencing low growth rates that even exhibited tendencies to decline. As a consequence, the EU introduced pre-accession aid programs to assist these and other potential member nations in their transition into the Union. This process of "catching up" began in 1989 with unilateral capital transfers from the EU through its Structural Funds Program, and subsequent programs were introduced in 1993 and 2000. These assistance programs tied the capital transfers to the accumulation of public capital, aimed at building up the infrastructure of the recipient nation, and thereby enabling it to maintain a growth rate compatible with that of the European Union.

[1] The World Bank (1994, 2004).

161

How investment in infrastructure is to be financed is important. A significant source for the financing of investment in public infrastructure in resource-constrained developing economies is external financing. Such financing could be in the form of borrowing from abroad, or through unilateral capital transfers, as in the case of the European Union. But at the same time, it is likely that external assistance and borrowing will not meet the total financial needs of public investment; hence domestic participation by both the government and the private sector is also important.

The objective of this chapter is to analyze the process of developmental assistance in the form of transfers to a small growing open economy. The model builds upon the various components developed in previous chapters, particularly Chapter 4, and has the following key characteristics. First, the assistance may be tied to the accumulation of public capital, which is therefore an important stimulus for private capital accumulation and growth. Second, we assume that public investment in infrastructure is financed both by the domestic government and by international transfers, thereby incorporating the important element of domestic co-financing, characteristic of the European Union. The international transfers are assumed to be tied to the scale of the recipient economy and therefore are consistent with maintaining an equilibrium of sustained (endogenous) growth. The model is sufficiently general to allow the possibility of a third source of financing public infrastructure, the private sector of the economy. By taxing private firms, and spending a fixed proportion of those taxes in financing new infrastructure, the government can ensure the private sector's participation in building up the economy's stock of infrastructure.[2] We assume that the small open economy faces restricted access to the world capital market in the form of an upward-sloping supply curve of debt, of the form introduced in Chapter 4.

One general issue of concern for both donors and recipients is how foreign aid should be spent in an economy with scarce resources. This has given rise to a long-standing debate, both in academic and policy circles, as to whether international transfers should be "tied" ("productive") or "untied" ("pure"). As Bhagwati (1967) points out, tied external assistance can take several forms. It may be linked to (i) a specific investment project, (ii) a specific commodity or service, or (iii) procurement in a specific country. Recent studies by the World Bank point out that over time, a larger proportion of foreign aid has become "untied" with respect to requirements for procuring

---

[2] The efficient use of infrastructure is a further important issue. For example, Hulten (1996) shows that inefficient use of infrastructure accounts for more than 40% of the growth differential between high- and low-growth countries.

goods and services from the donor country, but it has become more "tied" in the sense of being linked to investments in public infrastructure projects (telecommunications, energy, transport, water services, etc). Between 1994 and 1999, for example, the proportion of official development assistance that was "untied" in the sense of not being subject to restrictions by donors on procurement sources rose from 66 percent to about 84 percent. At the same time, between two-thirds and three-fourths of official development assistance was either fully or partially tied to public infrastructure projects (see note 1).

This chapter contributes to the general discussion of foreign aid in several important directions. First, most of the existing development literature, which examines the possible effects of aid on saving and investment in developing countries, has been based mainly on static models and therefore does not address two important issues. The first is the effect of aid on investment and capital accumulation and the second is the fact that most development assistance is temporary in nature; both of these require the use of an explicit dynamic framework.[3]

Second, since it is likely that external assistance and borrowing will fail to meet the total financial needs for public investment, domestic participation by both the government and the private sector is also important. Recently, in an influential article, Burnside and Dollar (2000) find that foreign aid is most effective when combined with a positive policy environment in the recipient economy. In earlier works, Gang and Khan (1991) and Khan and Hoshino (1992) report that most bilateral aid for public investment in less developed countries (LDCs) is tied and is given on the condition that the recipient government invests certain resources into the same project. We specifically characterize the consequences of domestic co-financing of public investment and outline the tradeoffs faced by a recipient government when it responds optimally to a flow of external assistance from abroad.

Third, the question we shall address is closely related to the "transfer problem," one of the classic issues in international economics, dating back to Keynes (1929), Ohlin (1929), Pigou (1932), and Samuelson (1952, 1954). This early literature was concerned with "pure" transfers, which could be in the form of unrestricted gifts or as debt-relief. It suggested that in a two-country world with stable markets and no distortions, international transfers, through their effects on the terms of trade, impoverish the donor and enrich

---

[3] A key early reference is Chenery and Stroud (1966). See Cassen (1986) and, more recently, Brakman and van Marrewijk (1998) for a survey of this literature. Two exceptions are Djajic, Lahiri, and Raimondos-Moller (1999) and Hatzipanayotou and Michael (2000), who examine the effects of transfers in an intertemporal context.

the recipient.[4] While our analysis focuses primarily on "productive" transfers, the use of which is tied to public investment, we parameterize the transfer so that we can conveniently identify pure and productive transfers as polar cases.

The analysis of this chapter adapts and applies the previous models to an important policy issue. But by combining various components, it becomes too complex for detailed formal analysis and consequently most of the analysis is conducted numerically. In general, the impact of a transfer on the economy depends crucially upon (i) whether or not it is "pure" or "tied" to public investment, and (ii) how the government responds. The main results of our model include the following. With inelastic labor supply (the assumption adopted in this chapter), a permanent pure transfer has no intertemporal effects; it simply raises current consumption instantaneously, raising welfare correspondingly. By contrast, a tied transfer generates a dynamic adjustment. But whether it benefits or harms the economy depends upon its initial stock of public capital. In the most relevant case, where the economy is under-endowed with public capital, a tied transfer will raise the growth rate per-manently and will raise welfare by a larger amount than if the transfer is pure. However, if the recipient economy is relatively well endowed with public capital, a tied transfer may reduce the growth rate and be harmful. In that case, the economy can still be made better off with a pure transfer. In any event, the economy can always convert a tied transfer to a pure transfer, by a corresponding reduction in its own participation. Furthermore, we show how the government can maximize the benefits of the tied transfer by the appro-priate coordinated determination of its expenditure and tax rates. On the other hand, we show that if it responds by choosing its policy instruments to maximize the growth rate, it can be made worse off by the tied transfer. There is thus a sharp tradeoff between welfare maximization and growth maxi-mization, not present in the basic Barro (1990) model, but characteristic of the Futagami, Morita, and Shibata (1993) model.

Both a temporary pure transfer and a temporary productive transfer gen-erate transitional dynamics, though of a sharply contrasting nature. Tem-porary pure transfers have only modest short-run growth effects, which impact most directly on private capital, causing the dynamics, as represented by the public–private capital and debt–private capital ratios, to decline in the short run. These adjustments are then reversed after the temporary pure

---

[4] Subsequent work has extended this early research in various directions. These include extensions to a multilateral world (Bhagwati, Brecher, and Hatta, 1983, 1985), the role of distortions (Turunen-Red and Woodland, 1988), and the intertemporal dimensions (Galor and Polemarchakis, 1987; Haaparanta, 1989; and Brock, 1996).

transfer ceases and the economy reverts back to its original equilibrium. A tied transfer has much more potent short-run growth effects, and by impinging more directly on public capital and debt, yields precisely the opposite transitional dynamics. The public–private capital and debt–capital ratios now increase in the short run, and decline after the removal of the shock. By influencing the transitional growth rates, temporary transfers have *permanent* effects on the *levels* of key variables such as the capital stocks, output, and welfare, these gains being more significant for the productive transfer. One striking contrast between the two transfers is that a productive transfer leads to a substantial increase in the long-run debt of the recipient economy, whereas a pure transfer leads to unchanged long-run indebtedness. The increase in the former case is not a problem, since the country is able to finance the higher debt with its enhanced productive capacity.

7.2 The analytical framework[5]

7.2.1 Private sector

The economy is small and populated by an infinitely lived representative agent who produces and consumes a single traded commodity. Output, Y, of this commodity is produced using the Cobb–Douglas production function:

$$Y = a\left(\frac{K_G}{K}\right)^{\eta} K = aK_G^{\eta}K^{1-\eta}; \quad a>0, \quad 0<\eta<1 \qquad (7.1a)$$

where K denotes the representative agent's stock of private capital and K_G denotes the stock of public capital. Equation (7.1a) is of the form (4.18a) of Chapter 4, except for convenience we abstract from congestion, so that K_G is a pure public good.

The agent's utility function is of the familiar isoelastic form:

$$U \equiv \int_0^{\infty} \frac{1}{\gamma}C^{\gamma}e^{-\rho t}dt; \quad -\infty < \gamma < 1 \qquad (7.1b)$$

The accumulation of private physical capital remains unchanged, involving quadratic adjustment (installation) costs:

$$\Phi(I, K) = I + h_1\frac{I^2}{2K} = I\left(\frac{1+h_1}{2}\frac{I}{K}\right) \qquad (7.1c)$$

---

[5] This analysis is adapted from Chatterjee, Sakoulis, and Turnovsky (2003).

so that the net rate of capital accumulation is:

$$\dot{K} = I - \delta_K K \tag{7.1d}$$

where δ_K denotes the rate of depreciation of private capital. Since we employ extensive numerical simulations, the introduction of capital depreciation is important for the calibration to be plausible.

Agents may borrow internationally on a world capital market. As in Chapter 4, we assume that the creditworthiness of the economy influences its cost of borrowing from abroad. World capital markets assess an economy's ability to service debt costs and the associated default risk, the key indicator of which is the country's debt–capital (equity) ratio. As a result, the interest rate countries are charged on world capital markets increases with this ratio. This leads to the upward-sloping supply schedule for debt, expressed by assuming that the borrowing rate, $r(N/K)$, charged on (national) foreign debt, N, is of the form:

$$r(N/K) = r^* + \omega(N/K); \quad \omega' > 0 \tag{7.1e}$$

where r^* is the exogenously given world interest rate and $\omega(N/K)$ is the country-specific borrowing premium that increases with the nation's debt–capital ratio. As discussed previously, various formulations can be found in the literature, but the homogeneous specification adopted in (7.1e) is necessary to sustain a balanced growth equilibrium.[6]

The agent's decision problem is to choose consumption, and the rates of accumulation of capital and debt, to maximize intertemporal utility (7.1b) subject to the flow budget constraint:

$$\dot{Z} = C + r(N/K)Z + \Phi(I, K) - (1 - \tau)Y + \bar{T} \tag{7.2}$$

where Z is the stock of debt held by the private sector, τ is the income tax rate, and $\bar{T}$ denotes lump-sum taxes.[7] As noted previously, in performing his optimization, the representative agent takes the borrowing rate, $r(.)$, as given.

The optimality conditions with respect to C and I, are

$$C^{\gamma-1} = v \tag{7.3a}$$

---

[6] Chatterjee, Sakoulis, and Turnovsky (2003) employ the relationship $r(N/(K + K_G)) = r^* + \omega(N/(K + K_G))$, but this makes little difference.

[7] It is natural for us to assume $Z > 0$, so that the country is a debtor nation. However, it is possible for $Z < 0$ in which case the agent accumulates credit by lending abroad. For simplicity, interest income is assumed to be untaxed.

$$1 + h_1(I/K) = q \tag{7.3b}$$

where v now denotes the shadow value of wealth in the form of internationally traded bonds, q' is the shadow value of the agent's private capital stock, and $q = q'/v$ is defined as the market price of private capital in terms of the (unitary) price of foreign bonds. These equations are familiar and require no further comment (cf. [4.4a] and [4.4b]). Solving (7.3b) yields:

$$\frac{\dot{K}}{K} \equiv \phi_K = \frac{q-1}{h_1} - \delta_K \tag{7.3b'}$$

which is also unchanged.

Applying the standard optimality conditions with respect to Z and K implies the standard arbitrage relationships:

$$\rho - \frac{\dot{v}}{v} = r\left(\frac{N}{K}\right) \tag{7.4a}$$

$$\frac{(1-\tau)(1-\eta)aK_G^{\eta}K^{-\eta}}{q} + \frac{\dot{q}}{q} + \frac{(q-1)^2}{2h_1 q} - \delta_K = r\left(\frac{N}{K}\right) \tag{7.4b}$$

which again require no further discussion. Finally, in order to ensure that the agent's intertemporal budget constraint is met, the usual transversality conditions must hold:

$$\lim_{t \to \infty} vZe^{-\rho t} = 0; \quad \lim_{t \to \infty} q'Ke^{-\rho t} = 0. \tag{7.4c}$$

7.2.2 Public capital, fiscal transfers, and national debt

We assume that the gross accumulation of public capital, G, is also subject to convex costs of adjustment, similar to that of private capital:

$$\Psi(G, K_G) = G(1 + (h_2/2)(G/K_G)) \tag{7.5a}$$

In addition, the stock of public capital depreciates at the rate δ_G so that the net rate of public capital accumulation is:

$$\dot{K}_G = G - \delta_G K_G \tag{7.5b}$$

The resources for accumulation of public capital come from two sources: domestically financed government expenditure on public capital, $\bar{G}$, and a program of fiscal transfers, *TR*, from the rest of the world. We therefore postulate

$$G \equiv \bar{G} + \lambda TR \qquad 0 \leq \lambda \leq 1 \qquad (7.6)$$

where λ represents the degree to which the flow of transfers from abroad is tied to investment in the stock of public infrastructure.[8] The case $\lambda = 1$ implies that transfers are completely tied to investment in public capital, representing a "productive" transfer. The other polar case, $\lambda = 0$, implies that incoming transfers are not invested in public capital and hence represent a "pure" transfer, of the Keynes–Ohlin type. In order to sustain an equilibrium of on-going growth, both domestic government expenditure on infrastructure ($\bar{G}$) and the flow of transfers from abroad must be tied to the scale of the economy:

$$\bar{G} = \bar{g}Y, \quad \text{and} \quad TR = \sigma Y, \quad 0 < \bar{g} < 1, \quad \sigma > 0, \quad 0 < \bar{g} + \sigma < 1$$

We can therefore rewrite (7.5b) in the following form:

$$\dot{K}_G = G - \delta_G K_G = gY - \delta_G K_G = (\bar{g} + \lambda\sigma)Y - \delta_G K_G; \quad g = \bar{g} + \lambda\sigma > 0$$
$$(7.5b')$$

and dividing (7.5b') by K_G, the growth rate of public capital is given by:

$$\frac{\dot{K}_G}{K_G} \equiv \phi_G = (\bar{g} + \lambda\sigma)\frac{Y}{K_G} - \delta_G. \qquad (7.5b'')$$

The government faces the flow budget constraint:

$$\dot{A} = \Psi(G, K_G) + r(N/K)A - \tau Y - TR - \bar{T} \qquad (7.7)$$

This equation states that the excess of domestic government expenditure on public infrastructure and interest payments on debt over tax and transfer receipts, is financed by accumulating debt (*A*). Note that if $\lambda = 0$, the transfer results in an equivalent reduction in government debt. If $\lambda = 1$ a unit increase in transfers raises the flow of government purchases correspondingly. In the absence of installation costs ($h_2 = 0$) this will leave the stock of government

---

[8] Note that there are different ways of specifying how aid is tied. The specification (7.5a) relates aid to the accumulation of new public capital. An alternative formulation is to tie the aid to total investment costs, inclusive of installation costs. As noted by Chatterjee, Sakoulis, and Turnovsky (2003), the differences between these specifications are minor, and since there is no compelling evidence favoring one formulation over the other, we adopt (7.5b), which turns out to be marginally simpler.

debt unchanged. But to the extent that public investment involves installation costs, which require domestic resources, a unit increase in transfers will actually require the government to issue additional debt to finance the installation component of the investment. In addition we require that the government satisfy its intertemporal budget constraint specified as:

$$\lim_{t \to \infty} A e^{-r(\cdot)t} = 0 \tag{7.7'}$$

National debt is the sum of private debt and public debt, $N = Z + A$. Thus combining (7.7) and (7.2) we get the national budget constraint (the nation's current account):

$$\dot{N} = r(N/K)N + C + \Phi(I, K) + \Psi(G, K_G) - Y - TR \tag{7.8}$$

Equation (7.8) states that the economy accumulates debt to finance its expenditures on public capital, private capital, consumption and interest payments net of output produced and transfers received. It is immediately apparent that higher consumption or investment raises the rate at which the economy accumulates debt. On the other hand, higher transfers affect the growth rate of debt in two offsetting ways. The direct effect of a larger unit transfer on the growth rate of debt is given by $(\lambda - 1) + (h_2/K_G)\lambda G$. An interesting observation is that the more transfers are tied to public investment (the higher λ), the lower the decrease in the growth rate of debt. When transfers are completely tied to investment in infrastructure, i.e. $\lambda = 1$, debt increases on account of higher installation costs. However, the indirect effects induced by the change will still need to be taken into account.

7.2.3 Macroeconomic equilibrium

The steady-state equilibrium we shall derive has the characteristic that all real quantities grow at the same constant rate and that q, the relative price of capital, is constant. Thus we shall express the core dynamics of the system in terms of the following stationary variables, normalized by the stock of private capital, $c \equiv C/K$, $k_g \equiv K_G/K$, $n \equiv N/K$, and q. The equilibrium system is derived as follows.

First, taking the time derivative of k_g and substituting (7.5b'') and (7.3b') yields:

$$\frac{\dot{k}_g}{k_g} \equiv \phi_G - \phi_K = (\bar{g} + \lambda\sigma)ak_g^{\eta-1} - \frac{(q-1)}{h_1} - (\delta_G - \delta_K) \tag{7.9a}$$

Next, dividing (7.8) by N, and substituting, we can rewrite this equation as:

$$\frac{\dot{N}}{N} \equiv \phi_N = r(n)$$

$$+ \frac{1}{n}\left[\{(\bar{g} + \lambda\sigma) - (1 + \sigma)\}ak_g^\eta + a^2\frac{h_2}{2}(\bar{g} + \lambda\sigma)^2 k_g^{2\eta-1} + \frac{(q^2 - 1)}{2h_1} + c\right] \tag{7.8'}$$

Taking the time derivative of n and combining with (7.3b′) leads to:

$$\frac{\dot{n}}{n} \equiv \phi_N - \phi_K$$

$$= r(n) + \frac{1}{n}\left[\{(\bar{g} + \lambda\sigma) - (1 + \sigma)\}ak_g^\eta + a\frac{h_2}{2}(\bar{g} + \lambda\sigma)^2 k_g^{2\eta-1} + \frac{(q^2 - 1)}{2h_1} + c\right]$$

$$- \left(\frac{q-1}{h_1}\right) + \delta_K \tag{7.9b}$$

Third, from (7.3a) and (7.4a), we derive the growth rate of consumption:

$$\frac{\dot{C}}{C} \equiv \phi_C = \frac{r(n) - \rho}{1 - \gamma} \tag{7.3a'}$$

Taking the time derivative of c and combining with (7.3b′) leads to:

$$\frac{\dot{c}}{c} \equiv \phi_C - \phi_K = \frac{r(n) - \rho}{1 - \gamma} - \frac{(q - 1)}{h_1} + \delta_K \tag{7.9c}$$

Finally, rewriting (7.4b) implies:

$$\dot{q} = r(n)q - (1 - \tau)(1 - \eta)ak_g^\eta - \frac{(q-1)^2}{2h_1} + \delta_K q \tag{7.9d}$$

Equations (7.9a)–(7.9d) provide an autonomous set of dynamic equations in K_g, n, c, and q, from which the evolution of government debt can be derived.

7.2.4 Steady-state equilibrium

The economy reaches steady state when $\dot{k}_g = \dot{n} = \dot{c} = \dot{q} = 0$, implying that $\dot{K}/K = \dot{K}_G/K_G = \dot{N}/N = \dot{C}/C \equiv \tilde{\phi}$, the steady-state growth rate of the economy. The steady state can thus be described as follows:

$$(\bar{g} + \lambda\sigma)a\tilde{k}_g^{\eta-1} - \delta_G = \frac{\tilde{q} - 1}{h_1} - \delta_K \tag{7.10a}$$

$$r(\tilde{n}) - \frac{1}{\tilde{n}}\left[\{1 - \bar{g} + (1 - \lambda)\sigma\}a\tilde{k}_g^{\eta} - a\frac{h_2}{2}(\bar{g} + \lambda\sigma)^2\tilde{k}_g^{2\eta-1} - \frac{(\tilde{q}^2 - 1)}{2h_1} - \tilde{c}\right]$$
$$= \left(\frac{\tilde{q} - 1}{h_1}\right) - \delta_K \tag{7.10b}$$

$$r(\tilde{n})\tilde{q} - (1 - \tau)(1 - \eta)a\tilde{k}_g^{\eta} - \frac{(\tilde{q} - 1)^2}{2h_1} + \delta_K\tilde{q} = 0 \tag{7.10c}$$

$$\frac{r(\tilde{n}) - \rho}{1 - \gamma} = \frac{(\tilde{q} - 1)}{h_1} - \delta_K = \tilde{\phi} \tag{7.10d}$$

Equations (7.10a)–(7.10d) determine the steady-state equilibrium in the following recursive manner. First, equations (7.10a), (7.10c), and (7.10d) jointly determine $\tilde{k}_g$, $\tilde{q}$, and $r(\tilde{n})$, from which the steady-state growth rate, $\tilde{\phi}$, immediately follows. These quantities are independent of (i) the adjustment cost of public capital, h_2, and (ii) the sensitivity of the country-specific borrowing cost, as reflected by $r'(\tilde{n})$. Having determined $\tilde{r}$, the equilibrium stock of debt–capital ratio, $\tilde{n}$, is obtained from (7.1e). In particular, a higher interest sensitivity of borrowing costs lowers the equilibrium stock of debt to the point that the interest rate remains unchanged. Given $\tilde{k}_g$, $\tilde{q}$, $r(\tilde{n})$, and $\tilde{n}$, the equilibrium consumption–capital ratio, $\tilde{c}$, is obtained from the current account equilibrium condition (7.10b). Provided $\tilde{r} > \tilde{\phi}$ (which we shall show below is required for the transversality condition to hold) higher marginal borrowing costs reduce total interest payments, raising the consumption–capital ratio. Also, higher installation costs, h_2, reduce the amount of output available for consumption, $\tilde{c}$.

Since this system is highly non-linear, it need not be consistent with a well-defined steady-state equilibrium with $\tilde{k}_g > 0$, $\tilde{c} > 0$. Our numerical simulations, however, yield well-defined steady-state values for all plausible specifications of all the structural and policy parameters of the model.[9]

---

[9] A rigorous discussion of the issues giving rise to non-existent or multiple equilibria in a related model is provided by Turnovsky (1997c).

7.2.5 Equilibrium dynamics

Equations (7.9a)–(7.9d) form the dynamics of the system in terms of k, n, q, and c. Linearizing these equations around the steady-state values of k_g, n, q, and c obtained from (7.10a)–(7.10d), we obtain

$$
\begin{pmatrix} \dot{k}_g \\ \dot{n} \\ \dot{c} \\ \dot{q} \end{pmatrix} = \begin{pmatrix} \eta a(\bar{g}+\lambda\sigma)\tilde{k}_g^{\eta-1}-\delta_G-\tilde{\phi} & 0 & 0 & -(\tilde{k}_g/h_1) \\ a_{21} & r'(\tilde{n})\tilde{n}+r(\tilde{n})-\tilde{\phi} & 1 & (1/h_1)(\tilde{q}-\tilde{n}) \\ 0 & r'(\tilde{n})\tilde{c}/(1-\gamma) & 0 & -(\tilde{c}/h_1) \\ -\eta a(1-\tau)(1-\eta)\tilde{k}_g^{\eta-1} & r'(\tilde{n})\tilde{q} & 0 & r(\tilde{n})-\tilde{\phi} \end{pmatrix} \begin{pmatrix} k_g-\tilde{k}_g \\ n-\tilde{n} \\ c-\tilde{c} \\ q-\tilde{q} \end{pmatrix}
$$

$$(7.11)$$

where

$$
a_{21} \equiv -\eta\left\{1-\bar{g}+(1-\lambda)\sigma\tilde{k}_g^{\eta-1}\right\}+(2\eta-1)a^2(h_2/2)(\bar{g}+\lambda\sigma)^2 k_g^{2\eta-2}
$$

The determinant of the coefficient matrix of (7.11) is positive under the condition that $r(\tilde{n}) > \tilde{\phi}$, i.e. the steady-state interest rate facing the small open economy must be greater than the steady-state growth rate of the economy.[10] Imposing the transversality condition (7.4c), we see that this condition is indeed satisfied. Since (7.11) forms a fourth-order system, a positive determinant implies that there could be zero, two, or four positive (unstable) roots and correspondingly four, two, or zero negative (stable) roots. Imposing the following sufficiency conditions: (i) $-1/2 < \gamma < 0$, (ii) $\delta_G \leq \delta_K$, and (iii) $\tilde{q} > \tilde{n}$, we are able to rule out the cases of zero or four positive roots.[11] Conditions

---

[10] The determinant of the coefficient matrix in (7.11) is given by

$$
\frac{(1-\eta)(\tilde{q}-1)r'(\tilde{n})}{h_1}\left[\frac{\tilde{c}\tilde{q}}{h_1}+\frac{\tilde{c}}{1-\gamma}\left\{r(\tilde{n})-\frac{\tilde{q}-1}{h_1}+\delta_K\right\}\right]
$$

$$
+\frac{\tilde{k}_g r'(\tilde{n})}{h_1}\frac{\tilde{c}}{1-\gamma}\eta(1-\tau)(1-\eta)a\tilde{k}_g^{\eta-1}>0 \qquad \text{if } r(\tilde{n}) > \tilde{\phi}
$$

[11] Let μ be the vector of characteristic roots of the system in (7.11). Then, the characteristic equation is a fourth-order polynomial of the form $\mu^4+\pi_1\mu^3+\pi_2\mu^2+\pi_3\mu+\pi_4=0$, where π_i ($i = 1, 2, 3, 4$) are functions of the terms in the coefficient matrix in (7.11). By the determinantal condition, $\pi_4 > 0$. Imposing (i) $-1/2 < \gamma < 0$, and (ii) $\delta_G < \delta_K$, we can show that $\pi_1 > 0$. Condition (iii) $\tilde{q} > \tilde{n}$, leads to $\pi_2 < 0$. Then, by applying Descartes' rule of signs, we can show that there is a maximum of two positive roots. Also, condition (i) implies that the trace of the matrix in (7.11) is positive, which rules out the case of zero positive roots. Hence the system has two positive roots and two negative roots. Note that conditions (i) and (ii), together with (iii) $\tilde{q} > \tilde{n}$, are only sufficient conditions for saddlepoint stability. Conditions (ii) and (iii) are quite plausible, the latter asserting that the net asset position of the domestic private sector is positive. Other more complex (but less restrictive) sufficiency conditions can also be derived. Numerical solutions yield saddlepoint behavior in all cases and do not require the imposition of these sufficient conditions.

(i) and (ii) impose restrictions on the structural parameters γ, δ_K, and δ_G and (iii) states that in steady state the value of the capital stock in the economy must be greater than the value of its outstanding stock of debt. Under these conditions the dynamic system (7.11) can be shown to be saddlepoint-stable with two positive (unstable) and two negative (stable) roots. We denote the two stable roots by μ_1 and μ_2, with $\mu_2 < \mu_1 < 0$.

7.3 Long-run effects of transfers and fiscal shocks

Table 7.1a summarizes the long-run effects of a permanent transfer on the key equilibrium variables, including the public to private capital ratio. These results imply that a permanent transfer tied to public capital will raise the long-run ratio of public to private capital. This increases the productivity of private capital, thereby raising its relative price and the equilibrium growth rate. Financing the higher investment expenditures for the accumulation of private capital increases the agents' holdings of debt and thus increases the steady-state stock of national debt relative to private capital. The resulting effect (not reported) on the steady-state stock of consumption relative to private capital is ambiguous. We can show that the effect on consumption is a weighted average of two terms, the weights being λ and $(1 - \lambda)$. The first is applied to two components, one representing the effect of a higher ratio of public to private capital, the other the increase in the market price of private capital. A higher stock of public relative to private capital raises output relative to private capital and therefore tends to increase consumption relative to private capital. On the other hand, higher investment in public capital increases its installation costs and this leads to a crowding out of private consumption. Moreover, the increase in the market price of private capital, and the consequent increase in private investment, makes the agent substitute away from consumption and this tends to reduce steady-state consumption. Depending on which component dominates, this first effect on consumption (which is proportional to λ) could either go up or down. The second term represents the effect of that part of transfers not tied to public investment, and hence is scaled by $(1 - \lambda)$. Since a fraction $(1 - \lambda)$ of resources is freed up with the inflow of higher transfers, it contributes toward increasing consumption. The overall effect on consumption is thus ambiguous.

Two critical factors in determining these long-run responses are (i) λ, the degree to which transfers are tied to investment in public infrastructure, and (ii) $r'(n)$, the extent to which borrowing costs are tied to the nation's debt

Table 7.1. *Steady-state effects of changes in transfers and fiscal shocks*

(a) Permanent increase in transfers

$$\frac{d\tilde{k}_g}{d\sigma} = \frac{\lambda a r'(\tilde{n})}{J} \left[\frac{\tilde{q}}{h_1} + \frac{r(\tilde{n}) - (\tilde{q}-1)/h_1}{(1-\gamma)}\right] \tilde{k}_g^{\eta-1} > 0$$

$$\frac{d\tilde{q}}{d\sigma} = \frac{\lambda a^2 r'(\tilde{n})}{J} \frac{\eta(1-\tau)(1-\eta)}{(1-\gamma)} \tilde{k}_g^{2\eta-2} > 0$$

$$\frac{d\tilde{n}}{d\sigma} = \frac{\lambda a^2}{J} \frac{\eta(1-\tau)(1-\eta)}{h_1} \tilde{k}_g^{2\eta-2} = \frac{(1-\gamma)}{h_1 r'(\tilde{n})} \frac{d\tilde{q}}{d\sigma} > 0$$

(b) Permanent increase in domestic government spending

$$\frac{d\tilde{k}_g}{d\bar{g}} = \frac{a r'(\tilde{n})}{J} \left[\frac{\tilde{q}}{h_1} + \frac{r(\tilde{n}) - (\tilde{q}-1)/h_1}{(1-\gamma)}\right] \tilde{k}_g^{\eta-1} = \frac{1}{\lambda} \frac{d\tilde{k}_g}{d\sigma} > 0$$

$$\frac{d\tilde{q}}{d\bar{g}} = \frac{a^2 r'(\tilde{n})}{J} \frac{\eta(1-\tau)(1-\eta)}{(1-\gamma)} \tilde{k}_g^{2\eta-2} = \frac{1}{\lambda} \frac{d\tilde{q}}{d\sigma} > 0$$

$$\frac{d\tilde{n}}{d\bar{g}} = \frac{a^2}{J} \frac{\eta(1-\tau)(1-\eta)}{h_1} \tilde{k}_g^{2\eta-2} = \frac{1}{\lambda} \frac{d\tilde{n}}{d\sigma} > 0$$

(c) Permanent increase in the income tax rate

$$\frac{d\tilde{k}_g}{d\tau} = \frac{a r'(\tilde{n})(1-\eta)\tilde{k}_g^{\eta}}{J h_1 (1-\gamma)} > 0$$

$$\frac{d\tilde{q}}{d\tau} = -\frac{a^2(1-\eta)^2 r'(\tilde{n})(\bar{g}+\lambda\sigma)\tilde{k}_g^{2\eta-2}}{J(1-\gamma)} < 0$$

$$\frac{d\tilde{n}}{d\tau} = -\frac{(1-\eta)^2 a^2 \tilde{k}_g^{2\eta-2}}{J h_1} < 0$$

$$J \equiv a(1-\eta) r'(\tilde{n}) \left[(\bar{g}+\lambda\sigma)\left\{\frac{\tilde{q}}{h_1} + \frac{r(\tilde{n})-(\tilde{q}-1)/h_1}{1-\gamma}\right\} + \frac{\eta(1-\tau)\tilde{k}_g}{h_1(1-\gamma)}\right] \tilde{k}_g^{\eta-2} > 0$$

---

position. In the extreme case of a pure transfer ($\lambda = 0$) there is no effect on either the steady-state public–private capital ratio, the growth rate, or the nation's debt–capital ratio. All that happens is that the consumption–capital ratio increases. Furthermore, this adjustment occurs instantaneously and raises welfare unambiguously. In the limiting case where $r'(n) = 0$, the growth rates of the production side and the consumption side diverge. The (common) growth rate of public and private capital is enhanced by productive transfers, while the growth rate of consumption remains unaffected. In this respect the present model reduces to the model with public capital discussed in Chapter 4.

In Table 7.1b we see that the effects of an increase in the domestic rate of participation, $\bar{g}$, on $\tilde{k}_g$, $\tilde{q}$, and $\tilde{n}$ are identical to those of a productive transfer. Thus to the extent that the domestic government matches the tied transfer, the effects are reinforcing. Table 7.1c describes the effects of a higher distortionary tax rate. By having a contractionary effect on private capital accumulation, this also raises the ratio of public to private capital, while reducing the equilibrium growth rate and therefore the equilibrium interest rate, and thus the equilibrium debt to capital ratio.

7.4 Optimal responses

As our numerical results will show, the effect of the capital transfer on the domestic economy depends in part upon the corresponding response (if any) of the domestic government. In this respect we see that a *tied* or "productive" fiscal transfer of a given amount, coupled with an equivalent *decrease* in government expenditure, is equivalent to an *untied* transfer of an equivalent amount. Here, we briefly discuss two other responses: (i) the growth-maximizing fiscal response, and (ii) the welfare-maximizing fiscal response.

7.4.1 Growth-maximizing fiscal response

Suppose that the government sets its expenditure rate, $\bar{g}$, and its tax rate, τ, so as to balance the costs of the net purchase of capital, given the transfers, namely:

$$\tau = \bar{g} - (1 - \lambda)\sigma \qquad (7.12)$$

Installation costs are thus financed by issuing new debt or by lump-sum taxes in accordance with the flow constraint (7.7):

$$\dot{A} + \bar{T} = r(.)A + (h_2/2)(G^2/K_G)$$

Using (7.12), together with the results from Tables 7.1b and 7.1c, we can then establish that the steady-state growth rate will be maximized if $\bar{g}$ and τ are set in accordance with:[12]

$$\hat{\bar{g}} = \eta - \sigma(\lambda - \eta); \quad \hat{\tau} = \eta - \sigma(1 - \eta) \qquad (7.13)$$

In the absence of foreign transfers, equations (7.13) reduce to the growth-maximizing tax (= expenditure) rate $\hat{\tau} = \hat{\bar{g}} = \eta$, obtained originally by Barro (1990) in his flow model, and later by Futagami, Morita, and Shibata (1993) in their stock model. But the presence of foreign transfers ($\sigma > 0$) leads to a divergence between the growth-maximizing tax and expenditure rates, except in the case where the transfers are fully tied to investment in public capital. Both also deviate from η, in contrast to Barro (1990) and Futagami, Morita, and Shibata (1993). Having the fraction, σ, of income coming from abroad, permits the tax rate to be lowered, so that $\hat{\tau} \leq \eta$. To the extent that the transfers are untied, $\hat{\bar{g}}$ must exceed $\hat{\tau}$, and in fact it will exceed η if $\lambda < \eta$.

---

[12] To establish this we set $dq/d\bar{g} = \partial q/\partial\tau \cdot \partial\tau/\partial\bar{g} + \partial q/\partial\bar{g} = 0$ where $\partial\tau/\partial\bar{g} = 1$ from (7.12) and then substitute for $\partial q/\partial\tau, \ \partial q/\partial\bar{g}$ from Table 7.1.

Substituting (7.13) into the dynamic system (7.9a)–(7.9d) we see that the equilibrium dynamics, including the steady state, are independent of λ. In other words, if the government sets its expenditure and tax rates to maximize the growth rate, the transitional dynamics and the long-run equilibrium are rendered independent of the extent to which the transfers are tied to investment.

7.4.2 Welfare-maximizing fiscal response

A second response is to determine constant fiscal responses, constrained by (7.12), that maximize the welfare gains generated by the transfer, namely:

$$\Delta(W) = \int_0^\infty \frac{1}{\gamma} \left[(C(t))^\gamma - (\tilde{C}(t))^\gamma \right] e^{-\beta t} dt \qquad (7.14)$$

where $\tilde{C}$ is the consumption along an initial equilibrium balanced growth path. Evaluating this quantity numerically, we find that the welfare-maximizing choices of τ and $\bar{g}$, subject to (7.12), are less than the growth-maximizing values, as in Futagami, Morita, and Shibata (1993) and Turnovsky (1997b). Moreover, setting τ and $\bar{g}$ in this way, we again find that the equilibrium path (7.9a)–(7.9d) is independent of λ. This is an important result, since it implies that by combining the transfer with the appropriate expenditure and tax mix, the recipient economy can choose its equilibrium path and associated level of welfare, which is independent of any constraints imposed by the donor country.

7.5 Numerical analysis of transitional paths

Further insights into the effects of transfers are obtained by analyzing the model numerically. We begin by calibrating a benchmark economy using the set of parameters representative of a small open economy reported in Table 7.2, which we assume starts out from an equilibrium with zero transfers.

Our choices of preference parameters, ρ and γ, and depreciation rates, δ_K and δ_G, and the world interest rate, r^*, are standard, while a is a scale variable.[13] The productive elasticity of public capital $\eta = 0.2$ is consistent

---

[13] A convenient source for conventional choices of parameters for calibration is provided by Cooley (1995).

Table 7.2. *The benchmark economy*

Preference parameters: $\gamma = -1.5$, $\rho = 0.04$
Production parameters: $a = 0.4$, $\eta = 0.2$, $h_1 = 15$, $h_2 = 15$
Depreciation rates: $\delta_K = 0.05$, $\delta_G = 0.04$
World interest rate: $r^* = 0.06$
Risk premium on borrowing: $a = 0.1$[a]
Policy parameters: $\tau = 0.15$, $g = 0.05$
Transfers: $\sigma = 0$, $\lambda = 0$

[a] The functional specification of the upward-sloping supply curve that we use is $r(n) = r^* + e^{an} - 1$. Thus, in the case of a perfect world capital market, when $a = 0$, $r = r^*$, the world interest rate.

with the empirical evidence (see Gramlich, 1994). The borrowing premium $a = 0.10$ is chosen to ensure a plausible equilibrium debt–output ratio. The tax rate is set at $\tau = 0.15$, while the rate of domestic government expenditure on public investment is assumed to be $\bar{g} = 0.05$. The choice of adjustment costs is less obvious and $h_1 = 15$ lies in the consensus range of 10 to 16.[14] Note also that the equality of adjustment costs between the two types of capital serves as a plausible benchmark.

These parameter values lead to the following plausible benchmark equilibrium, reported in row 1 of Table 7.3: the ratio of public–private capital is 0.29; the consumption–output ratio is 0.6; the debt to output ratio is 0.45, leading to an equilibrium borrowing premium of 1.4% over the world rate; the capital–output ratio is over 3, with the equilibrium growth rate being just under 1.4%. This equilibrium is a reasonable characterization of a small medium-indebted economy experiencing a modest steady rate of growth and having a relatively small stock of public capital. Rows 2–7 summarize key short-run and long-run changes to this equilibrium following the specified changes. The final column in the table summarizes the effects on economic welfare, measured by the optimized utility of the representative agent:

$$W = \int_0^\infty \frac{1}{\gamma} C^\gamma e^{-\beta t} dt$$

[14] For example, Origueira and Santos (1997) choose $h_1 = 16$ on the grounds that it generates a plausible speed of convergence. Auerbach and Kotlikoff (1987) assume $h_1 = 10$, recognizing that this is a low estimate value, while Barro and Sala-i-Martin (2000) propose a value above 10. In conducting the sensitivity analysis reported in Table 7.5, we have also assumed smaller values of h.

Table 7.3. Responses to permanent changes

	$\tilde{k}_g$	$\tilde{r}$ (%)	C/Y	$\tilde{N}/Y$	Y/K	$\phi_K(0)$ (%)	$\phi_G(0)$ (%)	$\phi_Y(0)$ (%)	$\phi_C(0)$ (%)	$\tilde{\phi}$ (%)	$\Delta(W)$ (%)
Benchmark $\sigma=0,\ \lambda=0,$ $g=0.05,\ \tau=0.15$	**0.291**	**7.423**	**0.601**	**0.452**	**0.312**	**1.37**	**1.37**	**1.37**	**1.37**	**1.37**	—
Pure transfer $\sigma=0.05,\ \lambda=0,$ $g=0.05,\ \tau=0.15$	0.291	7.423	0.651	0.452	0.312	1.37	1.37	1.37	1.37	1.37	+8.32
Tied transfer $\sigma=0.05,\ \lambda=1,$ $g=0.05,\ \tau=0.15$	0.610	8.845	0.561	0.774	0.362	1.701	6.739	2.71	1.37	1.938	+9.83
Bond-financed gov. exp. increase $\sigma=0,\ \lambda=0,$ $g=0.10,\ \tau=0.15$	0.610	8.845	0.511	0.774	0.362	1.71	6.739	2.72	1.37	1.938	+0.30
Co-financing $\sigma=0.05,\ \lambda=1,$ $g=0.10,\ \tau=0.15$	0.943	9.738	0.474	0.929	0.395	2.176	13.69	4.16	1.37	2.295	+4.71
Growth-max. gov. response $\sigma=0.05,\ \lambda=1,$ $g=0.16,\ \tau=0.16$	1.362	10.41	0.379	1.013	0.425	2.57	18.55	5.77	1.37	2.562	−8.63
Welfare-max. gov. response $\sigma=0.05,\ \lambda=1,$ $g=0.02,\ \tau=0.02$	0.376	9.31	0.545	0.989	0.329	2.82	3.52	2.96	1.37	2.12	+10.49

where C is evaluated along the equilibrium path. These welfare changes are calculated as the percentage change in the initial stock of capital necessary to maintain the level of welfare unchanged following the particular shock.

7.5.1 Permanent shocks

Row 2 reports the effects of a permanent *pure transfer* equal to 5% of the recipient country's GDP. While $\sigma = 0.05$ is arbitrary, it is approximately the average rate of foreign aid offered by the European Union under its aid program to prospective members in the early 1990s and thus serves as a reasonable benchmark. It represents a pure wealth effect, which from (7.10a)–(7.10d) has no effect on $\tilde{k}_g, r(\tilde{n}), \tilde{n}$, and $\tilde{\phi}$, and therefore no effect on the transitional adjustments. All that happens is that the transfer leads to an immediate and permanent increase in consumption, raising the consumption–output ratio from 0.60 to 0.65, and leading to an increase in welfare of 8.3%.

Row 3 describes the impact of a permanent *productive transfer*, fully tied to investment in public capital, which is also 5% of the economy's GDP. In the new steady state the ratio of public to private capital increases from 0.29 to 0.61, thereby generating a huge investment boom in infrastructure. The increase in the stock of public capital increases the marginal productivity of private capital, thereby leading to a positive, though lesser, accumulation of private capital. Although the transfer stimulates consumption through the wealth effect (like the pure transfer), the higher long-run productive capacity has a greater effect on output, leading to a decline in the long-run con-sumption–output ratio from 0.60 to 0.56. The higher productivity raises the long-run growth rate to 1.94%, while long-run welfare improves by 9.8%, as indicated in the last column of row 3. The increased accumulations of both private and public capital lead to a higher demand for external borrowing as a means of financing new investment in private capital and the installation costs of public capital. This results in an increase in the steady-state debt–output ratio from 0.45 to 0.77, raising the borrowing premium to over 2.8%. How-ever, this higher debt relative to output is sustainable since it is caused by higher investment demand rather than higher consumption demand. The long-run increase in the economy's productive capacity (as measured by the higher stocks of public and private capital, and output) ensures that the higher debt is sustainable. This view has also been expressed by Roubini and Wachtel (1998).

The transitional dynamic paths are depicted in Figure 7.1. Figure 7.1a illustrates the stable adjustment locus in k_g-n space, indicating how k_g and n increase almost proportionately during the transition. The contrasting

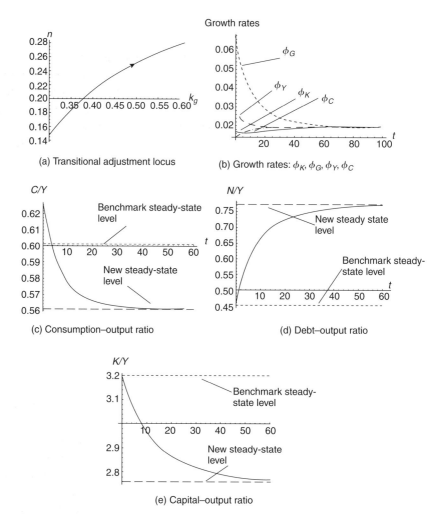

Figure 7.1 Transitional adjustment to a permanent productive transfer shock:
$\lambda = 1$; $\sigma = 0.05$

transitional paths of the four growth rates ϕ_K, ϕ_G, ϕ_Y, and ϕ_C toward their common long-run growth rate are shown in Figure 7.1b. The stimulus to public capital raises its initial growth rate to over 6.7%, after which it declines monotonically. By contrast, private capital adjusts only gradually. Indeed, after increasing on impact to 1.78%, it declines marginally, before the stimulating effect of the higher public capital has its full impact and eventually raises its growth rate toward the equilibrium. The growth rate of output is an average of the growth rates of the two capital stocks. The fact that the growth rate of output initially doubles from 1.37% to 2.77% is of interest and is consistent with the experiences of some of the recipient countries in the European Union. Finally, the growth rate of consumption is unaffected on impact, but responds only gradually. The reason for this is evident from (7.3a′) and the fact that it depends upon the sluggishly evolving debt–capital ratio, n.[15] Figures 7.1c–7.1e illustrate the transition paths for the consumption–output ratio, the debt–output ratio, and the capital–output ratio, respectively. The capital–output ratio declines monotonically over time, while the debt–output ratio increases. This is because the accumulation of public capital raises the average productivity of private capital, while the accumulation of both types of capital raises the need to borrow from abroad. By contrast, the consumption-output ratio initially increases before declining through time. This is because the wealth effect associated with the transfer raises consumption immediately, while the effect on the economy's productive capacity, through capital accumulation, takes time.[16]

Row 4 reports the effects of a bond-financed (or equivalently lump-sum tax financed) government expenditure increase on infrastructure in the absence of transfer flows. In order to draw a comparison with the case of a transfer shock, the magnitude of the government expenditure shock is equal to that of the transfer. We find that the two shocks have identical effects on the economy's long-run equilibrium in all but two respects. First, the government expenditure shock causes a larger crowding out of private consumption than does a transfer shock, with the consumption–output ratio declining to 0.51. This is because in contrast to the transfer of resources from abroad, the higher domestic government expenditure entails a direct appropriation of the economy's output, thereby decreasing the amount available for consumption. Second, as a consequence, the welfare gains from the higher government expenditure are also smaller than those from productive transfers. Welfare improves by only 0.3% in this case as against a 9.8% improvement from the transfer shock. The dynamics are generally similar qualitatively and are not illustrated. There is a minor change in the initial growth rate of private capital, which in turn is reflected in the initial growth rate of output, both of which rise marginally. This is a consequence of the reduction in private

---

[15] Much of the recent literature on growth theory has emphasized the speed of convergence, that is the speed at which the economy converges to its steady state. We obtain an asymptotic speed of convergence of around 6% which is plausible for an open economy. The speed is fairly insensitive to the form of the transfer and the form of policy response.

[16] We have also considered the time path for the instantaneous utility and find that it is uniformly higher at each instant of time with the tied transfer.

consumption stemming from the higher financing costs (either lump-sum taxation or borrowing).[17]

7.5.2 Domestic co-financing and welfare gains

Rows 5 to 7 deal with the issue of domestic co-financing in response to a transfer shock, a feature that is common to all of the EU's structural funds programs. Row 5 requires the domestic government to match fully the contribution from abroad. The interesting point here is that this reduces the welfare gain to 4.7%, the reason being that this forces the domestic government to devote 15% of output to public investment, making the public sector too large. If, instead, the transfer were untied, while forcing the equal co-financing, welfare would again be 9.83%.

Alternatively, suppose that the domestic government accommodates the transfer shock by setting its own participation so as to maximize the long-run growth rate. That is, the tax and expenditure rates are set in accordance with (7.13). Assuming without any loss of generality that $\lambda = 1$, this implies $\hat{\tau} = \hat{\hat{g}} = 0.16$ (i.e. $\hat{g} = 0.21$). Notably, this response causes the steady-state growth rate to nearly double from the benchmark value of 1.37% to 2.56%. The short-run growth rates of public and private capital undergo similar large increases to nearly 3% and over 18% respectively, with the short-run growth rate of output increasing to over 6%. This emphasis on growth and capital accumulation implies that there is less output available for consumption and, indeed, the consumption–income ratio drops to 0.38. This is undesirable from an intertemporal welfare point of view; indeed, welfare drops by 8.6% relative to the benchmark.[18]

Row 7 describes the final response, namely where the government sets its tax and expenditure rates so as to maximize the welfare gains resulting from the transfer. Again, without loss of generality, setting $\lambda = 1$, the welfare-maximizing response is to set $g = \tau = 0.02$, these values being obtained as solutions to (7.14) from numerical simulations of the model. This leads to a long-run growth rate of 2.1%, with the short-run growth rates of public capital, private capital, and output, being moderated to 3.5%, 2.8%, and 3% respectively. The consumption–output ratio is also correspondingly higher at

---

[17] The case where the increase in government investment is financed by a higher distortionary tax rate leads to generally similar responses, since with the externalities, the distortions are relatively small.

[18] This specific result does depend upon the magnitude of the adjustment costs. If, instead, $h_1 = h_2 = 8$, we find that the growth-maximizing response is also welfare-improving relative to the benchmark.

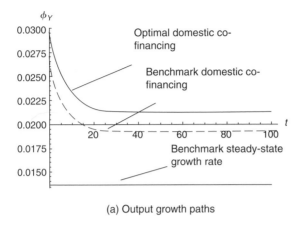

(a) Output growth paths

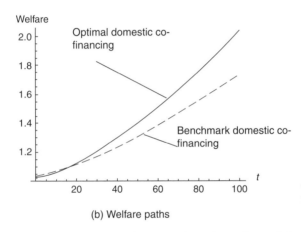

(b) Welfare paths

Figure 7.2 Growth and welfare paths under alternative regimes of domestic co-financing

0.55, with the corresponding intertemporal gain in welfare being 10.5%. Comparing 6 and 7 we see that there is a dramatic tradeoff between growth maximization, on the one hand, and welfare maximization, on the other.

The dynamic adjustments with active co-financing are qualitatively similar to that illustrated in Figure 7.1 where the government responds passively. But there are some minor differences, which are brought out in Figure 7.2. Figure 7.2a compares the time paths of the growth rate of output under two regimes: (i) where the domestic government responds passively to the productive transfer, and (ii) where the domestic government sets its participation at the welfare-maximizing level. We see that the time path of the growth rate of output is uniformly higher in the latter case. Figure 7.2b illustrates the time

Table 7.4. *Alternative benchmarks*

	$\tilde{k}_g$	$\tilde{N}/Y$	$\tilde{\phi}$ (%)	$\Delta(W)$ (%)
Benchmark II: $\sigma=0$, $\lambda=0$, $g=0.12$, $\tau=0.15$	**0.742**	**0.846**	**2.096**	—
Pure transfer: $\sigma=0.05$, $\lambda=0$, $g=0.12$, $\tau=0.15$	0.742	0.846	2.096	+10.50
Tied transfer: $\sigma=0.05$, $\lambda=1$, $g=0.12$, $\tau=0.15$	1.077	0.972	2.410	−1.65
Bond-financed gov. exp. increase: $\sigma=0$, $\lambda=0$, $g=0.17$, $\tau=0.15$	1.077	0.972	2.410	−12.76
Co-finance: $\sigma=0$, $\lambda=0.05$, $g=0.17$, $\tau=0.15$	1.417	1.054	2.651	−16.54
Benchmark III: $\sigma=0$, $\lambda=0$, $g=0.02$, $\tau=0.15$	**0.109**	**−0.103**	**0.069**	—
Pure transfer: $\sigma=0.05$, $\lambda=0$, $g=0.02$, $\tau=0.15$	0.109	−0.103	0.069	+7.56
Tied transfer: $\sigma=0.05$, $\lambda=1$, $g=0.02$, $\tau=0.15$	0.417	0.618	1.634	+31.62
Bond-financed gov. exp. increase: $\sigma=0$, $\lambda=0$, $g=0.07$, $\tau=0.15$	0.417	0.618	1.634	+21.46
Co-finance $\sigma=0$, $\lambda=0.05$, $g=0.07$, $\tau=0.15$	0.742	0.846	2.096	+36.55

paths of welfare gains (relative to the benchmark) for these two regimes. Here we see that there is a weak intertemporal tradeoff. By devoting more resources to investment in the short run, the optimal response reduces short-run consumption and utility in return for a significantly higher permanent growth rate and more consumption in the future (beyond fifteen years).

7.5.3 Some sensitivity analysis

While the above parameters represent a plausible description of a small poorly endowed economy, some of the results are dependent upon this characteriza-tion. Tables 7.4 and 7.5 conduct some sensitivity analysis. Table 7.4 considers two alternative benchmark economies, corresponding to $g=0.12$ (large domestic government investment) and $g=0.02$ (small domestic government investment). In the first case (Benchmark II), a tied transfer leads to a small welfare loss of 1.65%, while additional domestically financed government expansion leads to a large welfare loss of 12.8%. Furthermore, equal co-financing is even worse, leading to a welfare loss of 16.5%, which is more than the sum of its two components. By contrast, the untied transfer is highly desirable, improving welfare by 10.5%. The reason for this is that such an economy is characterized by an overly large stock of public capital relative to private capital and a large foreign debt. It is clearly better off by reducing its debt and is only made worse off by increasing its stock of public capital.

Table 7.5. *Welfare sensitivity to installation costs and capital market imperfections ($\sigma = 0$ to $\sigma = 0.05$)*

	$h_2 = 1$		$h_2 = 15$		$h_2 = 40$	
	$\lambda = 0$	$\lambda = 1$	$\lambda = 0$	$\lambda = 1$	$\lambda = 0$	$\lambda = 1$
$a = 0.03$	8.99%	20.85%	9.3%	13.16%	9.92%	-1.89%
$a = 0.10$	8.06%	16.26%	8.32%	9.83%	8.81%	-2.39%
$a = 10$	7.73%	15.32%	7.96%	9.47%	8.41%	-1.5%

For Benchmark III things are reversed. The country has only a small ratio of public to private capital and actually is a foreign creditor. Both the tied transfer and the domestically financed government expenditure improve welfare dramatically (31.6% and 21.5% respectively), and co-financing is even better. With small debt, the pure transfer is now only moderately welfare-improving, and indeed less so than for Benchmark II.

A natural question concerns the extent to which the gains from a foreign transfer depend upon (i) the installation costs associated with public capital (h_2), and (ii) the degree of imperfection of the world capital market (measured by a). Table 7.5 presents these gains for the two cases $\lambda = 0$ and $\lambda = 1$, for three values of each of these parameters, in the case that the domestic government acts passively. The values of $h_2 = 1$, 15, and 40 correspond to low, medium, and high installation costs, while $a = 0.03$, 0.10, and 10 correspond to high, medium, and virtually no access to the world capital market. The percentage changes reported in the table refer to the benchmark that would correspond to the associated combination of parameters. Thus, for example, the figures in the top left-hand corner imply that an economy for which $a = 0.03$, $h_2 = 1$ will enjoy an 8.99% improvement in welfare if it experiences a 5% pure transfer, and a 20.85% welfare gain if the transfer is tied to investment in public capital. From this table we can make the following observations:

(i) For a given degree of imperfection in the world capital market (i.e. given a) an increase in the installation costs of public capital (h_2) leads to larger welfare gains from a pure transfer of a given magnitude, but a decrease in welfare gains if the transfer is tied to public capital.

(ii) For given installation costs, an increase in the degree of imperfection in world capital markets in general leads to lower long-run welfare gains from the transfer.

(iii) For very high installation costs the economy is better off with a pure transfer: a tied or productive transfer is welfare-reducing in the long run, irrespective of the nature of world capital markets. However, in all other cases, welfare gains from productive transfers are higher than those from pure transfers.

The result in (iii) that under very high adjustment costs, a tied transfer is welfare-reducing is interesting. Intuitively, it reflects the fact that by tying the transfers, the donor country is committing the recipient country to devote a large portion of its resources to the costly task of installation, thereby making it worse off.

7.6 Temporary transfers

Most transfer programs, whether pure or productive, are only temporary. Thus it is important to analyze the consequences of a temporary transfer. As before, we assume that the magnitude of the transfer is 5% of the recipient country's GDP, and we focus on the polar cases of a pure transfer ($\lambda = 0$) and a fully tied productive transfer ($\lambda = 1$), respectively. We assume that the duration of the transfer is ten years, consistent with the average length of the EU's structural funds programs.

The results of our experiments are reported in Table 7.6, and their dynamics are illustrated in Figures 7.3–7.5. The first four columns of Table 7.6 report the instantaneous impact of a temporary transfer on the growth rates of private and public capital, output, and consumption, respectively. Rows 1 and 2 describe the type of transfer shock, i.e. whether it is pure or tied in nature.

7.6.1 Pure transfers

We turn first to the pure transfer, reported in row 1. Neither the growth rate of consumption nor debt responds immediately. In the case of consumption, the reason for this remains as for the permanent transfer; its growth rate is tied via the borrowing rate to the debt–capital ratio, n, which is constrained to evolve continuously over time. Similarly, when $\lambda = 0$, (7.5b″) implies that the growth rate of public capital responds to the productivity of public capital, Y/K_G, which also evolves only gradually. By contrast, the growth rate of private capital, being determined by q, does respond on impact, increasing from 1.37% to 1.58%. This is because with the transfer being only temporary, the initial response in the consumption–output ratio is dampened from 0.65, if it were permanent, to just over 0.63, thereby freeing some domestic output, which then becomes available for investment in private capital. The short-run higher

Table 7.6. *Key responses to a temporary transfer shock*
Benchmark steady state: $\lambda = 0$; $\sigma = 0$; $g = 0.05$; $\tau = 0.15$; $T = 10$ years

	Initial response of growth rates of key variables					Permanent gains/losses (relative to the benchmark) across steady states (benchmark = 1)					
	$\phi_K(0)$ (%)	$\phi_g(0)$ (%)	$\phi_C(0)$ (%)	$\phi_Y(0)$ (%)	$\tilde{\phi}$ (%)	K	K_g	C	N	Y	W (%Δ)
Pure transfer $\lambda = 0$; $\sigma = 0.05$	1.58	1.37	1.37	1.54	1.37	1.03	1.03	1.03	1.04	1.03	4.39
Productive transfer $\lambda = 1$; $\sigma = 0.05$	1.74	6.74	1.37	2.74	1.37	1.07	1.10	1.07	0.64	1.08	4.97

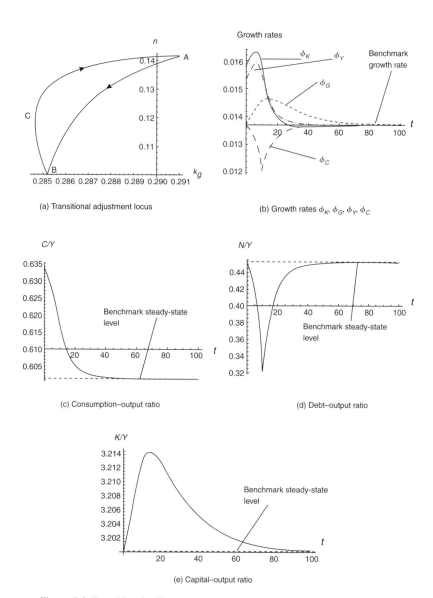

Figure 7.3 Transitional adjustment to a temporary pure transfer shock: $\lambda = 0$; $\sigma = 0.05$; duration of shock $= 10$ years

growth rate of private capital raises the short-run growth rate of output to 1.54%, this reflecting the relative importance of private capital in production.

In contrast to the permanent pure transfer, the adjustments are characterized by transitional dynamics. These can be understood by considering Figure 7.3a, the phase diagram describing the dynamic adjustments of the ratio of public capital to private capital, k_g and the debt–capital ratio n, in conjunction with the growth rates for K and K_G illustrated in Figure 7.3b, and N (not illustrated).[19] Suppose that the economy starts out from the equilibrium point A in Figure 7.3a. Since the transfer has no impact on the initial growth of public capital, while leading to more private investment, the ratio of public capital to private capital, k_g, begins to decline. At the same time, while the untied transfers reduce the accumulation of debt, the higher investment and consumption has the opposite effect. On balance, the former effect dominates, and the initial growth rate of debt falls from its benchmark value of 1.37% to 0.5%, so that the debt–capital ratio, n, begins to decline as well. The economy therefore begins to move along the locus AB in Figure 7.3a. During the early stages of the decline in k_g and n, the growth rate of private capital continues to increase, though at a declining rate, reaching a peak at about 1.64% after six periods, after which it too begins to decline. This is because the initial jump in q, together with the decline in k_g reduces the rate of return on private capital, requiring $\dot{q} > 0$, to ensure that the return on capital equals the cost on debt, which initially declines at a slower rate. The increase in the private capital stock raises the growth rate of output, thereby gradually increasing the growth of public capital and thus slowing the decline in k_g. By contrast, as n declines, the decline in the growth rate of debt accelerates dramatically, due primarily to the lower interest costs. After ten periods, when the transfer ceases, the economy is at B. At that point, the growth rates of K, k_g, and N are respectively 1.57%, 1.46%, and − 7.80%. However, the removal of the transfer immediately raises the growth rate of debt to 7.75%, so that the debt–capital ratio starts to increase. By contrast, with private capital still being accumulated at a faster rate than public capital, K_G continues to decline, though with the former declining and the latter increasing, this decline ceases at time 15, when the economy is at C. Thereafter, the reduced relative stock of public capital raises its productivity, encouraging public investment, so that the economy returns to its original equilibrium along CA, with both k_g and n increasing. From Figure 7.3b the growth rate of output is seen to be an average of that of the two capital stocks, while the time path for the consumption growth rate reflects that of the time path of n.

---

[19] The reason for not illustrating the growth rate of N is one of scale. Its growth rate is much larger (in magnitude) than that of Y, a fact that can be inferred from the N/Y ratio illustrated in Figure 7.3c. Critical values are as follows: during the duration of the temporary pure transfer $\dot{N}/N$ declines from 0.5% to −7.8% at $t = 10$, when it immediately jumps to 7.75% before converging back to the steady-state value of 1.37%.

Figures 7.3c–7.3e illustrate the dynamic time paths of the consumption–output, debt–output, and capital–output ratios, respectively. These all mirror the differential growth rates as set out in Figure 7.2. Thus, for example, the K/Y ratio is increasing or decreasing, as long as the ratio k_g is falling or rising. Likewise the fact that C/Y falls rapidly at first is because during this period Y is rising while C is falling; the decline is more gradual when the two growth rates are close to converging.

7.6.2 Tied transfers

Row 2 of Table 7.6 reports the impact of a temporary tied (productive) transfer. Again, the growth rate of consumption does not respond instantaneously. However, the growth rates of all other variables respond instantaneously, with the magnitudes of these initial jumps being significantly higher than for a pure transfer. Thus, the growth rate of private capital increases on impact to 1.74% as compared to 1.58% for a pure transfer. With the transfer being tied to public investment, the growth rate of public capital increases to 6.7%, a sharp contrast to its sluggish response to a pure transfer. As a result, the growth rate of output goes up to 2.74% as against 1.54% for a pure transfer. It is interesting to observe that when compared to the corresponding jumps for a permanent productive transfer shock (see Table 7.3, columns 6–9), we find that a temporary productive transfer induces marginally larger initial responses in growth rates than does a permanent shock of equal magnitude. Thus, in the short run, while the transfer program is in effect, strong positive differentials are created in growth rates relative to the benchmark. This result vindicates the objectives of the EU's temporary transfer programs; empirically the magnitude is consistent with the growth rates experienced by Spain and Portugal as recipients in the EU transfer program.

The dynamics can be understood by considering Figure 7.4a in conjunction with the growth rates illustrated in Figures 7.4b. These indicate a dramatic contrast with those of the pure transfer; indeed the time paths for most variables are generally reversed.[20] Suppose that the economy starts out at point A in Figure 7.4a. With the dramatic increase in the growth rate of public capital, far exceeding that of private capital, the ratio of public to private capital begins to rise. At the same time, with the tied transfers being unavailable for debt

---

[20] Again, the growth rate of N cannot be conveniently illustrated in Figure 7.4b, because of differences in magnitude, which are now even more dramatic. Critical values are now as follows. During the duration of the temporary tied transfer $\dot{N}/N$ declines from 24% to 1.8% at $t = 10$, when it immediately jumps to -5.8% before converging back to the steady-state value of 1.37%.

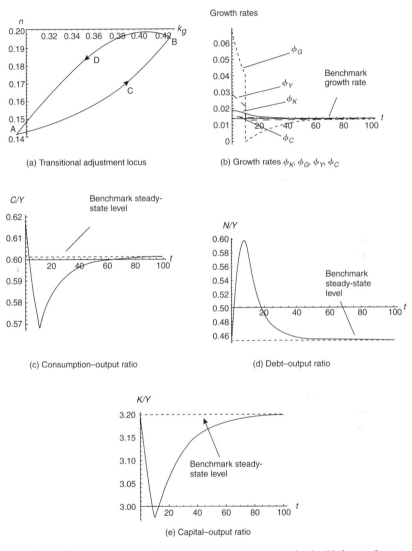

Figure 7.4 Transitional adjustment to a temporary productive/tied transfer shock: $\lambda = 1$; $\sigma = 0.05$; duration of shock $= 10$ years

reduction, the higher consumption and investment leads to a similar dramatic increase in the growth rate of debt, which increases at the rate of 24% on impact, so that the debt–capital ratio begins to rise sharply as well. The economy therefore begins to move along the locus ACB in Figure 7.4a. As k_g and n both increase, the growth rates of both public capital and debt decline dramatically, the latter more so, with the economy reaching B after ten periods. The permanent elimination of the transfer at that time reverses the dynamics, taking the economy back to its original equilibrium along the locus BDA.

From Figure 7.4b, we see that following the initial jump, the growth rates of public and private capital, and of output, start declining toward the benchmark growth rate. The growth rate of consumption, although unaffected initially, increases slightly in transition. At the end of the program, when the transfer flows cease, the growth rate of public capital jumps down below its benchmark level, after which it then increases back to its (unchanging) equilibrium level.

Figures 7.4c–7.4e present the dynamic paths of the consumption–output, debt–output, and capital–output ratios respectively. These are all generally opposite to those for the pure transfer, reflecting the reversal in the dynamics of k_g and n. One interesting difference arises with respect to the consumption–output ratio, which falls below its benchmark during the period the transfer is in effect. This is due to a short-run substitution of consumption for capital accumulation. However, the end of the transfer program causes a reverse substitution toward consumption, and the ratio increases to its benchmark in the long run. The general picture which emerges in comparing Figures 7.3 and 7.4 is that the particular nature of the incoming transfer has important implications for the economy's dynamic adjustment, in both the short run and the long run. In our case, the transitional dynamics of a pure transfer are very different from those of a productive transfer.

7.6.3 Permanent effects of a temporary transfer shock

In this section we show how a temporary transfer program, by altering the growth rate during the transition, can have permanent effects on the *levels* of key variables such as the capital stock, output, and consumption of the recipient economy. In addition we show how the type of incoming transfer (pure or tied) affects the magnitude and direction of the permanent effects. Figure 7.5 and the last six columns of Table 7.6 report the permanent effects of temporary transfers. Specifically, we normalize the benchmark steady-state level to unity and express the new steady-state levels relative to the normalized benchmark. Thus, the ratio of 1.10 across steady states implies a 10% increase in levels relative to the benchmark.

Formally, we may let the after-shock time path of a variable X be:

$$X(t) = X(0)\exp[\int_0^T \phi_X(s)ds + \int_T^t \phi_X(s)ds]$$

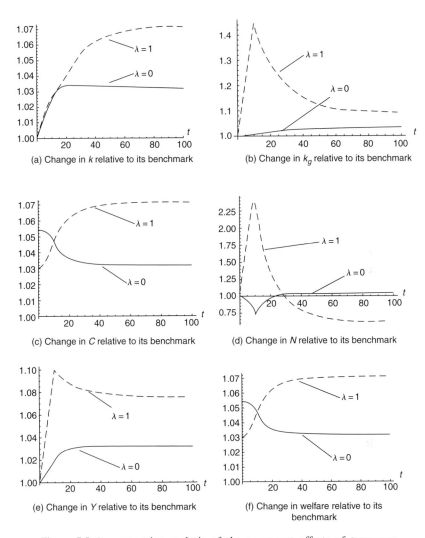

Figure 7.5 A comparative analysis of the permanent effects of temporary productive and pure transfer shocks (benchmark levels = 1)

where $\phi_X(t)$ is the growth rate of variable X, at time t, and follows different paths while the temporary policy is in effect (until time T) and after it is removed. The corresponding time path of X in the absence of the shock (the benchmark path) is then given by:

$$X_b(t) = X_{b,0} \exp\left(\phi_b t\right)$$

where X_b and ϕ_b denote the benchmark level of X and ϕ respectively. Then the long-run impact of the temporary shock on the level of X relative to its benchmark is given by:

$$\frac{X(t)}{X_b(t)} = \frac{X(0)}{X_{b,0}} \exp \left[\int_0^T (\phi_X(s) - \phi_b) ds + \int_T^t (\phi_X(s) - \phi_b) ds \right]$$

while in the long run the growth rate of $X(t)$ returns to its original benchmark level, ϕ_b, the accumulated effect of the differential growth rate during the transition on the level of $X(t)$ is permanent and may be significant.[21]

For our experiments, $X = K$, K_g, C, N, Y, and the level of long-run welfare, denoted by W. From columns 6–11 in Table 7.6 we see that temporary transfers do indeed have permanent effects on the levels of key economic variables. However, as the results reveal, the magnitude of the effects is different, depending upon the specific nature of the transfer. From Row 1 we see that a temporary pure transfer leads to only a 3% long-run improvement in the stocks of private and public capital and in the levels of consumption and output. However, the debt position of the economy worsens by 4% in the long run. On the other hand, the long-run effects of a productive transfer are less uniform and larger in magnitude. Row 2 indicates that a temporary productive transfer increases the long-run stocks of private and public capital by 7% and 10% respectively. Consumption and output increase by 7% and 8% respectively. For both types of transfer, the effects on intertemporal welfare are substantial, being 4.4% and 5% respectively. The relatively small difference is due to the fact that the greater benefits associated with the tied transfer occur through time and are therefore discounted. The long-run debt position of the economy actually improves by 25%. This is in contrast to the result for pure transfers: a temporary productive transfer improves the current account permanently, while a pure transfer causes a permanent deterioration of the current account. This is due to the fact that the increase in long-run productive capacity, as measured by the long-run changes in the stock of private and public capital, and the level of output, is much larger for a productive shock. The higher long-run productive capacity enables the economy to improve its long-run debt position. The above results are graphically represented in Figure 7.5.

---

[21] Note that K, K_g, Y, and N evolve continuously at $t = 0$, so that for these variables $X(0)/X_{b,0} = 1$. In contrast, C and W undergo jumps at time 0. These differences are illustrated in Figure 7.5.

7.7 Conclusions

In this chapter we have addressed an important topical issue, namely the impact of a program of tied transfers, such as those implemented recently by the EU, on the growth and macroeconomic performance of a recipient country. The effects of both permanent and temporary transfers have been considered, the former serving as a benchmark, the latter being a closer representation of actual policies.

The main general conclusion to emerge is that there is a sharp contrast between the effects of pure transfers of the traditional Keynes–Ohlin type and those of transfers tied to public investment. A permanent pure transfer has no growth or dynamic consequences. It is always welfare-improving, the gains varying positively with the size of the government, when the stock of debt and the benefits of debt reduction increase. In contrast, a tied transfer generates dynamic adjustments, as public capital is accumulated in the recipient economy. Its effect on the long-run growth rate, and the extent to which this is beneficial, depends upon the size of the infrastructure in the economy, as well as the co-financing arrangements, if any, imposed on that economy, and how its government chooses to react to the additional flow of resources. For what we consider to be the most applicable case of an economy relatively poorly endowed with public capital, a tied transfer will both raise the long-run growth rate and yield greater intertemporal benefits than does a pure transfer. However, the benefits from an equal co-financing, similar to that proposed by the European Union, are substantially smaller than if no such arrangement is imposed. If the economy is relatively well endowed with government capital, a tied transfer is welfare-reducing, and is particularly harmful if it involves domestic co-financing.

These distinctions also apply for temporary transfers. The transitional dynamics in the two cases are in sharp contrast. Whereas a temporary pure transfer has only modest short-run growth effects, the productive transfer has significant impacts on short-run growth, thus validating the position taken by the European Union. Both transfers, although only temporary, have permanent effects on levels, with those of the tied shock being significantly greater. For example, for the benchmark economy we find that a ten-year tied transfer of 5% of the recipient economy's GDP raises long-run output by 10% and its welfare by nearly 5%, values we find to be significant.

8

Foreign aid, capital accumulation, and economic growth: some extensions

The analysis of Chapter 7 has been based on two plausible, but critical, assumptions, namely the Cobb–Douglas production function and inelastic labor supply. It turns out that the relative merits of tied versus untied aid are highly sensitive to both these assumptions. Accordingly, this final chapter is devoted to exploring these sensitivity issues in further detail.

8.1 Generalization of model[1]

The model is virtually identical to that of Chapter 7 and hence our description is brief. The economy is small and populated with an infinitely lived representative agent who produces and consumes a single traded good. The agent has one unit of time, a fraction l of which is devoted to leisure, and the balance, $1 - l$, to labor supply. Output, Y, is produced using the constant elasticity of substitution (CES) production function

$$Y = a\left(\frac{K_G}{\bar{K}}\right)^{\varepsilon} [\eta\{(1-l)K_G\}^{-\kappa} + (1-\eta)K^{-\kappa}]^{-1/\kappa}, \quad \varepsilon \geq 0, \quad -\infty < \kappa < 1$$

(8.1a)

where K denotes the representative agent's stock of private capital, $\bar{K}$ is the average stock of private capital, and K_G denotes the stock of public capital. The production function has two components. In the first, public capital interacts with the agent's labor supply to yield labor measured in efficiency units, $(1-l)K_G$, which in turn combines with private capital. Thus $s \equiv 1/(1+k)$ is the elasticity of substitution between private capital and

---

[1] This chapter is based on material first presented in Chatterjee and Turnovsky (2007).

196

"efficiency units of labor" in production. The second element is an externality provided by public capital, incorporated in the term $(K_G/\bar{K})^\varepsilon$. Here, K_G enhances general productivity by offsetting congestion effects associated with the aggregate private capital stock, $\bar{K}$; see e.g. Barro and Sala-i-Martin (1992a), Eicher and Turnovsky (2000). The production function has constant returns to scale in both the private factors of production, K and $(1 - l)$, and the accumulating factors, $K, \bar{K}$, and K_G, enabling it to support an equilibrium of ongoing (endogenous) growth with both private factors being paid their respective marginal physical products.[2]

As in Chapter 3, the agent consumes the traded good at the rate C, yielding utility over an infinite horizon represented by the isoelastic utility function:

$$U \equiv \int_0^\infty \frac{1}{\gamma}(Cl^\theta)^\gamma e^{-\rho t}dt \qquad (8.1b)$$

where θ represents the relative importance of leisure in utility.

The agent's specification of capital accumulation, and access to the world financial market remains as specified by equations (7.1c)–(7.1e), and the agent's optimization problem is to choose C, l, I, $\dot{N}$, and $\dot{K}$ to maximize (8.1b) subject to the flow budget constraint

$$\dot{N} = C + r(N/K)N + \Phi(I, K) - (1 - \tau)Y + \bar{T} \qquad (8.2)$$

where all quantities are as defined previously. Since we shall assume (see [8.5] below) that the government maintains a balanced budget, the private sector's debt coincides with national debt.

The relevant optimality conditions are as before and require no further comment, except to note the modification to (8.4b), reflecting the more general production function:

$$C^{\gamma-1}l^{\theta\gamma} = v \qquad (8.3a)$$

$$\theta C^\gamma l^{\theta\gamma-1} = v(1-\tau)\frac{\partial Y}{\partial(1-l)} \qquad (8.3b)$$

$$1 + h_1(I/K) = q \qquad (8.3c)$$

---

[2] Chatterjee and Turnovsky (2004) assume $\varepsilon = 0$ and we shall treat this as our benchmark case as well. A natural alternative specification to (8.1a) is $Y = a(K_G/\bar{K})^\varepsilon[\eta\{(1-l)\bar{K}\}^{-\rho} + (1-\eta)K^{-\rho}]^{-1/\rho}$, which simply augments the Romer (1986) model to include the "congestion-offsetting" externality effect of public capital.

$$\rho - \frac{\dot{v}}{v} = r(N/K) \tag{8.4a}$$

$$\frac{a^{-\kappa}(K_G/\bar{K})^{-\varepsilon\kappa}(1-\tau)(1-\eta)(Y/K)^{1+\kappa}}{q} + \frac{\dot{q}}{q} + \frac{(q-1)^2}{2h_1 q} - \delta_K = r(N/K)$$

$$\tag{8.4b}$$

The usual transversality conditions also apply.

The specification of public capital accumulation and transfers remain as specified in Section 7.2.2. The only difference, already alluded to, is that government sets its tax and expenditure parameters to maintain a balanced budget.[3] Expressing this in the form:

$$\bar{T} = \Psi(G, K_G) - \tau Y - TR \tag{8.5}$$

$\bar{T}$ determines the lump-sum tax necessary to balance the current budget, given by the right-hand side of (8.5). The national budget constraint (the current account) is obtained by combining (8.5) and (8.2):

$$\dot{N} = r(N/K)N + C + \Phi(I, K) + \Psi(G, K_G) - Y - TR \tag{8.6}$$

8.2 Macroeconomic equilibrium

The steady-state equilibrium of the economy has the characteristic that all real aggregate quantities grow at the same constant rate, and that the labor allocation, l, and the relative price of capital, q, are constant. We show in the appendix to this chapter how the equilibrium dynamics of the system can be conveniently expressed in terms of the following stationary variables: $y \equiv Y/K$, $k_g \equiv K_G/K$, $n \equiv N/K$, l, and q. Since all agents are identical, we shall focus on a symmetric equilibrium in which $K = \bar{K}$. Thus we obtain:

$$\frac{\dot{k_g}}{k_g} = (\bar{g} + \lambda\sigma)\frac{y}{k_g} - \delta_G - \left(\frac{(q-1)}{h_1} - \delta_K\right) \tag{8.7a}$$

---

[3] As noted in Chapter 7, several aid programs call for co-financing by the government of the recipient economy, which is required to match the foreign aid to some degree; in that chapter we also consider growth-maximizing and welfare-maximizing government responses. Since the main consequences of co-financing arrangements are only marginally affected by the elasticity of labor supply, there is no need to consider this aspect further here.

$$\frac{\dot{n}}{n} = r(n) + \frac{1}{n}\left[c + \frac{q^2 - 1}{2h_1} + \{(\bar{g} + \lambda\sigma) - (1 + \sigma)\}y + \frac{h_2}{2}(\bar{g} + \lambda\sigma)^2\frac{y^2}{k_g} \right]$$
$$- \left(\frac{(q - 1)}{h_1} - \delta_K \right)$$

(8.7b)

$$\dot{l} = \left(\frac{\{1 + \Omega\}\{\rho - r(n)\} + (1 - \gamma)\{[\Omega(1 + \kappa) - (1 + \Omega)\varepsilon]\psi_K + [1 + \kappa + (\varepsilon - \kappa)(1 + \Omega)]\psi_G\}}{[\{\gamma(1 + \theta) - 1\}\{1 + \Omega\} - (1 - \gamma)(1 + \kappa)\Omega(\frac{l}{1-l})]} \right) l$$

(8.7c)

$$\dot{q} = r(n)q - \frac{1}{a^\kappa k_g^{\varepsilon\kappa}}a(1 - \tau)(1 - \eta)y^{1+\kappa} - \frac{(q - 1)^2}{2h_1} + \delta_K q$$

(8.7d)

where

$$\Omega \equiv \Omega(k_g, l) \equiv ((1 - \eta)/\eta)\left[(1 - l)k_g\right]^\kappa$$

(8.8a)

$$\frac{Y}{K} \equiv y = y(k_g, l) = ak_g^\varepsilon\left[(1 - \eta) + \eta\{(1 - l)k_g\}^{-\kappa}\right]^{-1/\kappa}$$

(8.8b)

$$\frac{C}{K} \equiv c = c(k_g, l) = \frac{(1 - \tau)}{\theta}\left(\frac{l}{1 - l}\right)\left(\frac{1}{1 + \Omega}\right)y$$

(8.8c)

$$r(n) = r^* + \omega(n)$$

(8.8d)

and the growth rates of the two types of capital are:

$$\frac{\dot{K}}{K} \equiv \psi_K = \frac{q - 1}{h_1} - \delta_K$$

(8.9a)

$$\frac{\dot{K}_G}{K_G} \equiv \psi_G = (\bar{g} + \lambda\sigma)\frac{y}{k_g} - \delta_G.$$

(8.9b)

Equations (8.7a)–(8.7d) provide an autonomous set of dynamic equations in k_g, n, l, and q, of which two (k_g and n) are state variables and the others (q and l) are "jump" variables, free to respond instantaneously to new information as it becomes available. Once k_g and l are known, the output–capital ratio and the consumption–output ratio are determined by (8.8b) and

(8.8c). The parallels between this system and (7.9a)–(7.9d) for the basic model of foreign aid should be clear.

The economy reaches steady state when $\dot{k}_g = \dot{n} = \dot{l} = \dot{q} = 0$. Applying these conditions to (8.7a)–(8.7d) we can solve for the steady-state values $\tilde{k}_g, \tilde{q}, \tilde{n}$, and $\tilde{l}$. Given these quantities, (8.8b)–(8.8d) and either (8.9a) or (8.9b) determine $\tilde{y}$ and $\tilde{c}$, the steady-state interest rate, $\tilde{r}$, and the long-run growth rate, $\tilde{\psi}$, respectively.[4] Linearizing (8.7a)–(8.7d) around the steady state yields an approximation to the underlying dynamic system. This system (not reported) is analogous to (7.11) and forms the basis for our dynamic simulations. To be saddlepoint-stable, we require that there be two unstable roots to match the two jump variables. For all plausible sets of parameter values our numerical simulations yield the required pattern of eigenvalues, namely two positive (unstable) and two negative (stable) roots, the latter being denoted by μ_1 and μ_2, with $\mu_2 < \mu_1 < 0$.

Equations (8.7) and (8.8) represent "core" dynamic equations from which other key variables, in particular the various growth rates, may be derived. In addition to the growth rates of the two capital goods reported in (8.9a) and (8.9b), the growth rates of consumption and output are given by

$$\frac{\dot{C}}{C} \equiv \psi_C = \frac{r(n) - \rho + \gamma\theta(1/l)\left[F(k_g, n, q, l)/G(k_g, l)\right]}{1 - \gamma} \tag{8.9c}$$

$$\frac{\dot{Y}}{Y} \equiv \psi_y = \frac{1}{1 + \Omega(k_g, l)}\left[\Omega(k_g, l)\psi_K + \psi_G - \frac{\dot{l}}{1-l}\right] + \varepsilon[\psi_G - \psi_k] \tag{8.9d}$$

where $F(.)$ and $G(.)$ are defined in the Appendix. Although the growth rates diverge during the transition, they ultimately converge to the common equilibrium rate $\tilde{\psi}_K = \tilde{\psi}_G = \tilde{\psi}_C = \tilde{\psi}_Y = \tilde{\psi}$.

8.3 The dynamic effects of foreign aid: a numerical analysis

The introduction of labor supply, while a simple conceptual extension, complicates the formal analysis significantly. Accordingly, all of our substantive analysis is undertaken using numerical simulations. We begin by calibrating a benchmark economy, using the parameters summarized in Table 8.1, representative of a small open economy, which starts out from an

---

[4] The solution for the steady-state equilibrium is set out in the Appendix. As for the simpler model of Chapter 7, numerical simulations always yield well-defined steady-state values for all plausible parameter specifications.

Table 8.1. *The benchmark economy*

Preference parameters:	$\gamma = -1.5$, $\rho = 0.04$, $\theta = 1$
Production parameters:	$a = 0.6$, $\eta = 0.2$, $\varepsilon = 0$, $h_1 = 15$, $h_2 = 15$
Elasticity of substitution in production:	$s = 1$
Depreciation rates:	$\delta_K = 0.05$, $\delta_G = 0.05$
World interest rate:	$r^* = 0.06$
Premium on borrowing:	$a = 0.15^a$
Policy parameters:	$\tau = 0.15$, $\bar{g} = 0.05$
Transfers:	$\sigma = 0$, $\lambda = 0$

^{a} The functional specification of the upward-sloping supply curve that we use is $r(n) = r^* + e^{an} - 1$. Thus, in the case of a perfect world capital market, when $a = 0$, $r = r^*$, the world interest rate.

equilibrium without any transfers or aid from abroad. As already noted, the productive elasticity of public capital $\eta = 0.2$ is consistent with the empirical evidence (see Gramlich, 1994). But given the introduction of labor in efficiency units, this implies that the productive elasticity of labor is also 0.2, while that of private capital is 0.8.[5] Setting $k = 0$, i.e. $s = 1$, yields the Cobb–Douglas technology, which serves as a reasonable benchmark.[6] The public good externality parameter is set at $\varepsilon = 0$.

Substituting these base parameters into the steady-state equations (8.A.7a)–(8.A.7f), (see Appendix), (8.9a) and the functional form for (8.10d), yields the following benchmark equilibrium values: $\tilde{k}_g = 0.253$, $\tilde{n} = 0.141$, $\tilde{q} = 1.997$, $\tilde{y} = 0.337$, $\tilde{y} = 0.337$, $\tilde{c} = 0.202$, $\tilde{r} = 0.0813$, and $\tilde{\psi} = 0.0165$. Table 8.2, Row 1 summarizes these in a more convenient form. Thus the benchmark

---

[5] An inevitable feature of calibrating a Romer (1986)-type AK model is that keeping the size of the externality plausible, while maintaining the assumption of constant returns to scale in the private factors, imposes constraints on the elasticities of labor and private capital. In order to reconcile these elasticities with the empirical evidence on the income shares of labor and private capital, it is necessary to interpret K as an amalgam of physical and human capital, with $(1 - l)$ describing "raw" unskilled labor; see Rebelo (1991).

[6] As justification for the Cobb–Douglas functional form, Berndt's (1976) early comprehensive study is often cited. For the preferred methods of estimation, using superior data, he finds estimates of the elasticity of substitution to range from around 0.8 to 1.2. However, recent authors have argued that the treatment of technological change has biased the estimates toward unity, and that modifying the econometric specification leads to significantly lower estimates of the elasticity, in the range 0.5–0.7, thus rejecting the Cobb–Douglas specification; see e.g. Antràs (2004) and Klump, McAdam, and Willman (2007). Duffy and Papageorgiou (2000) estimate the elasticity of substitution using cross-sectional data and find that the Cobb–Douglas production function is an inadequate representation of technology across countries. Their evidence suggests that the elasticity of substitution exceeds unity for rich countries, but is less than unity for developing countries.

Table 8.2. *Permanent foreign aid shock*
Benchmark equilibrium: Cobb–Douglas production function $(s = 1)$

(a) Long-run effects

	$\tilde{K}_G/\tilde{K}$	$\tilde{r}$ (%)	$\tilde{i}$	$\tilde{C}/\tilde{Y}$	$\tilde{K}/\tilde{Y}$	$\tilde{N}/\tilde{Y}$	$\tilde{\psi}$ (%)	$\Delta(W)$ (%)
Benchmark equilibrium ($\sigma=0, \lambda=0, \bar{g}=0.05, \tau=0.15$)	**0.253**	**8.13**	**0.780**	**0.602**	**2.969**	**0.416**	**1.65**	–
Tied aid ($\sigma=0.05, \lambda=1, \bar{g}=0.05, \tau=0.15$)	0.542	9.77	0.768	0.563	2.523	0.622	2.31	7.96
Untied aid ($\sigma=0.05, \lambda=0, \bar{g}=0.05, \tau=0.15$)	0.252	7.99	0.793	0.653	3.011	0.396	1.60	7.71

(b) Short-run effects

	$l(0)$	$\frac{C(0)}{Y(0)}$	$\psi_K(0)$ (%)	$\psi_G(0)$ (%)	$\psi_Y(0)$ (%)	$\psi_C(0)$ (%)	$\Delta(W(0))$ (%)
Benchmark equilibrium ($\sigma=0, \lambda=0, \bar{g}=0.05, \tau=0.15$)	**0.780**	**0.602**	**1.65**	**1.65**	**1.65**	**1.65**	–
Tied aid ($\sigma=0.05, \lambda=1, \bar{g}=0.05, \tau=0.15$)	0.777	0.594	1.95	8.33	3.48	1.87	-1.53
Untied aid ($\sigma=0.05, \lambda=0, \bar{g}=0.05, \tau=0.15$)	0.7925	0.650	1.55	1.57	1.54	1.64	8.32

equilibrium yields a steady-state ratio of public to private capital of 0.25, a consumption–output ratio of 0.60, and a debt–output ratio of 0.42, yielding an equilibrium borrowing premium of 2.13% over the world rate of 6%. The capital–output ratio is 2.97, and 78% of the agent's time is allocated to leisure, consistent with empirical evidence, yielding a long-run growth rate of 1.65%. The equilibrium is a reasonable characterization of a small medium-indebted economy, experiencing a modest steady growth rate and having a relatively small stock of public capital.

This equilibrium is based on several specific assumptions and therefore it is important to conduct some sensitivity analysis. The critical parameters upon which we focus are (i) the elasticity of substitution in production, s, (ii) the elasticity of leisure in utility, θ, (iii) the externality parameter, ε, and (iv) the domestic fiscal policy parameters, $\bar{g}$ and τ.

8.3.1 A permanent increase in the flow of foreign aid: long-run effects

We now introduce a permanent foreign aid flow to the above benchmark economy. Specifically, the inflow of foreign aid is tied to the scale of the recipient economy, and increases from 0% of GDP in the initial steady state to 5% of GDP in the new steady state (an increase in σ from 0 to 0.05). This aid may be tied to new investment in public capital ($\lambda = 1$), representing a "productive" transfer, or it may be untied ($\lambda = 0$), in which case it is a "pure" transfer. The long-run and short-run responses of key variables in the recipient economy are reported in rows 2 and 3 of Tables 8.2a and 8.2b. In addition, the final columns in the tables summarize the effects on long-run welfare (ΔW), and short-run welfare ($\Delta W(0)$), both measured by the optimized utility of the representative agent, where C and l are evaluated along the equilibrium path. These welfare changes are measures of equivalent variation, calculated as the percentage change in the initial stock of capital necessary to maintain the level of welfare unchanged following the particular shock. The differences between the effects of the two types of transfer are dramatic.

We first consider the long-run effects of an increase in foreign aid (Table 8.2a) and then discuss the short-run transitional dynamics generated by this shock (Table 8.2b and Figure 8.1).

Tied aid

The long-run impact of a tied foreign aid shock is reported in row 2 of Table 8.2a. Since the aid is tied directly to public investment, in the new steady state the ratio of public to private capital more than doubles, increasing from 0.25 to

0.54, as a consequence of the investment boom in infrastructure. The larger stock of public capital increases the marginal productivity of private capital and labor, leading to a positive, though lesser, accumulation of private capital, and increasing employment time from 0.220 to 0.232. Although the transfer stimulates consumption through a wealth effect, the enhanced productive capacity has a greater effect on output, leading to a decline in the long-run consumption–output ratio from 0.60 to 0.563. The higher productivity raises the long-run growth rate to 2.31%, while long-run welfare improves by 7.96%. The increased accumulation of both private and public capital leads to a higher demand for external borrowing as a means of financing the new investment in private capital and the installation costs of public capital. This results in an increase in the steady-state debt–output ratio from 0.42 to 0.62, raising the borrowing premium to nearly 3.8%. However, this higher debt relative to output is sustainable since it is caused by higher investment demand rather than by higher consumption demand. The long-run increase in the economy's productive capacity (as measured by the larger stocks of public and private capital, and output) ensures that the additional debt is sustainable.

Untied aid

A permanent untied aid shock, i.e. an aid flow not tied to any investment activity, has precisely the opposite qualitative effects, as illustrated in row 3 of Table 8.2a. Apart from consumption and leisure, the changes are much smaller. Being untied, the transfer is devoted to debt reduction, thereby allowing an increase in consumption. The debt–output ratio declines to 0.396 and the consumption–output ratio rises to around 0.65. The increase in consumption raises the marginal utility of leisure, increasing the fraction of leisure time from 0.78 to 0.793. Since the aid no longer favors public investment, the ratio of public to private capital remains virtually unchanged. With the shift toward more consumption and leisure, productivity of both types of capital declines and the equilibrium growth rate is marginally reduced from 1.65% to 1.60%, leading to an overall increase in welfare of around 7.71%, marginally less than for the tied transfer.

8.3.2 Transitional dynamics

Tied aid

The transitional adjustment paths following the increase in tied aid are illustrated in Figure 8.1a for the benchmark economy. Figure 8.1a illustrates the stable adjustment locus in k_g-n space, indicating how k_g and n both generally increase together during the transition.

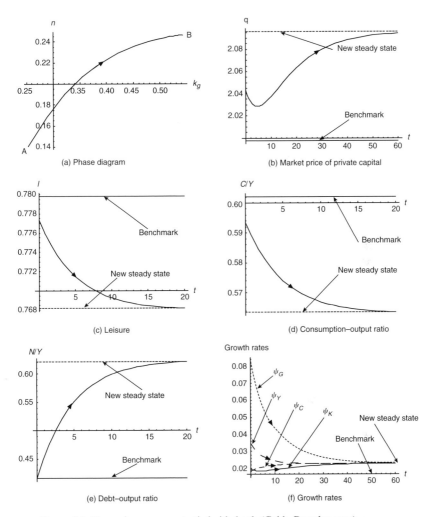

Figure 8.1 Dynamic responses to tied aid shock (Cobb–Douglas case)

The immediate effect of the tied aid shock is to raise the growth of public capital, to above 8%, thereby raising the productivity of both private capital and labor; see Table 8.2b, row 2. Given the cost of borrowing, the higher return to capital causes an instantaneous upward jump in the shadow price of private capital, q, from its initial benchmark level of 2 to 2.04, thereby inducing a corresponding increase in private investment. At the same time, the higher productivity of labor induces an immediate, but slight, decline in leisure from 0.780 to 0.777. While the upward jump in q reduces the rate of return on private capital, the increase in labor raises the return. On balance, the former slightly dominates and immediately after its initial increase, q begins to drop slightly, to around 2.03 after the first five periods. Leisure drops steadily toward its new equilibrium level of 0.768, so that after a few periods its positive productivity effect dominates, and q begins to rise monotonically toward its new equilibrium level of 2.10; see Figures 8.1b and 8.1c.

The introduction of the tied transfer leads to an initial short-run decline in the consumption–output ratio (Figure 8.1d). This is because the short-run substitution from leisure to labor both increases output and reduces the marginal utility of consumption. Thereafter, as the larger capital stocks are reflected in more output, the consumption–output ratio continues to decline monotonically toward its new steady-state value. Also, note that leisure and the consumption–output ratio move together. The contrasting time paths of the four growth rates, ψ_k, ψ_G, ψ_Y, and ψ_C during the transition toward their common long-run growth rate of 2.31% are strikingly illustrated in Figure 8.1f. With public capital being directly stimulated by the transfer, its growth rate jumps initially to over 8.3% before gradually declining. By contrast, private capital increases only very gradually from 1.95% to 2.31% during transition, as the accumulation of public capital enhances its productivity. As a result, the ratio of public to private capital increases at a steady monotonic rate. The growth rate of output is a weighted average of the growth rates of the two capital stocks plus the temporary growth of labor and therefore immediately increases sharply to 3.5% with the transfer. On the other hand, the only influence on the initial growth rate of consumption is the effect that operates through the labor supply and the labor–leisure choice, raising its growth rate from 1.65% to 1.87%. Thereafter it responds only gradually, in response to the accumulation of assets in the economy. It always lies below the growth rate of output, so that C/Y is falling, as noted in Figure 8.1d. However, the level of consumption is still growing, albeit at a modest rate.

The final aspect of the dynamics concerns the debt–output ratio. Starting at 0.42, the short-run increase in output leads to a slight initial decline in the debt–output ratio, after which it increases monotonically through time. This is because the accumulation of public capital raises the average productivity of private capital, while the accumulation of both types of capital raises the need to borrow from abroad to finance new investment and installation costs. But as noted previously, the higher debt, being backed by higher productive capacity through the tied transfer, is sustainable.

Untied aid

The transitional dynamics following an untied aid shock are illustrated in Figure 8.2. Three points should be made at the outset, which distinguish our results

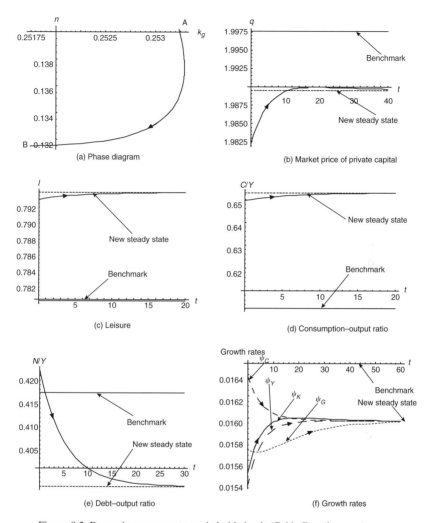

Figure 8.2 Dynamic responses to untied aid shock (Cobb–Douglas case)

from earlier findings. First, the existence of transitional dynamics following an untied aid shock depends crucially upon the endogeneity of labor supply. If labor supply is inelastic, then untied foreign aid has no dynamic or growth effects and the economy moves instantaneously to its new steady state via a once-and-for-all increase in the consumption–output ratio; see Chatterjee, Sakoulis, and Turnovsky (2003). Second, the dynamics in response to untied aid are in sharp contrast to those generated by tied aid, being more or less the reverse. This reflects the fact, noted in Table 8.2, that the long-run responses of the economy to the two types of aid are generally opposite in nature. Third, the dynamic adjustment generally occurs much more rapidly than in response to the tied aid shock.

Figure 8.2a illustrates the transitional adjustment paths for the two state variables, debt/private capital and public capital/private capital. We see that on receipt of the aid, these move in opposite directions, implying that on impact the debt–capital ratio begins to decline, while the public–private capital ratio begins to increase. Indeed, the untied transfer is initially applied primarily to debt reduction, which allows an immediate substantial increase in consumption, increasing the marginal utility of leisure, and thereby inducing an immediate sharp reduction in labor supply.

The main impact of an untied transfer is on consumption, leisure, and debt reduction, as illustrated in Figures 8.2c, 8.2d, and 8.2e. Its initial impact is to raise the marginal utility of leisure, causing a reduction in labor supply, and hence in the productivity of private and public capital, and in q. The receipt of the untied transfer has a slightly less adverse short-run effect on the growth rate of public capital, reducing it to 1.57%, slightly above that of private capital. As k_g increases, the productivity of public capital declines relative to private capital, causing their relative growth rates to reverse. After just over two periods the growth rate of private capital exceeds that of public capital and k_g begins to decline with n. The decline in q is partially reversed during the subsequent transition as the relative stock of public to private capital declines.

8.4 Sensitivity analysis

The contrast between the effects of tied and untied foreign aid is striking. It is therefore important to determine how sensitive this comparison is to the chosen parameter values for the benchmark economy. This is explored in Tables 8.3–8.6, along the various dimensions noted earlier.[7]

8.4.1 Elasticity of substitution in production versus flexibility in labor supply

Table 8.3 presents a grid summarizing the changes in key variables in response to equal amounts of tied aid and untied aid, respectively, as the

---

[7] In Chapter 7, with fixed labor supply, we conducted sensitivity analysis with respect to the adjustment costs of public capital as well as the degree of capital market imperfection. We have also addressed these aspects here, but since the conclusions are basically unchanged from those obtained previously, we omit them from our discussion.

Table 8.3. *Sensitivity of permanent responses to the elasticities of substitution (s) and leisure (θ)*

$\tilde{N}/Y$	s = 0.8					s = 1					s = 1.2					s = 1.6				
	$d\tilde{I}$	$d(\tilde{C}/\tilde{Y})$	$d(\tilde{N}/\tilde{Y})$	$d(\tilde{K}/\tilde{Y})$	$d\tilde{\psi}$	$d\tilde{I}$	$d(\tilde{C}/\tilde{Y})$	$d(\tilde{N}/\tilde{Y})$	$d(\tilde{K}/\tilde{Y})$	$d\tilde{\psi}$	$d\tilde{I}$	$d(\tilde{C}/\tilde{Y})$	$d(\tilde{N}/\tilde{Y})$	$d(\tilde{K}/\tilde{Y})$	$d\tilde{\psi}$	$d\tilde{I}$	$d(\tilde{C}/\tilde{Y})$	$d(\tilde{N}/\tilde{Y})$	$d(\tilde{K}/\tilde{Y})$	$d\tilde{\psi}$
(a) Tied aid shock: σ increases from 0 to 0.05, λ = 1																				
θ = 0	0	−0.065	0.194	−0.35	1.03	0	−0.047	0.103	−0.30	0.741	0	−0.036	0.053	−0.266	0.566	0	−0.024	0.003	−0.227	0.375
θ = 1	0.009	−0.054	0.419	−0.630	0.984	**−0.012**	**−0.039**	**0.206**	**−0.446**	**0.657**	−0.026	−0.029	0.101	−0.327	0.446	−0.041	−0.024	0.019	−0.192	0.223
θ = 2	0.007	−0.046	0.572	−0.814	0.939	−0.007	−0.035	0.254	−0.507	0.608	−0.015	−0.028	0.111	−0.327	0.385	−0.017	−0.025	0.017	−0.147	0.158
(b) Untied aid shock: σ increases from 0 to 0.05, λ = 0																				
θ = 0	0	0.05	0	0	0	0	0.05	0	0	0	0	0.05	0	0	0	0	0.05	0	0	0
θ = 1	0.014	0.052	−0.038	0.055	−0.069	**0.014**	**0.051**	**−0.020**	**0.042**	−0.053	0.013	0.05	−0.011	0.032	−0.039	0.010	0.049	−0.002	0.018	−0.020
θ = 2	0.009	0.052	−0.058	0.080	−0.073	0.008	0.051	−0.028	0.053	−0.055	0.007	0.05	−0.012	0.034	−0.037	0.004	0.050	−0.002	0.014	−0.015

elasticity of substitution in production, s, varies between 0.8 and 1.6, while θ varies between 0 and 2. One interesting feature is that the effects of tied aid on the growth rate are highly sensitive to even minor deviations from the benchmark value of $s = 1$ (Cobb–Douglas). Thus, for example, if a researcher estimates $s = 1$ with a standard error of 0.1 – a tight estimate – and if $\theta = 1$, then, with 95% probability the implied increase of 0.66 percentage points in the growth rate could be as high as 0.98 or as low as 0.45. A sustained difference in the growth rate of half a percentage point accumulates to a substantial difference in economic performance. This is seen from the spread on the implied welfare gain of 7.96%, which is even larger, ranging as high as 21.1% and as low as 0.53%; see Table 8.4.

Looking though the two parts of Table 8.3, the following observations can be made.

(i) The tendency for tied and untied aid to have opposite long-run effects on economic activity is robust to variations in s and θ.

(ii) Tied aid has substantially greater long-run effects on variables involving asset accumulation (capital aid and foreign debt) than does untied aid. The effects on consumption and leisure are comparable in magnitude (though opposite in direction).

(iii) Increasing the elasticity of substitution, s, reduces the positive effect of tied aid on the growth rate, while reducing the negative effect on the consumption–output and capital–output ratios. On the other hand, a higher s primarily reduces the adverse effect of an untied aid shock on the debt–output ratio, while decreasing the positive effects on the capital–output and consumption–output ratios, the latter only mildly. The net effect is to reduce the adverse effect on the growth rate.

Intuitively, the larger the elasticity of substitution, the more the increased productivity of private capital resulting from the tied transfer induces substitution toward private capital. As a result, the Y/K ratio rises less, so that the increased productivity of private capital is reduced, thus reducing its rate of accumulation, and mitigating the fall in consumption. For untied aid, a higher elasticity of substitution means that the reduction in the productivity of private capital resulting from the reduction in labor supply is mitigated, so that the fall in the growth rate is moderated. Slower growth means less borrowing, lower borrowing costs, and thus a decline in the debt–output ratio.

(iv) Increasing the importance of leisure in utility, θ, reduces the positive effect of tied aid on the growth rate, and reduces the adverse effect on the consumption–output and capital–output ratios. It increases the adverse effect of untied aid on the growth rate, while reducing the positive effect on the capital–output ratio and the adverse effect on the debt–output ratio.

The intuition is as follows. The more the agent values leisure in utility, the less he is willing to reduce it in response to an increase in tied aid, the less the reduction in consumption, and the less the positive effect on the growth rate. In the case of untied aid, as θ increases and agents enjoy more leisure, the productivity of capital and the return on capital decline, so the adverse effect on the growth rate increases. However, there are some offsetting effects. As leisure increases, because of its diminishing marginal utility, agents increase their leisure at a diminishing rate. This mitigates the adverse effect of the untied aid on the growth rate, for sufficiently large θ.[8]

8.4.2 Welfare comparisons

The comparison of the overall intertemporal welfare gains for the two types of aid is particularly striking. Table 8.4 indicates that for the benchmark case, $s = 1$, $\theta = 1$, the net effects of the two types of aid on intertemporal welfare are more or less comparable; the gains from tied aid are 7.96%, while those from untied aid are 7.71%. But despite this similarity in the overall intertemporal welfare gains for the two forms of aid, the contrasting dynamic adjustments in the economy lead to sharp differences in the time profiles of the benefits they provide. For tied aid, the commitment toward public investment involves initial consumption losses and less leisure, leading to a short-run welfare loss of 1.53%. Over time, as the economy becomes more productive, consumption increases rapidly. Welfare increases dramatically, with subsequent gains dominating the initial losses, resulting in an overall intertemporal welfare gain. In contrast, the response to untied aid does not involve intertemporal tradeoffs. Instead, it results in an immediate and an almost constant increase in consumption, leisure, and therefore welfare, along the transition path.

Table 8.4 presents the sensitivity of the short-run and long-run welfare responses to the two types of aid shocks, for variations in s and θ. The following patterns emerge from the table.

---

[8] One result in Table 8.3 worth noting is the contrast in the response of leisure to an increase in tied aid as s increases from 0.8 to 1.6. As already noted, if $s = 1$, a tied transfer, by increasing labor productivity, encourages more work effort, an effect that is exacerbated as the elasticity of substitution increases beyond 1. For low s, however, this response is reversed. The intuition is seen most clearly by focusing on the polar case of the fixed coefficient production function, $s = 0$. In this case, private capital, K, and labor in efficiency units $(1 - \tau)K_g$, need to change proportionately. Since tied aid leads to an increase in the relative stock, $k_g \equiv K_g/K$, this must be accompanied by a decrease in labor for $(1 - l)k_g$ to remain constant and for production to remain efficient.

Table 8.4. *Sensitivity of short-run and long-run welfare responses to the elasticities of substitution (s) and leisure (θ)*

	$s=0.8$		$s=1$		$s=1.2$		$s=1.6$	
	$\Delta(W(0))$	$\Delta(W)$	$\Delta(W(0))$	$\Delta(W)$	$\Delta(W(0))$	$\Delta(W)$	$\Delta(W(0))$	$\Delta(W)$
(a) Tied aid: σ increases from 0 to 0.05, $\lambda=1$								
$\theta=0$	0.71	10.18	−3.97	6.00	−7.76	1.06	−13.04	−3.14
$\theta=1$	5.14	21.08	**−1.53**	**7.96**	−6.71	0.53	−12.56	−6.82
$\theta=2$	7.03	26.46	−0.69	9.15	−6.55	0.16	−12.52	−7.68
(b) Untied aid: σ increases from 0 to 0.05, $\lambda=0$								
$\theta=0$	8.24	8.24	8.66	8.66	8.94	8.94	9.28	9.28
$\theta=1$	7.49	6.47	**8.32**	**7.71**	8.94	8.55	9.70	9.52
$\theta=2$	7.22	5.89	8.21	7.50	8.94	8.54	9.78	9.64

(i) Both the short-run and the intertemporal welfare gains from an untied aid shock are remarkably insensitive to variations in both s and θ. For plausible ranges of the parameters, an untied aid flow equal to 5% of GDP leads to short-run welfare gains in the range 7–9% and long-run gains in the range 5–10%, both measured by an equivalent variation in the initial stock of capital. The long-run gains are typically within 1 percentage point of the short-run gains, suggesting a gradual increase over time.

(ii) In contrast, both the short-run and long-run welfare gains from tied aid of the same magnitude are highly sensitive to both parameters. For any given θ, the long-run welfare gains decline with s. On the other hand, welfare gains increase with θ for values of s less than 1. For high values of s, tied aid yields both short-run and long-run losses, the former being relatively independent of θ, and the latter increasing with θ. There is therefore a sharp contrast between the short-run and long-run welfare effects of tied aid.

Results (i) and (ii) from Table 8.4 are two key findings, and the following intuition may be provided. An untied aid flow has little effect on the stocks of public or private capital. The higher elasticity of substitution raises the level of output attainable from given stocks of capital, thereby raising consumption and welfare approximately uniformly. If the aid flow is tied, it increases the rate of investment in public capital. With a low elasticity of substitution this requires an approximately corresponding increase in private capital, leading to a large increase in output, consumption, and benefits. As the elasticity of substitution increases, the higher public capital is associated with a smaller increase in private capital, so that the increase in output, consumption, and welfare declines. This is exacerbated by the fact that for a high elasticity of substitution, the tied transfer generates a large increase in the real wage and its growth rate, leading to substantial substitution toward labor, which is further welfare-reducing.

The contrasting sensitivities of the welfare gains resulting from tied and untied transfers, respectively, to changes in s and θ, mean that the relative merits of the two forms of transfer, from a welfare standpoint, are also highly sensitive to these two critical parameters. To consider this, we shall focus on the benchmark case, $s = 1$, and consider variations in θ. As we have already noted, for $\theta = 1$, tied aid is marginally superior to untied aid from a long-run (intertemporal) welfare point of view. But as θ declines and leisure becomes less important in utility, untied aid is superior to tied aid. Indeed in the limiting case of inelastic labor supply, $\theta = 0$, an untied aid shock generates a long-run welfare gain of 8.66%, while the corresponding gain from a tied aid shock is much lower, at 6%. The less (more) important is leisure in utility, the more (less) tied aid crowds out private consumption, thus decreasing (increasing) the benefits relative to untied aid. This comparison is sensitive to even small variations in the elasticity of substitution. For example, if $s = 0.8$ tied aid dominates untied aid (intertemporally), irrespective of the importance of leisure (even for $\theta = 5$), while if $s = 1.2$ precisely the reverse is true.

8.4.3 Generalizations of the production function

Table 8.5 extends the comparison of the long-run welfare effects of tied and untied aid by allowing public capital to have the additional externality effect as introduced in (8.1a). The main message of these results is clear and unsurprising. While the benefits of untied aid are relatively insensitive to ε (being mildly negative), the benefits of tied aid are highly sensitive to this effect, so that the latter is heavily favored as ε increases. Take, for example, the benchmark case, $\theta = 1$, $s = 1$. Whereas tied aid is only marginally superior in the absence of this effect, it clearly dominates for $\varepsilon = 0.1$ (7.51% vs. 18.50%). Moreover, in cases where, for $\varepsilon = 0$, untied aid dominates tied aid, and where the latter is welfare-deteriorating, tied aid may now not only be positive from a welfare standpoint but may also be superior to untied aid. An example of this arises if $s = 1.6$ and $\varepsilon = 0.2$.[9]

---

[9] We have also conducted sensitivity analysis using the generalized Romer production function in note 2. If $\varepsilon = 0$ in that model, tied aid is clearly undesirable, since it is obliging the

Table 8.5. *Sensitivity of long-run welfare responses to the elasticities of substitution (s), leisure (θ), and the public capital externality (ε) (percentage changes in welfare, σ increases from 0 to 0.05)*

	$s=0.8$		$s=1$		$s=1.2$		$s=1.6$	
	$\lambda=0$	$\lambda=1$	$\lambda=0$	$\lambda=1$	$\lambda=0$	$\lambda=1$	$\lambda=0$	$\lambda=1$
(a) $\varepsilon=0.02$								
$\theta=0$	8.21	12.10	8.63	6.33	8.91	2.68	9.25	−1.68
$\theta=1$	6.44	23.46	**7.67**	**9.89**	8.51	2.24	9.47	−5.31
$\theta=2$	5.86	29.11	7.46	11.16	8.50	1.88	9.59	−6.16
(b) $\varepsilon=0.05$								
$\theta=0$	8.16	15.12	8.58	9.05	8.86	5.20	9.19	0.60
$\theta=1$	6.39	27.84	**7.61**	**12.94**	8.43	4.91	9.39	−2.93
$\theta=2$	5.82	33.34	7.40	14.34	8.42	4.57	9.50	−3.78
(c) $\varepsilon=0.1$								
$\theta=0$	8.08	20.57	8.49	13.93	8.77	9.70	9.09	4.65
$\theta=1$	6.30	34.21	**7.51**	**18.50**	8.32	9.73	9.25	1.33
$\theta=2$	5.75	41.17	7.31	20.18	8.32	9.46	9.37	0.51
(d) $\varepsilon=0.2$								
$\theta=0$	7.94	33.43	8.33	25.31	8.59	20.11	8.90	13.89
$\theta=0$	6.15	51.30	**7.31**	**31.90**	8.10	21.19	8.99	11.32
$\theta=0$	6.37	60.63	7.14	34.36	8.12	21.11	9.12	10.59

8.4.4 Sensitivity of transitional dynamics

We have recomputed the transitional paths for both types of aid to determine their sensitivity to variations in s and θ, as well as in ε. For untied aid, the time profiles retain the general qualitative characteristics, illustrated in Figure 8.2 for the benchmark $\theta=s=1$, as θ, s, and ε are varied. Many of the qualitative characteristics of the transitional paths following a tied aid shock also remain as illustrated in Figure 8.1, although there are some substantive differences, which are illustrated in Figures 8.3 and 8.4.

recipient economy to devote the resources to an unproductive use. But if ε is sufficiently large (e.g. around 0.2) it is again the case that tied aid is not only beneficial, but also superior to untied aid.

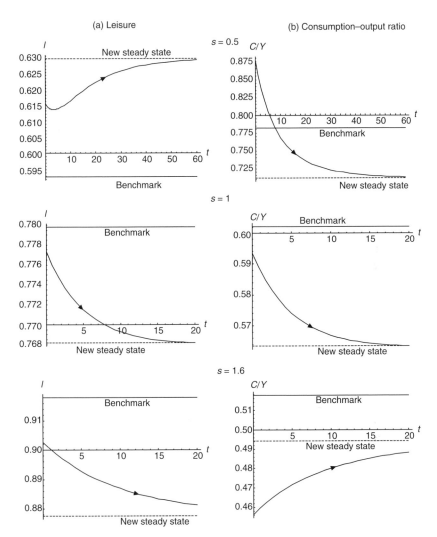

Figure 8.3 Sensitivity of dynamics of leisure–consumption to elasticity of substitution (tied aid)

The transitional time paths for leisure and the consumption–output ratio following a tied aid shock are sensitive to variations in the elasticity of substitution (s), and Figure 8.3 compares them for values of $s = 0.5$, 1, and 1.6, while θ remains at its benchmark value of unity. As already observed, for the benchmark economy, l and C/Y move together. For a low elasticity of substitution ($s = 0.5$), leisure generally increases, for reasons discussed in Section 8.4.1. The initial

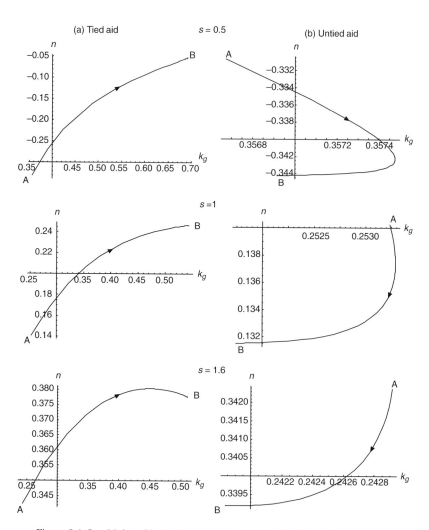

Figure 8.4 Sensitivity of basic dynamics to elasticity of substitution

increase in leisure increases the marginal utility of consumption, so that C/Y initially increases, after which it declines steadily. This implies that l and C/Y move in opposite directions throughout the transition. For a high elasticity of substitution, l initially declines and continues to decline during the transition, just as in the benchmark case. But in this case, the initial decline in l is sufficiently sharp to cause a sharp decline in initial consumption, $C(0)$. The C/Y ratio overshoots its long-run response, and thus rises during the transition, implying again that l and C/Y move in opposite directions throughout the transition.

Figure 8.4 illustrates the sensitivity of the dynamic adjustments of the basic state variables, k_g and n, to an increase in s. Figure 8.4a shows the case of tied transfers. As the elasticity of substitution increases, the curvature of the adjustment path increases. The higher the degree of substitution between the two types of capital, the more the transfer increases the initial growth rate of public capital relative to that of private capital.[10] At the same time, the rate of debt accumulation increases, raising borrowing costs. Over time, as the growth rate of public capital declines and that of private capital increases, foreign borrowing and borrowing costs fall. For a very high elasticity of substitution, we get very rapidly increasing debt and borrowing costs during the early phases of the transition. However, over time, these inhibit borrowing and debt eventually declines. In the limiting case where the two types of capital are perfect substitutes, n ultimately returns to its initial level.

Figure 8.4b shows the case of untied transfers. The main point to observe is that the initial period of an increasing public–private capital ratio, which prevails only briefly for the benchmark case, is much more prolonged for a low elasticity of substitution, while for a high elasticity of substitution k_g declines uniformly along with n.

8.5 Consequences for the government fiscal balance

One issue of debate in the aid–growth literature concerns the relationship between the effectiveness of foreign aid and "good" government policy. Recently, in a panel study of fifty-six developing countries and six four-year periods (1970–93), Burnside and Dollar (2000) argue that aid is most effective when complemented by "sound" or "good" economic policy making by the recipient government.[11] Consequently, their conclusions call for greater selectivity on the part of donor countries when making aid decisions. Burnside and Dollar's (2000) influential findings have now become an effective weapon for donor-countries and aid agencies to persuade prospective recipients to enforce more disciplined fiscal and monetary policies in order to receive aid; see Easterly (2003). However, several papers, including Collier and Dehn (2001), Dalgaard and Hansen (2001), and Easterly, Levine, and Roodman

---

[10] Care must be exercised in comparing the slopes of the n-k_g loci in Figures 8.1a and 8.2a, as the units differ.

[11] "Good" policy includes practices like low inflation, low government deficits, and fostering openness. A useful discussion of the role of fiscal policy for development, in general, and for the Millennium Development Goals, in particular, is provided by Gupta, Clements, and Inchauste (2004).

(2004) have shown that Burnside and Dollar's (2000) empirical results are not robust to the definitions of "aid," "good policy," and "growth." They show that broader definitions of these terms and extended data sets weaken the link between aid and the quality of policy, and consequently economic growth.

Despite the lack of consensus with regard to the empirical evidence, the issue of good government policy is obviously important and our model gives some insight on the role of the government budget deficit, one of the key elements of the Burnside–Dollar analysis, in the aid–growth process.

Recalling equation (8.5), T represents the amount of lump-sum taxation (or transfers) necessary to finance the primary deficit and is therefore a measure of *current* fiscal imbalance. Defining:

$$V \equiv \int_0^\infty \frac{\bar{T}(t)}{Y(t)} e^{-\int_0^\tau r(n)ds} d\tau$$

$$= \int_0^\infty \frac{1}{Y(t)} [\Psi(G, K_G) - \tau Y - TR] e^{-\int_0^\tau r(n)ds} d\tau$$

V measures the present discounted value of the lump-sum taxes per unit of current output necessary to balance the government budget over time, and thus provides a measure of the *intertemporal* fiscal imbalance; see Turnovsky (2004). Substituting for the appropriate quantities from Section 8.2, yields:

$$V = \int_0^\infty \left((\bar{g} + \lambda\sigma) \left[1 + (h_2/2)(\bar{g} + \lambda\sigma) \frac{y(t)}{k_g(t)} \right] - (\tau + \sigma) \right) e^{-\int_0^\tau r(n)ds} d\tau$$

(8.10)

The issue then is the effect of tied and untied aid on this measure. Table 8.6 summarizes the effects of tied and untied aid on both intertemporal welfare, W, and the government's intertemporal balance, V, for varying domestic fiscal configurations. The following important insights emerge from Table 8.6a.

(i) The welfare benefits from untied aid are relatively insensitive to substantial variations in both the tax rate and the rate of government spending, decreasing mildly with the former and increasing mildly with the latter. In addition, untied aid always improves the government's intertemporal fiscal balance and thus is beneficial from that standpoint.

(ii) The welfare benefits from tied aid increase slightly with the tax rate but decrease dramatically with the rate of government spending. This is because the benefits from tied aid depend critically upon the level of domestic government spending ($\bar{g}$) on public capital relative to the socially optimal level which, in turn, depends upon the tax rate. For example, for $\tau = 0.15$, the

Table 8.6. Sensitivity of foreign aid shocks to domestic fiscal structure (Cobb–Douglas production function, σ increases from 0 to 0.05)

| | $\bar{g}=0.02$ | | | | $\bar{g}=0.05$ | | | | | | | $\bar{g}=0.10$ | | | |
| | Tied aid ($\lambda=1$ is opt.) | | Untied aid ($\lambda=0$) | | Tied aid ($\lambda=1$) | | Untied aid ($\lambda=0$) | | Interior optimal mix | | | Tied aid ($\lambda=1$) | | Untied aid ($\lambda=0$ is opt.) | |
	ΔW	ΔV	ΔW	ΔV	ΔW	ΔV	ΔW	ΔV	ΔW	ΔV	φ	ΔW	ΔV	ΔW	ΔV
(a) $\varepsilon=0$															
$\tau=0.10$	26.97	0.87	7.26	-0.76	7.16	0.57	8.23	-0.58	8.89	0.13	0.39	-2.68	0.45	10.35	-0.48
$\tau=0.15$	27.73	1.09	6.87	-0.84	7.96	0.66	7.71	-0.64	8.92	0.07	0.53	-1.51	0.49	9.53	-0.52
$\tau=0.20$	28.45	1.37	6.51	-0.94	8.70	0.77	7.25	-0.70	9.12	0.32	0.68	-0.50	0.54	8.82	-0.56
(b) $\varepsilon=0.10$															
$\tau=0.10$	54.43	1.24	7.06	-1.14	17.69	0.63	7.98	-0.71				2.11	0.45	10.11	-0.51
$\tau=0.15$	55.35	1.77	6.71	-1.28	18.50	0.79	7.51	-0.78				3.27	0.50	9.34	-0.56
$\tau=0.20$	56.23	2.46	6.39	-1.45	19.26	0.99	7.08	-0.86				4.30	0.58	8.66	-0.61

socially optimal fraction of government spending in the absence of foreign aid is $\bar{g} = 0.098$.[12] If $\bar{g} = 0.02$, government investment is far below the optimum and clearly foreign aid tied to public investment is highly desirable; if $\bar{g} = 0.05$, the tied aid raises total public investment to 0.10, which is close to the social optimum and therefore still desirable. But if $\bar{g} = 0.10$, the rate of public investment is above the social optimum and any further tied aid is welfare-reducing.[13]

(iii) Tied aid always worsens the government's intertemporal deficit and is not desirable from that standpoint.[14] Thus for low rates of government expenditure tied aid involves a tradeoff in that increased wealth is accompanied by a higher intertemporal government deficit. For high rates of government expenditure, tied aid is unambiguously bad in that it is both welfare-reducing and also reduces the government's intertemporal balance. In contrast, untied aid always has a positive effect on both targets.

(iv) The larger the current government surplus, as parameterized by $\tau{-}\bar{g}$, the more (less) beneficial is tied (untied) aid. "Good" policy in the Burnside–Dollar sense thus favors tied aid.

(v) For extreme rates of expenditure, optimal policy (i.e. welfare-maximizing policy) involves corner solutions. Thus for $\bar{g} = 0.02$ tied aid is not only superior but maximizes welfare, while for $\bar{g} = 0.10$, untied aid is optimal. For $\bar{g} = 0.05$, the optimal policy is an interior mix. Thus for $\tau = 0.15$, the optimum is for 53% of the aid to be tied and the remainder untied. While this will take the economy to below the optimal rate of government investment, the losses from this are more than compensated by the fact that this is associated with a reduction in the government's intertemporal fiscal balance.

Table 8.6b yields a similar pattern in the case of a positive externality $\varepsilon = 0.10$. The main difference is that the existence of this externality raises the productivity of public capital. In this case the socially optimal rates of public investment are 0.120, 0.130, and 0.138, corresponding to $\tau = 0.10$, 0.15, and 0.20, respectively. Hence the tied transfer remains optimal even if $\bar{g} = 0.05$.

---

[12] This is obtained numerically. For $\tau = 0.1$ and 0.2 the socially optimal expenditures are 0.091 and 0.106, respectively.
[13] Since the total rate of public investment is $\bar{g} + \lambda\sigma$, the benefits of tied aid also depend upon its size, σ, since like $\bar{g}$, too large an increase in σ will take $\bar{g} + \lambda\sigma$ beyond the social optimum rate of public investment. There is, in effect, a tradeoff between $\bar{g}$ and σ insofar as the benefit of tied foreign aid is concerned.
[14] This result can also be established analytically by considering (8.10) in the case $\lambda = 1$. An important element for this result is the fact that tied aid also imposes installation costs which the government needs to finance.

8.6 Conclusions

The link between foreign aid, economic growth, and welfare depends crucially on the mechanism through which a particular aid program, whether tied or untied, is absorbed by the recipient economy. In this chapter, we have extended the analysis of Chapter 7 to include additional crucial mechanisms. In particular, we highlight the importance of the endogeneity of labor supply as an additional margin along which foreign aid may influence macroeconomic performance. In doing so, we focus on (i) the role played by the interaction of labor supply and public capital, and (ii) externalities associated with public capital accumulation in determining an economy's response to foreign aid. We also emphasize the tradeoffs between flexibility of leisure in utility and flexibility of substitution in production.

We conclude with three comments. First, our results carry some important policy advice. The fact that the effects of the tied transfer are less certain than those of the pure transfer, depending upon the structural characteristics of the recipient economy, suggests that the donor economy must be careful to ensure that it has accurate information on the recipient economy. When donors decide on whether a particular aid program should be tied to an investment activity, careful attention should be paid to the recipient's opportunities for substitution in production, the elasticity of labor supply, and production externalities. Otherwise, it is perfectly possible for a tied transfer to have an unintended adverse effect on the recipient economy, if that economy is structurally different from what the donor perceives.

Second, we have abstracted entirely from any political economy factors relating to rent-seeking or corruption, which are clearly relevant issues in any foreign aid discussion. Recent work by Acemoglu and Robinson (2000) and others show that the existence of "political elites" and powerful interest groups in poor economies may be a deterrent to investment, technological change, and economic development. Further, the lack of institutions may also inhibit the effects of aid on growth. Clearly, the consequences of these are significant considerations for determining both the nature and composition of foreign aid and are important directions for future research.

Finally, we should note that we have focused on the effects of the transfer on the economic performance of a small recipient economy. Being small, this has no feedback to the donor economy. However, where such transfers are being proposed simultaneously for a number of prospective member nations, the collective feedback effects on the donor economy need no longer be negligible. A natural extension of this analysis is, therefore, to consider the transfer in a multi-country growth equilibrium setting.

Appendix

This appendix provides the detailed derivations of the macrodynamic equilibrium.

Derivation of the equilibrium relationships (8.7a)–(8.7d)

The production function we consider is:

$$Y = a\left(\frac{K_G}{\bar{K}}\right)^{\varepsilon}[\eta\{(1-l)K_G\}^{-\kappa} + (1-\eta)K^{-\kappa}]^{-1/\kappa} \qquad (8.1a)$$

The marginal rate of substitution between C and l is given by:

$$\frac{C}{Y} = \frac{\eta(1-\tau)}{A^{\kappa}\theta}\left(\frac{l}{1-l}\right)\left[\frac{Y}{(1-l)K_G}\right]^{\kappa} \qquad (8.A.1)$$

where $A \equiv a\ (K_G/K)\varepsilon$. Next, we recall the definition of $\Omega(k_g,\ l) \equiv \Omega = ((1-\eta)/\eta)[(1-l)k_g]^{\kappa}$ given in (8.8a). Substituting this into the production function (8.1a) and into (8.A.1) we can express the output–capital ratio and consumption–capital ratio in the form:

$$Y/K \equiv y = y(k_g, l) = ak_g^{\varepsilon}[(1-\eta) + \eta\{(1-l)k_g\}^{-\kappa}]^{-1/\kappa}$$
$$= ak_g^{\varepsilon}\left[(1-\eta)\frac{1+\Omega}{\Omega}\right]^{-\frac{1}{\kappa}} \qquad (8.A.2a)$$

$$\frac{C}{K} \equiv c = c(k_g, l) = \frac{(1-\tau)}{\theta}\left(\frac{l}{1-l}\right)\left[\frac{1}{1+\Omega}\right]y \qquad (8.A.2b)$$

Then, differentiating the optimality condition (8.3a), the marginal rate of substitution condition (8.A.1), the production function (8.1a), all with respect to time, and recalling (8.4a), yields:

$$(\gamma - 1)\frac{\dot{C}}{C} + \gamma\theta\frac{\dot{l}}{l} = \frac{\dot{v}}{v} = \rho - r(N/K) \qquad (8.A.3a)$$

$$\frac{\dot{C}}{C} - \frac{\dot{Y}}{Y} = \frac{\dot{l}}{l} + (1+\kappa)\frac{\dot{l}}{1-l} + \kappa\left(\frac{\dot{Y}}{Y} - \frac{\dot{K}_G}{K_G}\right) - \varepsilon\kappa\left(\frac{\dot{K}_G}{K_G} - \frac{\dot{K}}{K}\right) \quad (8.A.3b)$$

$$\frac{\dot{Y}}{Y} \equiv \psi_Y = \frac{1}{1+\Omega}\left[\Omega\frac{\dot{K}}{K} + \frac{\dot{K}_G}{K_G} - \frac{\dot{l}}{1-l}\right] + \varepsilon\left(\frac{\dot{K}_G}{K_G} - \frac{\dot{K}}{K}\right) \quad (8.A.3c)$$

Combining these four equations together with (8.9a) and (8.9b), we can eliminate the growth rates, $\dot{C}/C, \dot{K}/K, \dot{K}_G/K_G, \dot{Y}/Y$, and $\dot{v}/v$ from these equations and express the dynamics of labor supply by the following differential equation:

$$\dot{l} = \frac{F(k_g, n, q, l)}{G(k_g, l)} \quad (8.A.4)$$

where:

$$F(k_g, n, q, l) \equiv \left\{[1 + \Omega(k_g, l)][p - r(n)]\right.$$
$$\left. + (1-\gamma)\left(\begin{array}{c}[\Omega(k_g,l)(1+\kappa) - (1+\Omega(k_g,l))\varepsilon]\psi_K \\ +[1+\kappa+(\varepsilon-\kappa)\{1+\Omega(k_g,l)\}]\psi_G\end{array}\right)\right\}l$$

$$G(k_g, l) \equiv \left[\{\gamma(1+\theta) - 1\}\{1 + \Omega(k_g, l)\} - (1-\gamma)(1+\kappa)\Omega(k_g, l)\left(\frac{l}{1-l}\right)\right]$$

and:

$$\psi_K(q) \equiv \frac{\dot{K}}{K} = \frac{(q-1)}{h_1} - \delta_K \quad (8.A.5a)$$

$$\psi_G(z, l) \equiv \frac{\dot{K}_G}{K_G} = g\frac{Y}{K_G} - \delta_G$$
$$= ag(1-l)k_g^\varepsilon[\eta\{1+\Omega(k_g, l)\}]^{-1/\kappa} - \delta_G \quad (8.A.5b)$$

Using (8.A.3a) and (8.A.4) we can express the growth rate of consumption as:

$$\psi_C \equiv \frac{\dot{C}}{C} = \frac{r(n) - p + \gamma\theta(1/l)[F(k_g, n, q, l)/G(k_g, l)]}{1-\gamma} \quad (8.A.5c)$$

while (8.7d) follows directly from the optimality condition (8.4b).

The equilibrium dynamics can now be represented by the following autonomous system in the stationary variables, k_g, n, q, and l:

$$\frac{\dot{k}_g}{k_g} = \frac{\dot{K}_G}{K_G} - \frac{\dot{K}}{K} = (\bar{g} + \lambda\sigma)\frac{y}{k_g} - \delta_G - \left(\frac{(q-1)}{h_1} - \delta_K\right) \qquad (8.A.6a)$$

$$\frac{\dot{n}}{n} = \frac{\dot{N}}{N} - \frac{\dot{K}}{K} = r(n) + \frac{1}{n}\left[c + \frac{q^2-1}{2h_1} + \{(\bar{g} + \lambda\sigma) - (1+\sigma)\}y + \frac{h_2}{2}(\bar{g} + \lambda\sigma)^2\frac{y^2}{k_g}\right]$$
$$- \left(\frac{(q-1)}{h_1} - \delta_K\right) \qquad (8.A.6b)$$

$$\dot{q} = r(n)q - \frac{(1-\tau)(1-\eta)y^{(1+\kappa)}}{a^\kappa k_g^{\varepsilon\kappa}} - \frac{(q-1)^2}{2h_1} + \delta_K q \qquad (8.A.6c)$$

$$\dot{l} = \frac{F()}{G()}$$
$$= \frac{\left[(1+\Omega)(\rho - r(n)) + (1-\gamma)\left\{\begin{array}{l}[\Omega(1+\kappa) - (1+\Omega)\varepsilon]\psi_K \\ +[1+\kappa + (\varepsilon - \kappa)(1+\Omega)]\psi_G\end{array}\right\}\right]}{[\{\gamma(1+\theta) - 1\}\{1+\Omega\} - (1-\gamma)(1+\kappa)\Omega(l/(1-l))]}l \qquad (8.A.6d)$$

where, from above, $\Omega = \Omega(k_g, l)$, $y = y(k_g, l)$, $c = c(k_g, l)$, $\psi_K = \psi_K(q)$, and $\psi_G = \psi_G(k_g, l)$.

Steady-state equilibrium

Steady-state equilibrium is attained when $\dot{z} = \dot{n} = \dot{l} = \dot{q} = 0$, so that

$$\frac{\dot{C}}{C} = \frac{\dot{K}}{K} = \frac{\dot{K}_G}{K_G} = \frac{\dot{Y}}{Y} = \frac{\dot{N}}{N} = \tilde{\psi}$$

Setting $\dot{k}_g = \dot{n} = \dot{l} = \dot{q} = 0$ in (8.A.6a)–(8.A.6d) and recalling (8.A.2a), (8.A.2b), (8.A.5a), (8.A.5b), and the definition of $\Omega(k_g, l)$, we can summarize the steady-state in the following form:

$$(\bar{g} + \lambda\sigma)\frac{\tilde{y}}{\tilde{k}_g} - \delta_G = \frac{\tilde{q} - 1}{h_1} - \delta_K \qquad (8.A.7a)$$

$$r(\tilde{n}) + \frac{1}{\tilde{n}}\left[\tilde{c} + \frac{\tilde{q}^2-1}{2h_1} + \{(\bar{g} + \lambda\sigma) - (1+\sigma)\}\tilde{y} + \frac{h_2}{2}(\bar{g} + \lambda\sigma)^2\frac{(1-\tilde{l})\tilde{y}^2}{\tilde{k}_g}\right] = \frac{(\tilde{q}-1)}{h_1} - \delta_K \qquad (8.A.7b)$$

$$r(\tilde{n})\tilde{q} - \frac{(1-\tau)(1-\eta)\tilde{y}^{(1+\kappa)}}{a^{\kappa}\tilde{k}_g^{\varepsilon\kappa}} - \frac{(\tilde{q}-1)^2}{2h_1} + \delta_K\tilde{q} = 0 \qquad (8.A.7c)$$

$$\frac{r(\tilde{n}) - \rho}{1 - \gamma} = \frac{(q-1)}{h_1} - \delta_K \qquad (8.A.7d)$$

$$\tilde{y} = a\tilde{k}_g^{\varepsilon}\left[(1-\eta) + \eta\{(1-\tilde{l})\tilde{k}_g\}^{-\kappa}\right]^{-1/\kappa} \qquad (8.A.7e)$$

$$\tilde{c} = \frac{(1-\tau)}{\theta}\left(\frac{\tilde{l}}{1-\tilde{l}}\right)\left[\frac{1}{1 + ((1-\eta)/\eta)((1-\tilde{l})\tilde{k}_g)^{\kappa}}\right]\tilde{y} \qquad (8.A.7f)$$

These six equations can be solved for the steady-state values of $\tilde{k}_g, \tilde{n}, \tilde{l}, \tilde{q}, \tilde{c},$ and $\tilde{y}$, and consequently, the equilibrium growth rate, $\tilde{\psi}$.

References

Acemoglu, D., 2008, *Introduction to Modern Economic Growth*, Princeton University Press, Princeton, NJ.

Acemoglu, D. and J. A. Robinson, 2000, "Political Losers as a Barrier to Economic Development," *American Economic Review* 90, 126–130.

Aghion, P. and P. Howitt, 1992, "A Model of Growth through Creative Destruction," *Econometrica* 51, 323–351.

1998, *Endogenous Growth Theory*, MIT Press, Cambridge, MA.

Antràs, P., 2004, "Is the U.S. Aggregate Production Function Cobb–Douglas? New Estimates of the Elasticity of Substitution," *Contributions to Macroeconomics* 4, 1–34.

Arrow, K. J. and M. Kurz, 1970, *Public Investment, the Rate of Return, and Optimal Fiscal Policy*, Johns Hopkins University Press, Baltimore, MD.

Aschauer, D. A., 1988, "The Equilibrium Approach to Fiscal Policy," *Journal of Money, Credit, and Banking* 20, 41–62.

1989a, "Is Public Expenditure Productive?" *Journal of Monetary Economics* 23, 177–200.

1989b, "Does Public Capital Crowd Out Private Capital?" *Journal of Monetary Economics* 24, 171–188.

Auerbach, A. J. and L. Kotlikoff, 1987, *Dynamic Fiscal Policy*, Cambridge University Press, Cambridge, UK.

Backus, D., P. Kehoe, and T. Kehoe, 1992, "In Search of Scale Effects in Trade and Growth," *Journal of Economic Theory* 58, 377–409.

Balassa, B., 1964, "The Purchasing-Power Parity Doctrine: A Reappraisal," *Journal of Political Economy* 72, 584–596.

Baldwin, R. E. and R. Forslid, 1999, "Incremental Trade Policy and Endogenous Growth: A q-Theory Approach," *Journal of Economic Dynamics and Control* 23, 797–822.

2000, "Trade Liberalization and Endogenous Growth: A q-Theory Approach," *Journal of International Economics* 50, 497–517.

Bardhan, P. K., 1967, "Optimal Foreign Borrowing," in K. Shell (ed.), *Essays on the Theory of Optimal Economic Growth*, MIT Press, Cambridge, MA.

Barro, R. J., 1990, "Government Spending in a Simple Model of Endogenous Growth," *Journal of Political Economy* 98, S103–S125.

1991, "Economic Growth in a Cross Section of Countries," *Quarterly Journal of Economics* 106, 407–443.

Barro, R. J. and J. W. Lee, 1994, "Sources of Economic Growth," in A. H. Meltzer and C. I. Plosser (eds.), *Carnegie–Rochester Conference Series on Public Policy*, vol. 40, North-Holland, Amsterdam.

Barro, R. J. and X. Sala-i-Martin, 1992a, "Public Finance in Models of Economic Growth," *Review of Economic Studies* 59, 645–661.

1992b, "Convergence," *Journal of Political Economy* 100, 223–251.

2000, *Economic Growth*, 2nd edn., McGraw-Hill, New York, NY.

Baxter, M. and R. G. King, 1993, "Fiscal Policy in General Equilibrium," *American Economic Review* 83, 315–334.

Benhabib, J. and R. E. A. Farmer, 1994, "Indeterminacy and Increasing Returns," *Journal of Economic Theory* 63, 19–41.

Benhabib, J. and R. Perli, 1994, "Uniqueness and Indeterminacy: On the Dynamics of Endogenous Growth," *Journal of Economic Theory* 63, 113–142.

Bernard, A. B. and C. I. Jones, 1996, "Comparing Apples and Oranges: Productivity Consequences and Measurement across Industries and Countries," *American Economic Review* 86, 1216–1238.

Berndt, E. R., 1976, "Reconciling Alternative Estimates of the Elasticity of Substitution," *Review of Economics and Statistics* 58, 59–68.

Bhagwati, J. N., 1967, "The Tying of Aid," in J. N. Bhagwati and R. S. Eckaus (eds.), *Foreign Aid*, Penguin, Harmondsworth, UK.

Bhagwati, J. N., R. A. Brecher, and T. Hatta, 1983, "The Generalized Theory of Transfers and Welfare: Bilateral Transfers in a Multilateral World," *American Economic Review* 73, 606–618.

1985, "The Generalized Theory of Transfers and Welfare: Exogenous and Endogenous Distortions," *Quarterly Journal of Economics* 100, 697–714.

Bhandari, J. S., N. U. Haque, and S. J. Turnovsky, 1990, "Growth, External Debt, and Sovereign Risk in a Small Open Economy," *IMF Staff Papers* 37, 388–417.

Bils, M. and P. J. Klenow, 2000, "Does Schooling Cause Growth?" *American Economic Review* 90, 1160–1183.

Blanchard, O. J. 1985, "Debt, Deficits, and Finite Horizons," *Journal of Political Economy* 93, 223–247.

Blankenau, W., 2005, "Public Schooling, College Subsidies and Growth," *Journal of Economic Dynamics and Control* 29, 487–507.

Bond, E. W., P. Wang, and C. K. Yip, 1996, "A General Two-Sector Model of Endogenous Growth with Human and Physical Capital: Balanced Growth and Transitional Dynamics," *Journal of Economic Theory* 68, 149–173.

Brakman, S. and C. van Marrewijk, 1998, *The Economics of International Transfers*, Cambridge University Press, Cambridge.

Brock, P. L., 1988, "Investment, the Current Account, and the Relative Price of Nontraded Goods in a Small Open Economy," *Journal of International Economics* 14, 235–253.

1996, "International Transfers, the Relative Price of Non-traded Goods, and the Current Account," *Canadian Journal of Economics* 29, 163–180.

Brock, P. L. and S. J. Turnovsky, 1994, "The Dependent Economy Model with Traded and Nontraded Capital Goods," *Review of International Economics* 2, 306–325.

Bruno, M., 1976, "The Two-Sector Open Economy and the Real Exchange Rate," *American Economic Review* 66, 566–577.

Burmeister, E. and A. R. Dobell, 1970, *Mathematical Theories of Economic Growth*, Macmillan, New York.

Burnside, C. and D. Dollar, 2000, "Aid, Policies, and Growth," *American Economic Review* 90, 847–868.

Caselli, F., G. Esquivel, and F. Lefort, 1996, "Reopening the Convergence Debate: A New Look at Cross-country Empirics," *Journal of Economic Growth* 1, 363–390.

Cassen, R., 1986, *Does Aid Work?* Clarendon Press, Oxford, UK.

Chamley, C., 1986, "Optimal Taxation of Capital Income in General Equilibrium with Infinite Lives," *Econometrica* 54, 607–622.

Chatterjee, S., 2007, "Should the Private Sector Provide Public Capital?" *Macroeconomic Dynamics* 11, 318–346.

Chatterjee, S., G. Sakoulis, and S. J. Turnovsky, 2003, "Unilateral Capital Transfers, Public Investment, and Economic Growth," *European Economic Review* 47, 1077–1103.

Chatterjee, S. and S. J. Turnovsky, 2004, "Substitutability of Capital, Investment Costs and Foreign Aid," in S. Dowrick, R. Pitchford, and S. J. Turnovsky (eds.) *Economic Growth and Macroeconomic Dynamics: Recent Developments in Economic Theory*, Cambridge University Press, Cambridge, UK.

2007, "Foreign Aid and Economic Growth: The Role of Flexible Labor Supply," *Journal of Development Economics* 87, 507–533.

Chenery, H. B. and A. M. Stroud, 1966, "Foreign Assistance and Economic Development," *American Economic Review* 56, 679–733.

Chung, K. and S. J. Turnovsky, 2007, "Foreign Debt Supply in an Imperfect International Capital Market: Theory and Evidence," unpublished working paper, University of Washington.

Collier, P. and J. Dehn, 2001, "Aid, Shocks, and Growth," Working Paper no. 2688, World Bank.

Cooley, T. F. (ed.), 1995, *Frontiers of Business Cycle Research*, Princeton University Press, Princeton, NJ.

Corden, W. M., 1960, "The Geometric Representation of Policies to Attain Internal and External Balance," *Review of Economic Studies* 28, 1–19.

Dalgaard, C. and H. Hansen, 2001, "On Aid, Growth, and Good Policies," *Journal of Development Studies* 37, 17–41.

Deaton, A., 1981, "Optimal Taxes and the Structure of Preferences," *Econometrica* 49, 1245–1260.

Devarajan, S., D. and Xie, and H. Zou, 1998, "Should Public Capital be Subsidized or Provided?" *Journal of Monetary Economics* 41, 319–331.

Devereux, M. B. and D. R. Love, 1994, "The Effects of Factor Taxation in a Two-Sector Model of Endogenous Growth," *Canadian Journal of Economics* 27, 509–536.

Diaz-Alejandro, C., 1965, *Exchange-Rate Devaluation in a Semi-Industrialized Country: The Experience of Argentina 1955–1961*, Cambridge University Press, Cambridge, UK.

Dinopoulos, E. and P. Thompson 1998, "Schumpeterian Growth without Scale Effects," *Journal of Economic Growth* 3, 313–337.

Djajic, S., S. Lahiri and P. Raimondos-Moller, 1999, "Foreign Aid, Domestic Investment and Welfare," *Economic Journal* 109, 698–707.

Domar, E., 1946, "Capital Expansion, Rate of Growth, and Employment," *Econometrica* 14, 137–147.

Duffy, J. and C. Papageorgiou, 2000, "A Cross-country Empirical Investigation of the Aggregate Production Function Specification," *Journal of Economic Growth* 5, 87–120.

Easterly, W., 2003, "Can Foreign Aid Buy Growth?" *Journal of Economic Perspectives* 17, 23–48.

Easterly, W., R. Levine, and D. Roodman, 2004, "Aid, Policies, and Growth: Comment," *American Economic Review* 94, 774–780.

Easterly, W. and S. Rebelo, 1993, "Fiscal Policy and Growth: An Empirical Investigation," *Journal of Monetary Economics* 32, 417–458.

Eaton, J. and M. Gersovitz, 1989, "Country Risk and the Organization of International Capital Transfer," in G. Calvo, R. Findlay, P. Kouri, and J. Braga de Macedo (eds.), *Debt, Stabilization, and Development: Essays in Memory of Carlos Diaz-Alejandro*, Blackwell, Oxford, UK.

Edwards, J. H. Y., 1990, "Congestion Function Specification and the 'Publicness' of Local Public Goods," *Journal of Urban Economics* 27, 80–96.

Edwards, S., 1984, "LDC Foreign Borrowing and Default Risk: An Empirical Investigation 1976–80," *American Economic Review* 74, 726–734.

Eicher, T. S. and S. J. Turnovsky, 1999a, "Non-Scale Models of Economic Growth," *Economic Journal* 109, 394–415.

1999b, "International Capital Markets and Non-Scale Growth," *Review of International Economics* 7, 171–188.

2000, "Scale, Congestion, and Growth," *Economica* 67, 325–346.

Evans, P. 1997, "How Fast do Countries Converge?" *Review of Economics and Statistics* 79, 219–225.

Fischer, S. and J. A. Frenkel, 1972, "Investment, the Two-Sector Model and Trade in Debt and Capital Goods," *Journal of International Economics* 2, 211–233.

1974, "Economic Growth and Stages of the Balance of Payments," in G. Horwich and Paul A. Samuelson (eds.), *Trade, Stability and Macroeconomics: Essays in Honor of Lloyd A. Metzler*, Academic Press, New York, NY.

Fisher, W., 1995, "An Optimizing Analysis of the Effects of World Interest Rate Disturbances on the Open Economy Term Structure of Interest Rates," *Journal of International Money and Finance* 14, 105–126.

Fisher, W. H. and D. Terrell, 2000, "World Interest Shocks, Capital, and the Current Account," *Review of International Economics* 8, 261–274.

Fisher, W. H. and S. J. Turnovsky, 1998, "Public Investment, Congestion, and Private Capital Accumulation," *Economic Journal* 108, 339–413.

Frenkel, J. A., A. Razin, and C. W. Yuen, 1996, *Fiscal Policies and Growth in the World Economy*, MIT Press, Cambridge, MA.

Futagami, K., Y. Morita, and A. Shibata, 1993, "Dynamic Analysis of an Endogenous Growth Model with Public Capital," *Scandinavian Journal of Economics* 95, 607–625.

Galor, O., 1996, "Convergence? Inferences from Theoretical Models," *Economic Journal* 106, 1056–1069.

Galor, O. and H. M. Polemarchakis, 1987, "Intertemporal Equilibrium and the Transfer Paradox," *Review of Economic Studies* 54, 147–156.

Gang, I. N. and H. A. Khan, 1991, "Foreign Aid, Taxes, and Public Investment," *Journal of Development Economics* 34, 355–369.

Gavin, M., 1990, "Structural Adjustment to a Terms of Trade Disturbance: The Role of Relative Price," *Journal of International Economics* 28, 217–243.

Glomm, G. and B. Ravikumar, 1994, "Public Investment in Infrastructure in a Simple Growth Model," *Journal of Economic Dynamics and Control* 18, 1173–1187.

    1998, "Flat Taxes, Government Spending on Education and Growth," *Review of Economic Dynamics* 1, 306–325.

Gramlich, E. M., 1994, "Infrastructure Investment: A Review Essay," *Journal of Economic Literature* 32, 1176–1196.

Grier, K. B. and G. Tullock, 1989, "An Empirical Analysis of Cross-National Economic Growth, 1951–1980," *Journal of Monetary Economics* 24, 48–69.

Grossman, G. M. and E. Helpman, 1991, *Innovation and Growth in the Global Economy*, MIT Press, Cambridge, MA.

Guitan, M., 1998, "The Challenge to Manage International Capital Flows," *Finance and Development* 35, 14–18.

Gupta, S., B. Clements, and G. Inchauste, 2004, "Fiscal Policy for Development: An Overview," in S. Gupta, B. Clements, and G. Inchauste (eds.), *Helping Countries Develop: The Role of Fiscal Policy*, IMF, Washington, DC.

Guvenen, T., 2006, "Reconciling Conflicting Evidence on the Elasticity of Intertemporal Substitution: A Macroeconomic Perspective, *Journal of Monetary Economics* 53, 1451–1472.

Haaparanta, P., 1989, "The Intertemporal Effects of International Transfers," *Journal of International Economics* 26, 371–382.

Hall, R. E., 1988, "Intertemporal Substitution in Consumption," *Journal of Political Economy* 96, 339–357.

Harrod, R. F., 1939, "An Essay in Dynamic Theory," *Economic Journal* 49, 14–33.

Hatzipanayotou, P. and M. S. Michael, 2000, "The Financing of Foreign Aid and Welfare: Income versus Consumption Tax," *Review of Development Economics* 4, 21–38.

Hayashi, F., 1982, "Tobin's Marginal q, Average q: A Neoclassical Interpretation," *Econometrica* 50, 213–224.

Hulten, C. R., 1996, "Infrastructure Capital and Economic Growth: How Well You Use It May Be More Important Than How Much You Have," Working Paper 5847, NBER.

Ireland, P. N., 1994, "Supply-Side Economics and Endogenous Growth," *Journal of Monetary Economics* 33, 559–571.

Islam, N., 1995, "Growth Empirics: A Panel Data Approach," *Quarterly Journal of Economics* 110, 1127–1170.

Jones, C. I., 1995a, "R&D Based Models of Economic Growth," *Journal of Political Economy* 103, 759–784.

    1995b, "Time Series Tests of Endogenous Growth Models," *Quarterly Journal of Economics* 110, 495–527.

    1999, "Growth: With or Without Scale Effects," *American Economic Review, Papers and Proceedings* 89, 139–144.

Jones, L. E. and R. E. Manuelli, 1990, "A Convex Model of Equilibrium Growth: Theory and Policy Implications," *Journal of Political Economy* 98, 1008–1038.

Jones, L. E., R. E. Manuelli, and P. E. Rossi, 1993, "Optimal Taxation in Models of Endogenous Growth," *Journal of Political Economy* 101, 485–517.

Keynes, J. M., 1929, "The German Transfer Problem," *Economic Journal* 39, 1–7.

Khan, H. A., and E. Hoshino, 1992, "Impact of Foreign Aid on the Fiscal Behavior of LDC Governments," *World Development* 20, 1481–1488.

King, R. G. and S. Rebelo, 1990, "Public Policy and Economic Growth: Developing Neoclassical Implications," *Journal of Political Economy* 98, S126–S150.

Klump, R., P. McAdam, and A. Willman, 2007, "Factor Substitution and Factor-Augmenting Technical Progress in the United States: A Normalized Supply-Side System Approach," *Review of Economics and Statistics* 89, 183–192.

Kneller, R., M. F. Bleaney, and N. Gemmell, 1999, "Fiscal Policy and Growth: Evidence from OECD Countries," *Journal of Public Economics* 74, 171–190.

Ladrón-de-Guevara, A., S. Ortigueira, and M. S. Santos, 1997, "Equilibrium Dynamics in Two-Sector Models of Endogenous Growth," *Journal of Economic Dynamics and Control* 21, 115–143.

Laursen, S. and L. A. Metzler, 1950, "Flexible Exchange Rates and the Theory of Employment," *Review of Economics and Statistics* 32, 281–299.

Lee, Y., 1995, "The Effects of Fiscal Policy in a Two-Country World Economy: An Intertemporal Analysis," *Journal of Money, Credit, and Banking* 27, 742–761.

Lucas, R. E. 1988, "On the Mechanics of Economic Development," *Journal of Monetary Economics* 22, 3–42.

Lucas, R. E. and N. L. Stokey, 1983, "Optimal Fiscal and Monetary Policy in an Economy without Capital," *Journal of Monetary Economics* 12, 55–93.

Mankiw, N. G., D. Romer, and D. Weil, 1992, "A Contribution to the Empirics of Economic Growth," *Quarterly Journal of Economics* 107, 407–438.

McDougall, I. A., 1965, "Non-Traded Goods and the Transfer Problem," *Review of Economic Studies* 32, 67–84.

Meng, Q. 2003, "Multiple Transitional Growth Paths in Endogenously Growing Open Economies," *Journal of Economic Theory* 108, 365–376.

Mino, K., 1996, "Analysis of a Two-Sector Model of Endogenous Growth with Capital Income Taxation," *International Economic Review* 37, 227–251.

Morshed, M. and S. J. Turnovsky, 2004, "Intersectoral Adjustment Costs and Real Exchange Rate Dynamics in a Two-Sector Dependent Economy Model," *Journal of International Economics* 62, 147–177.

Mulligan, C. B. and X. Sala-i-Martin, 1993, "Transitional Dynamics in Two-Sector Models of Endogenous Growth," *Quarterly Journal of Economics* 108, 739–775.

Murphy, R. G., 1986, "Productivity Shocks, Non-Traded Goods and Optimal Capital Accumulation," *European Economic Review* 30, 1081–1095.

Mussa, M., 1978, "Dynamic Adjustment in the Heckscher–Ohlin–Samuelson Model," *Journal of Political Economy* 86, 775–791.

Obstfeld, M., 1982, "Aggregate Spending and the Terms of Trade: Is there a Laursen–Metzler Effect?" *Quarterly Journal of Economics* 97, 251–270.

1989, "Fiscal Deficits and Relative Prices in a Growing World Economy," *Journal of Monetary Economics* 23, 461–484.

Obstfeld, M. and K. Rogoff, 1996, *Foundations of International Macroeconomics*, MIT Press, Cambridge, MA.

Ohlin, B. G., 1929, "Transfer Difficulties, Real and Imagined," *Economic Journal* 39, 172–178.

Ortigueira, S. and M. S. Santos, 1997, "On the Speed of Convergence in Endogenous Growth Models," *American Economic Review* 87, 383–399.

Palivos, T. and C. K. Yip, 1995, "Government Expenditure Financing in an Endogenous Growth Model: A Comparison," *Journal of Money, Credit, and Banking* 27, 1159–1178.

Patterson, K. D. and B. Pesaran, 1992, "The Intertemporal Elasticity of Substitution in the United States and the United Kingdom," *Review of Economics and Statistics* 74, 573–584.

Pearce, I. F., 1961, "The Problem of the Balance of Payments," *International Economic Review* 2, 1–28.

Pecorino, P., 1993, "Tax Structure and Growth in a Model with Human Capital," *Journal of Public Economics* 52, 251–271.

Pigou, A. C., 1932, "The Effect of Reparations on the Ratio of International Interchange," *Economic Journal* 42, 532–543.

Prescott, E. C., 2004, "Why do Americans Work so Much More than Europeans?" *Federal Reserve Bank of Minneapolis Quarterly Review* 28, 2–13.

Quah, D., 1996, "Convergence Empirics across Economies with (some) Capital Mobility," *Journal of Economic Growth* 1, 95–124.

Razin, A., 1984, "Capital Movements, Intersectoral Resource Shifts, and the Trade Balance," *European Economic Review* 26, 135–152.

Razin, A. and C. W. Yuen, 1994, "Convergence in Growth Rates: A Quantitative Assessment of the Role of Capital Mobility and International Taxation," in L. Leiderman and A. Razin (eds.), *Capital Mobility: The Impact on Consumption, Investment, and Growth*, Cambridge University Press, Cambridge, UK.

1996, "Capital Income Taxation and Long-Run Growth: New Perspectives," *Journal of Public Economics* 59, 239–263.

Rebelo, S., 1991, "Long-Run Policy Analysis and Long-Run Growth," *Journal of Political Economy* 99, 500–521.

1992, "Growth in Open Economies," in A. H. Meltzer and C. I. Plosser (eds.), *Carnegie–Rochester Conference Series on Public Policy*, vol. 36, North-Holland, Amsterdam.

Romer, P. M., 1986, "Increasing Returns and Long-Run Growth," *Journal of Political Economy* 94, 1002–1037.

1990, "Endogenous Technological Change," *Journal of Political Economy* 98, S71–103.

1994, "The Origins of Endogenous Growth," *Journal of Economic Perspectives* 8, 3–22.

Roubini, N. and P. Wachtel, 1998, "Current Account Sustainability in Transition Economies," Working Paper 6468, NBER.

Sachs, J., 1984, *Theoretical Issues in International Borrowing*, Princeton Studies in International Finance, 54, Princeton University International Finance Section.

Salter, W. E. G., 1959, "Internal and External Balance: The Role of Price and Expenditure Effects," *Economic Record* 35, 226–238.

Samuelson, P. A., 1952, "The Transfer Problem and Transport Costs: The Terms of Trade when Impediments are Absent," *Economic Journal* 59, 181–197.

1954, "The Transfer Problem and Transport Costs II: Analysis of Effects of Trade Impediments," *Economic Journal* 64, 254–289.

1964, "Theoretical Notes on Trade Problems," *Review of Economics and Statistics* 46, 145–154.

Sandmo, A., 1970, "The Effect of Uncertainty on Savings Decisions," *Review of Economic Studies* 37, 353–360.

Segerstrom, P., 1998, "Endogenous Growth without Scale Effects," *American Economic Review* 88, 1290–1311.

Senhadji, A. S., 2003, "External Shocks and Debt Accumulation in a Small Open Economy," *Review of Economic Dynamics* 6, 207–239.

Solow, R. M., 1956, "A Contribution to the Theory of Economic Growth," *Quarterly Journal of Economics* 70, 65–94.

1994, "Perspectives on Growth Theory," *Journal of Economic Perspectives* 8, 45–54.

Stokey, N. L. and S. Rebelo, 1995, "Growth Effects of Flat-Rate Taxes," *Journal of Political Economy* 103, 519–550.

Swan, T. W., 1956, "Economic Growth and Capital Accumulation," *Economic Record* 32, 334–361.

1960, "Economic Control in a Dependent Economy," *Economic Record* 36, 51–66.

Takayama, A., 1963, "On a Two-Sector Model of Economic Growth: A Comparative Statics Analysis," *Review of Economic Studies* 30, 95–104.

Turnovsky, S. J., 1996a, "Optimal Tax, Debt, and Expenditure Policies in a Growing Economy," *Journal of Public Economics* 60, 21–44.

1996b, "Fiscal Policy, Growth, and Macroeconomic Performance in a Small Open Economy," *Journal of International Economics* 40, 41–66.

1996c, "Fiscal Policy, Adjustment Costs, and Endogenous Growth," *Oxford Economic Papers* 48, 361–381.

1996d, "Endogenous Growth in a Dependent Economy with Traded and Nontraded Capital," *Review of International Economics* 4, 300–321.

1997a, *International Macroeconomic Dynamics*, MIT Press, Cambridge, MA.

1997b, "Fiscal Policy in a Growing Economy with Public Capital," *Macroeconomic Dynamics* 1, 615–639.

1997c, "Public and Private Capital in an Endogenously Growing Open Economy," in B. S. Jensen and K. -Y. Wong (eds.), *Dynamics, Economic Growth, and International Trade*, University of Michigan Press, Ann Arbor, MI.

1997d, "Equilibrium Growth in a Small Economy Facing an Imperfect World Capital Market," *Review of Development Economics* 1, 1–22.

1999, "Fiscal Policy and Growth in a Small Open Economy with Elastic Labor Supply," *Canadian Journal of Economics* 32, 1191–1213.

2000, "Fiscal Policy, Elastic Labor Supply, and Endogenous Growth," *Journal of Monetary Economics* 45, 185–210.

2002a, "Knife-Edge Conditions and the Macrodynamics of Small Open Economies," *Macroeconomic Dynamics* 6, 307–335.

2002b, "Intertemporal and Intratemporal Substitution and the Speed of Convergence in the Neoclassical Growth Model," *Journal of Economic Dynamics and Control* 26, 1765–1785.

2004, "The Transitional Dynamics of Fiscal Policy: Long-Run Capital Accumulation and Growth," *Journal of Money, Credit, and Banking* 36, 883–910.

Turunen-Red, A. H. and A. D. Woodland, 1988, "On the Multilateral Transfer Problem: Existence of Pareto Improving International Transfers," *Journal of International Economics* 25, 249–269.

Uzawa, H., 1961, "On a Two-Sector Model of Economic Growth," *Review of Economic Studies* 29, 40–47.

1968, "Time Preference, the Consumption Function and Optimum Asset Holdings," in J. N. Wolfe (ed.), *Value, Capital, and Growth: Papers in Honour of Sir John Hicks*, Aldine, Chicago, IL.

van der Ploeg, F., 1996, "Budgetary Policies, Foreign Indebtedness, the Stock Market and Economic Growth," *Oxford Economic Papers* 46, 382–396.

van der Ploeg, F. and G. S. Alogoskoufis, 1994, "Money and Endogenous Growth," *Journal of Money, Credit, and Banking* 26, 771–791.

Weder, M., 2001, "Indeterminacy in a Small Open Economy Ramsey Growth Model," *Journal of Economic Theory* 98, 339–356.

Weil, P., 1989, "Overlapping Families of Infinitely-lived Agents," *Journal of Public Economics* 38, 183–198.

World Bank, 1994, *World Development Report 1994: Infrastructure for Development*, Oxford University Press, New York, NY.

2004, *World Development Indicators*, CD-ROM, Washington, DC.

Young, A., 1998, "Growth without Scale Effects," *Journal of Political Economy* 106, 41–63.

Zhang, J., 1996, "Optimal Public Investment in Education and Endogenous Growth," *Scandinavian Journal of Economics* 98, 387–404.

Index